STEALING THE ENVIRONMENT

Social and Ecological Effects of Industrialization in Rourkela

Stealing the Environment

Social and Ecological Effects of Industrialization in Rourkela

RAJKISHOR MEHER

MANOHAR

First published 2022

ISBN 81-7304-572-0

Published by
Ajay Kumar Jain *for*
Manohar Publishers & Distributors
4753/23 Ansari Road, Daryaganj
New Delhi 110 002

Printed at
Lordson Publishers Pvt. Ltd.
Delhi 110 007

IN THE LOVING MEMORY
OF MY FATHER
SRI KRUPA MEHER

Contents

Tables

Figures

Preface

Industrialization is today a worldwide phenomenon. Economic development as a corollary to industrialization and urbanization as in the West demonstrated the potential for development of poorer countries. In recent years the harmful consequences of industrialization and urbanization have been realized. The concept of growth at all costs has led to the massive degradation of the environment and destruction of the symbiotic relationship existing between man and nature. For the purpose of growth a large number of industries are consuming fossil fuels and chemicals, which are not biodegradable. There is reckless exploitation of earth's resources for higher industrial gains. For the sake of material comforts, fossil fuels are burnt in large quantities; releasing harmful gases to the atmosphere and industrial effluents are poisoning rivers and oceans destroying marine life. There is overexploitation of mineral and other natural resources like forests and wildlife that are threatened to the point of near extinction. This sort of unplanned development has led to massive environmental pollution and ecological imbalance all over the globe and pauperization of large sections of people especially in the densely populated developing countries like India with an ascribed iniquitous social set up.

Hence, the present study entitled, *Stealing the Environment: Social and Ecological Effects of Industrialization in Rourkela*, attempts to explore the sociological and economic factors that affect the set patterns of symbiotic relationships between industry, ecology and society. The study starts with the premise that industrialization and urbanization generally accelerate the process of economic development thereby enriching man's materialistic form of life. However, the cravings for higher industrial gains lead to reckless exploitations of earth's resources, proliferation of undegradable chemicals into the biosphere resulting in massive pollution of land, water and air. Above all, large-scale concentration of human population in limited space as in urban centres puts lot of pressure on the ecology and sustaining capacity of the region. The large-scale migration of pauperized and unskilled population from the countryside towards the urban-industrial complex for livelihood exerts lot of pressure on the existing infrastructures and basic amenities, thereby resulting in irregular supply of such services to the various categories of urban population according to their socio-economic status. In a highly populated developing country like India having a poor capital base modern industrialization and urbanization leads to polarization of the economy into formal and informal economic sectors. The growth of formal and organized economy at a limited level provides an impetus to the massive proliferation of the unorganized and informal sector activities in urban areas because of the linkage and multiple effects generated by the large organized sector and heterogeneous wants created in an urban milieu. This further leads to proliferation of slums and squatters, inadequate supply of basic civic services for the poorer sections and general deterioration of quality of life in the city. Thus, the ecosystem, which provides various resources for the industry and society in general and absorbs the wastes generated by the latter ultimately, becomes sick if adequate steps are not taken to prevent the massive pollution exceeding its waste absorbing capacity.

This study has dealt with a number of aspects relating to the growth of industry, urban society and the consequences on the environment in the urban-industrial complex of Rourkela. In order to do this type of analysis of industrialization and the resulting urban social structure and their relationship with the ecology of the region, the study adopts a research based framework which views the problem from an inter-disciplinary perspective. The study needed the use of census data, government reports and gazetteers, and relevant published and unpublished research papers pertaining to industrialization, migration, urbanization and the state of ecology besides intensive survey of 316 households in selected localities of Rourkela with the help of a structured questionnaire. Also, by using both direct and indirect observation methods the behaviour and social interaction patterns of the people, economy, industry, land use and residential plan, and above all the relationships and impact of these systems on the urban ecology and environment were closely observed for more than a year. Thus, by adopting such methods it has been possible to depict broadly the nature of growth of industries, ecological dimensions of the city, spatial relationships of the internal structure of urban settlements, which has led to the formation of a particular type of morphological form and their consequent effects on the environment and ecosystem of the region.

In fact, the present study is a revised version of my Ph.D. thesis, 'Industrialization and the Urban Social Structure—A Sociological Study of Interrelationships between Industry, Ecology and Society in Rourkela' submitted to the School of Social Sciences, Jawaharlal Nehru University, New Delhi, in 1994. The work is an outcome of my seven years of research and discussions with my teachers, colleagues, friends and well-wishers. At the outset, I would like to place on record that I owe a great deal of intellectual and moral debts to my supervisor, Prof. M.N. Panini. I strongly feel that with out his guidance and encouragement I could not have finished this work on time. Besides, Prof. Panini, the comments of Prof. N.R. Sheth and Prof. Vinod K. Tewari as examiners of the doctoral thesis helped me to improve the work further. I will fail in my duty if I do not express my gratitude to them. I have benefited a lot from my discussions with Prof. Amitabh Kundu as he gave me lot of ideas to address the problem from an interdisciplinary perspective. By getting to work with him in a couple of research projects, I developed an aptitude for applied economic research and this helped me to utilize my limited knowledge of economics in this sociological study of Rourkela urban-industrial complex. I am indebted to him as he always found time despite his busy schedules.

I would also like to express my gratitude to Prof. T.K. Oommen, Prof. Yogendra Singh, Dr Nandu Ram and other faculty members of the Centre for the Study of Social Systems, JNU, New Delhi, from whom I learned the ABC of research. While I was in Delhi Prof. Girish K. Misra of the Indian Institute of Public Administration was also always a source of inspiration to me. It is he along with Prof. Kundu, who helped me a lot to overcome my financial crisis and the responsibility of looking after my old parents by providing me employment in temporary research projects off and on. So, I will be failing in my duty if I do not express my special thanks to him.

I strongly feel that I owe a great deal to my friend's parents and brother at Rourkela, late Shri Brundaban Sahu and his family members, who made my year long stay at Rourkela during field study highly comfortable and pleasant. So to say, during the period of my stay with them in their Rourkela house, I had become another son to them like my friend Shri Nabakrushna Sahu. Besides them, I would like to express my thanks to a good many friends at Rourkela namely, Mr Pradip K. Mishra, Mr Sanat Pradhan, Mr Prakash Ch. Das, Mrs Minati Mohapatra, Mr Sunil K. Panda, Mr Bijay K. Mishra and others who extended all cooperation to me during the course of my field study. My friend, Mr Prakash Ch. Das and his wife Mrs Minati Mohapatra of the personnel department in Rourkela Steel Plant helped me a great deal in establishing close rapport with the workers in the steel plant. Certainly, I will be failing in my duty if I do not place on record my special thanks and gratitude to my friend Shri Nabakrushna Sahu of Indian Economic Service, his wife Mrs Jyotsna Sahu and his younger brother Mr Rajkishore Sahu. My friend and his younger brother enlightened me a lot about the local conditions and formation of neighbourhoods and the complex ecological process of growth in Rourkela.

I also wish to record my thanks to Prof. Baidyanath Misra, ex-Chairman and Founder Director and Prof. L.K. Mahapatra, and Prof. K.K. Mohanti, the former Directors of Nabakrushna Choudhury Centre for Development Studies, Bhubaneswar, who encouraged me to complete my thesis at an early date. It is because of their cooperation I could complete the work and did not feel the strain of working in a research institute. Also, I wish to express my thanks to my colleagues at the Centre namely, Dr Radhamohan Mallik, Dr Shakti Prasad Padhi, Mr Paramanand Naik and to my teacher-cum-colleague Dr Kishor Ch. Samal from whom I have been benefited a lot while discussing with them the different aspects of industrialization, urbanization and the ecology. Besides them, I have been benefited a lot from the discussions held with my friends based in Delhi namely Dr Gopinath Pradhan, Dr Balgovind Baboo, Dr Chitrasen Pasayat, Dr Biswajit Ghosh, Dr Hrushikesh Panda, Mr Gajendra Bhujbal, Mr Ashok K. Tripathy and others.

It is obvious but needs to be mentioned that this sort of research work could not have been carried out without the help of the library staff in various libraries of Delhi and Bhubaneswar. I wish to record my thanks to all of them.

The earlier version of the Ph.D. thesis was neatly typed by Sri Harish Chandra Bisht and the technical help required for the purpose was extended by Sri Satyendra Kumar, a friend in JNU, New Delhi. However, Mrs Sujata Manjari Pani, Computer Operator, Nabakrushna Choudhury Centre for Development Studies, Bhubaneswar, took much pain while typing the corrected version of the manuscript. I am thankful to Mrs Pani for her diligence, patience and interest shown in neat typing of the manuscript.

Last but not the least, I will fail in my duty if I do not record my thanks to the sample respondents, people and officials in Rourkela, who made the field study a success.

My father was alive when the manuscript was given its present shape and he was anxious to see it in book form. However, he passed away all of a sudden. I am sure my old mother and my wife Sushama and daughters Pratiksha and Prajna will forget the agonies of my long years of negligence to them, the moment they see the manuscript in its final shape of the present book.

Nabakrushna Choudhury Centre
for Development Studies, Orissa,
Bhubaneswar

RAJKISHOR MEHER

CHAPTER 1

Introduction

Even though the modern system of industrial production has enriched the material base of society and has led to a universalistic, achievement-oriented social order, the growth of industries and increasing urbanization is affecting the ecosystem adversely. The tendency of developing countries to promote urban industrial growth at all costs and to allow market forces to determine the pace and pattern of the utilization of space has led to the destruction of the ecosystem on a massive scale. Moreover, the unequal distribution of income and assets under the capitalistic production system as well as a small percentage of the population controlling a sizeable portion of the production of various goods and services in the economy distorts the output structure and results in the misuse of the factors of production. While certain resources, like the labour force remain under-employed, causing social deprivation and poverty to a large section of the population, physical resources get overexploited resulting in environmental degradation. This distortion of the economy is reflected in urban settlement patterns as well. The alarming gap in income levels attracts workers from the less productive agriculture sector to urban areas, though it is difficult to get employment in the organized sector of the economy, partly because the urban population is itself growing at a rapid pace. Besides liquidation of non-agricultural activities in vast areas of the rural hinterland, modern, capital intensive industrialization has failed to absorb the displaced artisans, thereby causing a high rate of unemployment and an involuntary absorption of surplus labour in the primary sector. This leads to a rapid deterioration of the environment in rural areas. The high pressure of population on land as well as growing poverty and mass unemployment also push a large section of the able-bodied, lowly skilled population to industrial and urban areas in search of livelihood. However, as the absorption capacity of the intensively organized, manufacturing and service sector is limited for these lowly skilled cityward immigrants, they seek openings in the unorganized and informal sector of the economy in the city. The state of development of the technology and the labour surplus nature of the economy in many of the third world countries also encourages close linkages between the organized and unorganized sectors, generally in the interest of the former. The underdeveloped nature of the basic infrastructure and services in the city provides further scope for the proliferation of the informal sector. As a result, the cities of the third world continue to grow at an alarming rate with a dichotomous urban social and ecological structure.

Since the investible funds with the government and urban local bodies are limited, the desired level of environment is ensured only to a small section of the population. This results in the spatial segmentation of the population and the segregation of neighbourhoods within the city, operationalized through various landuse restrictions and building bye-laws. The infrastructural facilities and public amenities are also distributed unevenly and generally favour the relatively affluent localities. The process of industrialization and urbanization in developing countries, which have a capitalist market economy framework operates in such a way that it not only affects the ecosystem negatively, but the poor also are adversely affected largely due to an unequal distribution of resources (Roberts 1978: 137). Industry in general shapes the urban sociospatial structure. The relatively affluent and rich localities are infrastructurally well-designed and clean areas and situated far away from the poorer localities, which tend to be affected by industrial pollution. Ecological forces like competition, invasion, succession and adaptation operate in such a manner that in most cases rich and affluent sections reside in the better areas of the city which are free from air, water and sound pollution caused by industries and the city transport system, whereas the poor are forced to reside nearer to their place of employment such as industrial areas or the central district zones of the city as they cannot afford the high cost of transportation as well as the basic cost of services and the high rents of environmentally clean localities. Since industrial areas and business zones are the hub of economic activities in the city, the poor are forced to reside there. But unfortunately, these localities are also highly polluted due to a high population density, intensive movement of vehicles running on fossil fuels and the emission of poisonous gases and industrial effluents. Hence, although pollution has no boundary, the areas in which the poor and the rich reside are designed and shaped in such a way that the poor automatically become the worst victims of industrial pollution.

In a capital scarce and labour abundant economy governed by the capitalist ideology modern industrialization has evolved a dualistic socioeconomic set up. The organized industrial sector produces sophisticated capital goods, intermediate goods and durable luxury consumer items by using mechanized, capital intensive inputs rather than labour. The unorganized industrial sector having a close linkage and dependency upon the organized industries in the form of execution of job-works and labour required by the latter in a labour intensive set up, produces either expensive consumer goods or cheaper consumer goods of poor quality to cater to the needs of poor and lower middle class, by employing cheap labour at subsistence wages. Again because of supply scarcity and high labour productivity the organized sector workers are relatively better off than the informal sector workers. They are employees of large enterprises with regulated service conditions, reasonable remuneration and other facilities like accommodation, transport, gratuity, medical reimbursement, bonus, etc. However, the unorganized sector workers are either selfemployed or employed by small scale industries and other informal commercial and service establishments, where wages are very low; service is irregular and hardly provides any facility to the workers. These are the people, who reside in ramshackle huts built on unauthorized vacant land adjacent to industrial units or in and around the central business district, which are converted into slum and squatter settlements with minimum civic amenities. The existing regulating mechanisms are inadequate to force the employers of the informal and unorganized sector units to pay for the cost of housing, water supply, sewerage and transport of the poor workers employed by them. Also there is no legal provision to compel the large industrial units to provide housing and basic amenities for these workers even though they have virtually made themselves available for any kind of work in nearly all sections of the urban economy at minimum wages. Further, to add to the woes of these hapless people there are no proper municipal regulations to check and reduce the level of industrial pollution to which they are constantly exposed. The industrial units have virtually been given the freedom to discharge pollutants and other industrial effluents to the atmosphere and open fields, thereby exposing people and animals in the neighbourhood to serious health hazards.

The planned industrial towns of the country are also not free from such anomalies. The socio-cultural and economic forces ultimately shape the landuse pattern and segregate the residential areas of the rich and the poor. The ecological forces which generally determine spatial organization of people and their economic activities in the city, broadly get affected by the social and cultural stigmas and political forces as well. The populist politics of the political leaders lead to distortion of the city's Master Plan. Often with a plea to provide residential accommodation to the growing population and to accelerate the pace of industrial development, areas earmarked for green belts are also allowed to be encroached by the builders. Similarly, in busy market places of the city no space is clearly allotted for business transaction of the informal and small scale establishments, knowing fully well that they are an integral part of the urban economy in a densely populated developing country like India. As a result, informal sector establishments crop up in the residential areas and busy market places of the city by encroaching the footpaths and roads, thereby obstructing traffic and pedestrian movement and polluting the surrounding locality. Moreover, in order to manipulate votes of the urban poor, slums are allowed to come up in the heart of the city and often no regular provision is made for them to avail basic civic facilities such as water, electricity, public toilets and the like. The situation worsens and exploitation continues because these people are used as vote banks and the ruling party keeps on adopting *ad hoc* and piecemeal measures with a populist tinge to satisfy the people.

Since independence, despite planned efforts the growth of organized sector employment in the country is found to be very low. The employment share of the organized sector in the country is only around 8 to 10 per cent of the country's total workforce. This may be mainly due to capital scarcity and labour abundant situation. Benefits of industrialization and urbanization although reach the poor and underprivileged sections of society, they are mainly in the form of unorganized sector employment only. The rate of percolation or 'trickle down' process as expected from the country's present model of growth is so weak that there is hardly any chance for the large poorer section of the country's population to cross the barrier of poverty. Notwithstanding this, due to high pressure of population on land and lack of employment opportunities in the villages, the rural poor continue to migrate to the large and medium size cities of India. As there is very little opportunity for them to get absorbed in the modern organized sector, they seek their ecological niche in the informal sector economy of the city. In many cases, they continue with their earlier rural occupations like animal husbandry and dairy farming. In many towns and cities of Bihar, Madhya Pradesh, Orissa, Rajasthan and Uttar Pradesh, even the so-called posh localities are now invaded by the slum dwellers and the wide roads, parks, open green areas are rapidly becoming animal sheds and grazing grounds for domestic animals.

Owing to limited availability of resources with the local urban planning authorities, the implementation of various improvement schemes always lags behind the target. Further, the rate of inflow of distressed population to the large cities and commercial centres of India, is so high that only a small number of these people can find shelter in the better facilitated resettlement colonies. The rate of growth of slum population and multiplication of squatter colonies in the cities of the third world is alarming and within the existing resource base of the urban bodies, only a few of them can be converted to improved slum colonies or can be shifted to resettlement colonies. Further, the policy to relocate slums and squatter dwellers in the newly built resettlement colonies, located in the periphery of the city sometimes goes against the social and economic interests of the slum dwellers. Most of the slums are a replication of village community life and their location is nearer to the place of employment. Location of the resettlement colonies in the periphery of the city results in disruption of community life, loss of employment avenues for women resulting in decrease in the number of earning members in the household, increase in cost of transportation and therefore a sudden fall in the average income of the household. In Delhi, when the government in the mid-1970s, shifted a number of slum and squatter dwellers to the resettlement colonies in the periphery, for beautification of the city and improvement of the urban environment, many of the slum-dwellers reported a sudden loss of earning and disruption and break of community life. Ultimately malafide sale and transfer of the allotted plots took place on a large scale and quite a few of the allottees went back to their earlier homes in the city (Misra and Gupta 1981).

Besides, there is a seasonal cityward migration of rural agricultural labour especially from the rainfed and drought-prone areas, is a regular phenomenon in many parts of the country. As the urban local bodies and the city's shelter system do not have any stop-gap arrangement to accommodate these floating people, slums and squatters continue to sprawl in the heart of the towns and cities. Parks and other open fields get converted to defecation grounds and often the spacious footpaths and spaces under flyovers become temporary homes of these seasonal migrant population. This category of migration is more common in case of medium-sized cities in the backward regions of the country. As a result, despite the low level of industrialization, the surrounding environment of these towns and cities are also not free from massive land, air and water pollution.

All these observations clearly show that the very process of industrialization and urbanization accelerated in the country with much fanfare to achieve higher economic growth, has not only failed in its main objective, but also it has negatively affected the urban ecosystem. The main reasons of the present eco-crisis can be attributed to social, economic and political factors, which adversely affected the nature of urban growth and spatial organization of land and people, location of various industries and tertiary sector establishments in the city.

Modern industrial set-up has disturbed the ecology. The location and concentration of various industries in urban areas coupled with the growth in size and density of urban settlements has resulted in ruthless exploitation of natural resources, uprooting the people and depriving them of their traditional livelihood. It also resulted in conversion of agricultural lands into factory and residential quarters. This growth orientation coupled with a nonchallant attitude to environmental conservation leads to massive environmental pollution resulting from emission of poisonous gases and discharge of effluents by the domestic and factory sectors. The ecological degradation, destruction of natural vegetation and the symbiotic relationship between living and non-living world compound the problem of poverty.

Hence, it is imperative to explore in greater depth the interlinkages between industry, ecology and the urban social structure.

RESEARCH BACKGROUND AND THE LOCATION OF THE STUDY

Rourkela in Orissa is the selected site of one of the four steel plants the government established after independence, in order to promote industrialization in the country. The other three such sites are Bhilai, Bokaro and Durgapur. All the four present townships, viz., Rourkela, Bhilai, Bokaro and Durgapur, came up after the public sector steel plants were set up. Of these four townships, Bhilai is located in Madhya Pradesh, Bokaro in Bihar and Durgapur in West Bengal. These townships alongwith Jamshedpur and Chittaranjan, which existed before independence were grafted on the respective regions from the outside (Mohsin 1964: 1). Unlike the other towns and cities of India, which evolved in course of time due to social and economic forces operating within the region, these towns virtually came up in the wilderness, where only a few tribal hamlets existed. All the four industrial townships of Rourkela, Bhilai, Durgapur and Bokaro derived another advantage. Since they were literally built from scratch, they could be planned much the same way the city of Chandigarh was planned. So, in order to study the interrelationships between industry, ecology and society and the social and ecological effects of industrialization, in the modern urban centres of the country, the steel city of Rourkela has been selected for the present study.

The layout of Rourkela township began in the 1950s, when the Government of India decided to locate its first modern steel plant under the aegis of the public sector in that locality. The city came up on a spot which formerly consisted of 30 tribal hamlets and because of the existence of a small railway station, village Rourkela was more prominent among them. So, when the new township grew up in the wake of the location of the steel plant, it was named as Rourkela.

BROAD AIMS AND OBJECTIVES

The study of Rourkela attempts to grasp the shift from a natural regime of landuse pattern to the regime of man made machinery oriented pattern. After examining how the operation of various social, economic, cultural and ecological forces have affected the urban spatial structure of this town, an attempt has been made to study how industrialization is leading to massive environmental pollution and deterioration in the quality of life. It is believed that such an analysis will throw light on the working of basic ecological processes such as competition, concentration, segregation, invasion and succession under the influence of both planned and unplanned growth impulses. The study focuses on the relationships between inter-dependent layers of the urban-industrial complex of Rourkela, such as industry, ecosystem and the people. It also seeks to grasp the spatial distribution of different categories of population and the formation of the urban social structure.

THE STUDY DESIGN

The study is mainly based on direct and participatory observation of the various residential localities, at both the industrial and civil township of Rourkela, location and functioning of various industrial units in different areas of the city, including the giant public sector steel plant and also the main market complexes and government offices, from November 1987 to February 1989. In order to obtain a broad idea about the distribution of various categories of population such as castes, tribes, religions and linguistic groups, at an initial stage the electoral rolls of Rourkela City Assembly Constituency, was extensively studied to clear any ambiguities. Similarly, the information on the functioning of the various categories of large, medium and small industries of the city (with a total investment of more than Rs. 2 lakh on plant and machinery), was collected from the District Industries Centre at Rourkela. Then the working condition in the private sector industrial units (large, medium and small) of the city were broadly surveyed for a few days. In some cases informal interviews and discussions were held with the entrepreneurs, managerial staff and workers to get adequate understanding of the situation.

In Rourkela, the giant public sector steel plant is the pivot around which social, cultural, political and economic activities revolve. Hence, to acquire a broad based knowledge on the working process of the steel plant, its various aspects and utilization of several types of raw materials, production mix, by-products and their uses and above all the working conditions and the environmental surroundings, have been intensively observed. The various departments, such as production, raw material, fuel processing, administration have been observed and studied for more than a month or so. On all the occasions, both formal and informal discussions and interviews with the workers have been conducted during their leisure hours. Besides the workers, some of the members of the management were also interviewed informally.

Apart from that, a structured questionnaire was circulated in order to collect both quantitative and qualitative data at the primary level, with regard to the growth and development of the city, pattern of migration, socio-economic conditions of the workers, their state of health and the general environmental conditions. This questionnaire was evolved by adopting a similar method used in the influential study of Bangalore city, by Prakasa Rao and Tewari (1979). This questionnaire was proposed to be canvassed to various sample households in the selected localities of Rourkela steel township as well as civil township. The steel township is mainly resided by the employees of the steel plant; whereas others live in the civil township. It may be mentioned here that a part of the steel township has now been encroached upon by those who are not employed in the steel plant.

This structured questionnaire was framed with a purpose to examine the following features: (i) demographic features of the household and level of education, (ii) rate of work participation,

(iii) percentage of households living below the poverty line, (iv) inequality of income distribution across castes and communities, (v) housing conditions, (vi) incidence of sickness and types of diseases, (vii) fertility and mortality rates, (viii) solid waste and sewage disposal, (ix) water scarcity and pollution, (x) air pollution, (xi) pattern of migration, (xii) workers mobility pattern and the like. Each of the schedules was personally canvassed and filled up at the time of interview with the head of the sample households in selected localities. As it was a lengthy schedule and the respondents of the sample households had very little leisure time for discussion regarding their day-to-day problems besides providing necessary information for the questions, it was an uphill task to fill up even one or two schedules per day. Without sufficient networking in the locality, it was impossible to collect necessary information. So, initially without losing patience I kept on visiting the selected sample localities repeatedly and developed good rapport with the prominent persons of the locality. Although I knew very little about the city before the commencement of the field study, I could overcome several barriers after two/three months of my stay in the city because I personally hailed from the western part of Orissa and my ability to speak Oriya, the local Sambalpuri dialect, Hindi, and English helped me considerably.

SAMPLE PROCEDURE

Rourkela is a big class-I town with around 70,000 households according to the 1981 census. As it is very difficult for a single individual working for a doctoral thesis to cover all the localities of the two townships even by the simple random sampling method, it was decided to confine household survey sample in the six localities of the city, covering three localities from the civil township municipality area and three localities from the steel township Notified Area Council (NAC) area. The number of samples was kept to the manageable level of about 300 households. Before selecting these localities in the two townships, the matter was discussed with prominent citizens, well-acquainted with the spatial structure of the city. On the basis of such advice, the Oraon Para and some of the adjacent households of Udit Nagar area comprising

384 households, Malgodam slum area and a portion of Basanti Colony consisting of 1,311 households and Nala Road area consisting of Bhatti Road, Nala Road, Mohulpali, with a total of 1,298 households were considered. The total number of households in these localities were based on the voters' list of the Rourkela Assembly Constituency. In the civil township it was decided to cover 5 per cent of the households through random sampling. On this basis, 19 households of Udit Nagar and Oraon Para, 66 households of Malgodam-Basanti Colony and 65 households of Nala Road, Bhatti Road and Mahulpali area of the civil town were covered. Thus, the total number of the sample households covered in the civil township of Rourkela comes to 150 and for the sake of convenience it has been shown as civil township in the various tables used in the text (Fig. 1.1).

Similarly, in the case of the steel township NAC area, Sector-2 and Sector-3 localities and Modern India Labour Colony, Kalinga Auto Colony, etc., which form the Modern India Area located near the Fertilizer township was selected. From the voters' list and also from enquiry with the local residents, it was found that the total number of households in Sector-2 was 2,032, in Sector-3 it was 356 and in Modern India area it was 921. So, about 5 per cent random sample of the households was taken. On this basis, the sample households covered in Sector-2 is 102, in Sector-3, 18 and in Modern India, 46. Thus, the total number of households covered in the steel township NAC area is 166 and altogether a total of 316 households were considered in the sample for the purpose of the study (Fig. 1.1).

In addition to this, relevant secondary data on forested area, rainfall, health conditions of the people, provision of basic amenities, different categories of industries in large, medium and small size and the like from various sources such as State Government publications, Census publications and from the publications made by the Rourkela Steel Plant were collected. In order to obtain a general idea of the periphery some of the peripheral villages like Luakera, Pradhanpali, Tumkela, Hamirpur, Lathikata, etc., were also surveyed. Also the views of many political leaders, tribal leaders and heads of a few socio-cultural organizations were obtained in order to know their opinion about

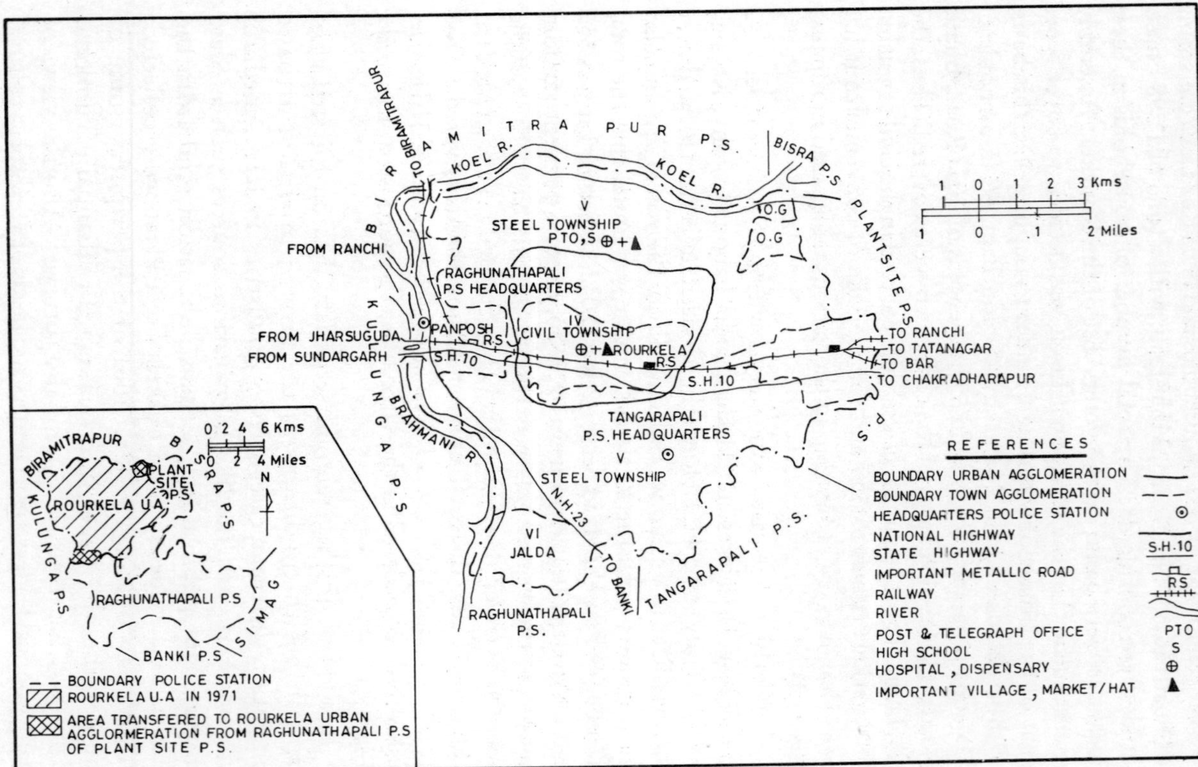

Fig. 1.1: Rourkela Urban Agglomeration

the quality of life in the city. The analysis and findings of primary, field study data alongwith the secondary data and information are reported in the subsequent chapters in accordance with the holistic framework devised for the present study.

ORGANIZATION OF THE STUDY

The study has been organized in the following manner. Chapter 1 starts with an introductory sketch of the industrialization and urbanization scenario in India. It then deals with the purpose and location of the study, its broad aims and objectives and the methodology used for surveying. In Chapter 2, a broad theoretical framework of the study has been developed. The review of the literature demonstrates that while some important insights can be gained from the various theories of urbanization and ecology, the magnitude of ecological crisis is such, that it cannot be adequately grasped by these theories only. Fortunately, some attempts have been made to theoretically grasp the emerging ecological crisis. These are evaluated, and they in turn are followed by an attempt to evolve a model for studying the interrelationships between industry, ecology and the society, which is the main concern of the present study. This is followed by a description of the preindustrial economy, society and the ecology of the region in which Rourkela is situated in Chapter 3. In Chapter 4, the history of the process of industrialization of Rourkela is described. This is followed in Chapter 5, by a detailed account of the spatial structure and settlement pattern and the emerging urban social structure. In Chapter 6, an attempt has been made to develop an integrated view of industrialization and its effects on social structure and ecology of Rourkela. Lastly the concluding chapter is devoted to a theoretical analysis of the linkages between urban society, industrialization and ecology according to the findings of this study.

CHAPTER 2

Industrialization, Urbanization and Ecology: Theoretical Considerations

Industrialization in a big way has made possible the development of urban centres in probably any part of the globe. Rapid improvement in transport and communication network has reduced the physical distance between various regions, thereby enabling people to settle down in any part of a country. It has been observed that with industrialization, besides utilizing the physical and economic resources of the immediate hinterland, aggregation of economic activities and large scale influx of people from various parts of the country also occur. Sovani (1981), rightly observes that industrialization has historically been the royal road to development and has been associated with urbanization both as a cause and as a consequence. Learning from the experience of economic development in the West, the developing countries pinned their hopes on industrialization and urbanization to stimulate socioeconomic development. In labour surplus developing countries Lewis's two sector model consisting of (i) a traditional rural subsistence sector characterized by zero or very low productivity of surplus labour and (ii) a highly productive urban industrial sector into which labour from the subsistence sector is gradually being transferred, has been influential in evolving strategies of development (Lewis 1954). One of the proponents of such a strategy has lauded the role of cities as growth poles in the regional economy since they act as the primary forces impelling rapid economic growth and as diffusion points of social change for developing countries (Breese 1969).

However, there is evidence to suggest that in India, the urban hierarchy reflects an extremely inefficient organization of space which often tends to cling to the regional economy as a parasite.

The large urban agglomerations have expanded beyond the limits of their economic base (Kundu 1980). Though the pace of industrialization has increased after independence, mainly because of planned economic development, the labour force are not sufficiently absorbed in the organized sector of the urban economy. The urban centres do not have the capacity to assimilate the migrants who are forced to move from one type of informal sector activity to another, in order to earn their livelihood. Many of the large and medium-sized cities in the country depict a scenario of congestion, overcrowded slums and filthy atmosphere. More than half of the population in many cities are not provided with minimum civic amenities. There is massive environmental pollution caused by unauthorized growth of industries, heavy traffic of different categories of vehicles plying on narrow and unsafe roads, odour of ripe garbage and untreated industrial effluents and domestic wastes flowing in uncovered drains and overloaded sewerage channels. The city no longer reflects the advancement of human civilization and prosperity of the people in general.

Considering such a scenario, it has become necessary to understand the ecology of the city, its economy and society from a holistic angle. How different subsystems of the economy, society and the urban ecosystem are interlinked with one another and how they are broadly formed and shaped by the infrastructural base of the region and in turn affecting the ecology of the region should be properly studied and understood. Therefore, to begin it is essential to assess the major theories of urbanization, ecology and growth of the city, which has been undertaken in the following sections.

INDUSTRY, ECOLOGY AND THE URBAN SOCIETY: A PERSPECTIVE

While inquiring into the causes of concentration of people in the cities, Adna Weber, concluded that this was primarily a product of economic forces which were of the kind that became significant with the industrial revolution (Weber 1899). Besides the primary economic causes, Weber identified a number of secondary causes of economic, political and social types. In a secondary economic sense the city grows not only because of the revolution in transport, finance, production and commerce, but also because of the lure of high wages and wider job opportunities. Various political factors like (i) legislation promoting free trade, (ii) legislation promoting freedom of migration, (iii) centralized administration with its location of persons in civic centres, and (iv) free forms of land tenure encourage the growth of the city. Among the social causes the city offers facilities for modern scientific education, amusements, higher standard of living, association of intellectuals and, institutions for the diffusion of knowledge and promotion of the values of city life. However, this theory of the city accounted only for the external aspects of the city, namely size, growth and location.

In contrast to Adna Weber's theory pertaining to growth, location and size of cities, his contemporary Josiah Strong, developed theoretical interest on the moral effects of the city. Strong thought that modern civilization is laid on materialistic orientation to life, in contrast to moral and spiritual aspects. According to him, this material growth is manifest in the development of the 'materialistic' city, whose phenomenal growth was attributed to a redistribution of population because of the development of scientific agriculture, mechanization and better transport facilities. He found the society undergoing an irreversible transformation from the farm to the city, making it highly incompatible with its intellectual and moral development. Among the basic problems the industrial revolution posed for the city was the adjustment of an aristocratic system co-existing with a democratic system. The complex form of city life has made the individual 'segmental and dependent', and any performance failure on the part of the individual becomes socially disastrous. According to Strong, homes are disappearing in the city at both the social extremes. The rich have substituted hotel and the club for home life; whereas the poor homeless reside in slums and footpaths in a condition of ignorance, vice and wretchedness (Strong 1896).

However, these theories developed in the aftermath of industrial revolution did not offer explanations for the trajectory of urban growth, the emerging territorial division of labour, landuse and settlement patterns and the social structure of the city. It was in fact, the Chicago School of Sociology, in the early part of the twentieth century, that laid the foundation of a systematic sociological theory of the city (Park, Burgess and Mckenzie 1925).

Researchers of the Chicago School observed that plant species adapt to their environment by distributing themselves over a localized area enabling them to engage in complementary uses of habitat resources. This led to an understanding of the growth and function of the burgeoning industrial city in an ecological perspective. The spatial organizations of the city and the settlement patterns were viewed as the result of competition among subpopulation of the city for spatial positions to perform diverse but complementary economic and social activities. Accordingly, the study of urban structure in its spatial aspects became identified with the human ecology.

Park provided the general framework for the ecological perspective. He put forward the view that the city is a 'natural habitat of civilized man' in the sense that it represents a 'cultural area' with peculiar cultural types. It obeys laws of its own and there is a limit to the arbitrary modifications, which can be made in its physical structure and moral order. Like the entire city, each of its subsections and neighbourhood reflects the qualities of its inhabitants and acquire its own historical continuity. In the city through isolation, the immigrant and racial colonies, or the socalled ghettoes and areas of segregated population tend to maintain themselves in isolation (Park et al., op. cit).

The flourishing trade and industry of the city encourage further division of labour and universalistic achievement oriented social structure. The older traditional social and economic structures based on particular ties such as family or religion, culture, caste and status breaks down in the face of an order based on occupation and vocational interests. The growth of the city is accomplished by a substitution of indirect 'secondary' relations for direct face-to-face 'primary' relations. Thus according to Park, the city represents an externally organized unit in space produced by laws of its own. However, it was Ernest W. Burgess, who made a lucid and precise statement of this external spatial organization of the city by his ecological theory and the systematic explanation of its intrinsic laws was put forward by Rodrick Mckenzie (ibid.).

Burgess treated the growth of the city in terms of its physical expansion and differentiation in space. He believed that the expansion of the city took the form of the development of a series of concentric rings, representing successive zones of urban expansion. According to him the natural growth of the city takes the form of radial expansion from its central business district, like the Chicago 'Loop'. This is the core area and is normally encircled by a transitory second area which is invaded by business and light manufacturing industry. This zone is characterized by poor housing, low rent and property being held for business use. Encircling this zone there is a third area, which is inhabited by the industrial workers who have escaped the pollution and deterioration, but have retained an easy access to their places of work. This area threatens to become the next slum. Beyond this zone is the 'residential area' of high-class apartment buildings or exclusive restricted area belonging to single family units. Still farther beyond the city limit, the fifth zone is the suburban area or satellite town cities from where commuters travel 30 to 60 minutes to the central business district or their workplace.

Park and Burgess had assumed that the city presented a physical portrait of typically specific areas and zones. They made numerous references to the laws, which established them. The fullest statement of these so-called 'laws' or 'processes', was made by their colleague R.K. Mckenzie. Mckenzie developed the concentric rings theory of the city using the concepts of plant ecologists. At the biotic level, the various processes recognized by the plant ecologists was translated into human terms, using concepts such as competition, dominance, segregation, invasion and succession. According to the ecological theorists of the city, the foremost fundamental concept is competition. In the city man competes with limited space and accessibility for the most desirable location for his residence and for his economic activities. Such competitive activity is reflected in land values, which through the price mechanism sorts out similar types of persons. Competition leads to differentiation and specialization of urban landuse, and this in turn leads to segregation of neighbourhoods. Consequently, different parts of the city such as the central business district, the areas of commerce and the residential areas come to be inhabited by different types of people.

The second process is that of dominance. Within different types of plant associations, one species dominates and controls the environmental conditions, which encourage or discourage other types of species. In a similar fashion the central business district exerts dominating influence within the whole urban complex. Competition between business concerns to get located in the area of maximum accessibility leads to rising land values in areas close to the city centre, and this further affects the disposition of other elements within the urban complex. Similarly, the industrial areas are dominated by the industries, which by their noxious character repel residential development in that zone.

Dominance in the ecological parlance is intimately connected with the concepts of invasion and succession. In the plant world, plants by their activities in changing the microenvironment in which they live, create conditions in which other less tolerant plants are also able to survive and gradually the other species begin to invade the environment. Eventually they establish themselves as dominant elements and as the process continues, form part of a succession of dominant elements. Lower status groups apply this process of invasion and succession to human communities in relation to invasion of residential areas by the commercial and business undertakings and of higher status residential areas by lower status groups. Burgess writes that in the expansion of the city a process occurs which sifts, sorts and relocates individuals and groups by residence and occupation. Thus within the 'main stem' appears the 'hobohemia' of homeless migratory men. In the zone of deterioration encircling the central business district are found the slums which are submerged regions of degradation, disease and the nefarious activities of underworld. However, as one moves outward the segregation and assemblage of other social groups are to be found.

Therefore, the major processes that form the city in order of importance are competition, concentration, centralization, segregation, invasion and succession. Their successive operation creates the 'natural areas' that form the physical structure of the city.

This ecological theory of the city propounded by the Chicago School of Sociology, in fact provided the methodological framework for several studies and surveys of urban life and structure in the 1920s and early 1930s. These included studies of whole communities such as Mckenzie's *The Neighbourhood: A Study of Columbus, Ohio.* Studies of certain types of areas within Chicago such as Louis Wirth's *The Ghetto* and Zorbaugh's *The Gold Coast and the Slum*, and studies of types of social groups or individuals relating social aspects to their environmental setting, such as Anderson's *The Hobo*, Trasher's *The Gang*, Cliffordshaw's *Delinquency Areas* or Cressey's *The Taxi Dance Hall*.

However, while the 1920s and early 1930s showed high enthusiasm and productive effort in the human ecology theory of the city, the middle and late 1930s, saw an increasing amount of criticism of the ecological stance on both theoretical and empirical fronts (Hoyt 1939; Mukerjee 1940). Critics like Homer Hoyt compiled the Federal Housing Administration's report, *The Structure and Growth of Residential Neighbourhoods in American Cities* on the basis of rental data collected from a large number of cities. Hoyt evolved a new model of urban structure, which was different from the zonal pattern of Burgess. Tracing the movement of the high status residential neighbourhood, he emphasized the importance of the radial routes outwards from the centre of the cities and showed the way by which the high status areas determined much of the other patterning within the city. Such areas themselves, once established in a certain sector of the city, would tend to grow or expand outwards within that sector. Other sectors, which begin to grow as low rent residential sectors, similarly retain the same character for long distances outwards, as the low rent housing extends with the process of urban expansion. Assigning prime importance to the high rent sector, Hoyt then suggested that the point of origin of this sector was determined by a number of considerations. Its growth proceeds along lines of travel, or towards another nucleus of buildings or trading centres. It progresses towards raised areas, free from the risk of flooding and along bay and water front areas, where such areas are not pre-empted by industrial development. Growth occurs along areas of open country avoiding 'dead-end' sections. Thus, Hoyt made a modification of the Burgess model, which called attention to occasional radial landuse sectors overlaying zones.

The Chicago School of Human Ecology confined its theory and investigation to sub-social, spatial and competitive aspects of human society. It was assumed that community ecology determined the structure of economic, political and moral life in the city. When this social ecology theory of urban industrial complex was gaining popularity in the West, the first constructive, systematic and theoretical work on social ecology was brought out by Radha Kamal Mukerjee in India. He defined social or human ecology as a 'synoptic study of plant, animal and human communities, which are systems of correlated working parts in the organization of the region' (Mukerjee 1940: vii). According to him, the region exhibits a complex pattern of adaptations between environmental factors and plant and animal communities including human societies. His interpretation and analysis of changes in the regional structure was based on the use of concepts like balance, competition, competitive cooperation, distribution, organization, stratification and succession.

Mukerjee's interpretation of social ecology was a major departure from the stand taken by the Chicago School of Sociology. First, he did not overemphasize the spatial aspects of regions. Second, he took into account not only competition but also cooperation. Also, he did not make the erroneous distinction between social and subsocial aspects of human life, and recognized the importance of culture in human ecological relations.

Hawley also differed from the classical concepts of human ecology theory and its preoccupation with subsocial and spatial aspects of human community and the concept of competition. According to him, the collective life of human beings, like all other organisms revolves around two axes simultaneously, one of which is symbiotic and the other commensalistic. Each represents a peculiar and complementary integrative force, and together they constitute the basis of community cohesion (Hawley 1950). Thus, Hawley's approach to ecology included social aspects of human community, i.e. the aspects of both cooperation and competition (symbiotic and commensalistic), and reduced the emphasis on spatial patterns. Another important aspect of Hawley's theory is his emphasis upon human possession of culture. He observed, 'each acquisition of a new technique or a new use of an old technique regardless of the sources of its origin alters man's relation with the organisms about him, and changes his position in the biotic community' (ibid). He regarded the technology and social organization as aspects of culture. In his view, it is the possession of culture, which enables human beings to develop the potentiality to modify the environment, recognizing thereby the essential difference between human ecology and biological ecology that his predecessors failed to make out. According to Hawley, human ecology deals with the functional system of relationships of a territorially based human population, i.e. the social organization of a local community. Thus, his approach distinguished itself from that of the earlier theorists, who were preoccupied with spatial configurations of human community. In considering that the realm of human ecology is the study of the form and the functioning of the community and of the development of the community, he discusses the nature of ecological organization in terms of three aspects: differentiation, community structure and spatial structure. For him ecological organization refers to the complex of functional interrelationships by which men live and community is the basic unit of ecological investigation. The difference between community and ecological organization is a matter of degree; the former is applied to a relatively small territory, whereas the latter may extend over an area of unlimited scope.

Using Hawley's theory, Duncan refined his own ecological theory, to make it more succinct and wider in scope. His framework of human ecology constitutes the four variables of population, environment, organization and technology (Duncan 1959). According to him, a spatially delimited human population enters into a process of continuous and dynamic interaction with environment to produce its sustenance. This interaction in terms of adjustment or adaptation is greatly facilitated and complicated by man's possession of culture. In this frame of reference, the two variables—social organization and technology become the focus of interest as aspects of culture. The concept of technology in human ecology refers not merely to a complex of art and artifact whose patterns are invented, diffused and accumulated, but to a set of techniques employed by the population to gain sustenance from its environment and to facilitate the organization of sustenance activity (Duncan 1959: 682).

Although, human ecology was initially developed as the study of urban community and its structure in spatial aspects, according to Hawley, it has developed along two related and distinguishable lines of investigation. One aspect pertains to the study of the form and development of urban organization, and the other with how human social systems of various types develop in different environmental settings (Hawley 1981). These are not totally distinct from one another—the first may be regarded as a special case of the latter. Notwithstanding many criticisms of the earlier ecological theory of the city, it has been noticed that Burgess's concentric zone concept still exhibits a remarkable persistence. The findings of many studies confirm that the distribution of housing types and the occupational, educational and family characteristics of the city residents exhibit a gradient pattern of variation from lower to higher values with increasing distance from the central business district.

The Western ecology model however, does not seem to account for the urbanization pattern in developing countries especially that of India. From his study of the Bangalore city in India, Noel P. Gist remarked that the part played by space and nature in patterning human habitat and in distributing social institutions therein can be characterized as limiting and not determining. Within a given frame of limitation it may be assumed that culture would play a positive role in shaping the human environment and arranging the human groups therein. In Western cities 'slum' is found to be an area in transition resulting from the interaction of the ecological processes of invasion and succession where a city's inhabitants and techno-economic agencies interact. Whereas in India, the slum is an integral part of urban structure with a fringe ward movement (Gist 1957). The available data on Indian cities reveal that these centres do not display any clear-cut functional division in their landuse. The same unit is often found being used for residential and business purposes (Breese 1966). According to Gist, the classical urban pattern of Indian cities may be summarised as follows: high income groups live nearer to the centre of the city, which is the social and institutional heart of the community, whereas the residence of the low income groups are located near the periphery. Economic establishments tend to be dispersed throughout the city, instead of getting highly centralized and suburban growth from residential decentralization is limited (Gist 1957).

URBAN STUDIES IN INDIA

Gist's observation has been followed by several other studies on the internal structure of urban settlements in India. These studies highlight the spatial relationships between the economic and sociocultural organizations, which gives rise to typical morphological forms. While several of them are simple descriptions of the morphological patterns of urban complexes like Ranchi-Dhurwa, Durg-Bhilai, Begusarai and Chittaranjan (Ahmad and Srivastava 1976; Agarwal 1976; Anal 1972; Bhattacharjee and Basak 1970), others attempt to account for the urban morphological patterns. Sardar Singh Dhabriya's study of several towns in Rajasthan, S.P. Mathur's study of Dehradun and R.L. Singh's study of Varanasi, regard local history as accounting for the urban ecology (Dhabriya 1973; Mathur 1973; Singh 1973 and 1976). Again Bijit Ghosh and K.C. Mago's study of Srirangam shows how the town is structured around its holy temple (Ghosh and Mago 1971).

Some scholars have attempted to adopt a comparative method of study to highlight the uniqueness of urban morphology in India. Manzoor Alam in his study of Hyderabad city points out that although the socio-economic structure of this city is typical of most Indian cities, it is distinct from the ecological pattern of Western cities (Alam 1976). Viswanadham's comparative study of the ecological structures of Hyderabad and a few large urban centres of the United States show more differences than similarities in the internal structure of Indian and Western cities (Viswanadham 1977). The above view is substantiated by the American urban geographer John E. Brush, according to whom the Indian city patterns are too complicated to be subsumed under any single theoretical model. According to him, the Indian city patterns may be regarded as representing a transitional stage between the pre-industrial and the industrial models of urban development (Brush 1970 and 1977).

Another approach attempts to explain the patterns of the Indian cities by relating the population distribution and formation of ethnic pockets in cities to their morphological patterns. In this regard Brush's study has been highly influential. He noted that the Indian city reveals a unique distribution of population density to the pattern (Brush 1968 and 1973). The study of Indian metropolitan cities such as Kolkata, Chennai and Mumbai by using the techniques of Shevky-Bell Social Area Analysis by Berry and Rees, Weinstein, Narain and Jain and the delineation of broad ecological pattern in terms of ethnic and socio-economic features of population in Aurangabad city by

Kulkarni and a few other Indian cities by Tewari et al. may be classified under the above category (Berry and Rees 1969; Weinstein 1974; Narain and Jain, 1976; Kulkarni 1976; Tewari et al. 1986). Among such studies, Prakasa Rao and Tewari's study of Bangalore has thrown several interesting insights about urban morphology and urban social structure. The study shows that urban settlement patterns also reveal caste and class gradients. While the upper castes are located in the city centre, gradually with the expansion of the city they are moving towards the periphery and leaving the poor in the degraded interstices between the periphery and centre (Prakasa Rao and Tewari 1979).

Most of the sociological studies of urbanization have not, however, been influenced by the Chicago School. These studies have focussed on migration patterns, slums and related problems such as urban poverty and crime, studies of selected communities in cities, social mobility and the like (D'Souza 1970 and 1978; de Souza 1978; Singh 1978; Rao 1986 and 1974; Muttagi 1976; Ross 1969; Punekar 1970; George 1971; Saberwal 1976 and 1978). These studies have thrown light on several important social dimensions of urbanization and it can be said that migration to urban areas follow the paths opened by caste, community and kinship ties (Rao 1974, 1976 and 1986; Holmstrom 1985). Such patterning of urban migration also determines the social composition of urban neighbourhoods and have highlighted the fact that these clusters of caste and ethnic communities have accounted for the continued influence of caste and other ethnic factors in the urban society (Rao 1974; Saberwal 1978; Panini 1986; Bose 1968; Patel 1963; Mythili 1974).

The growing international concern over environmental pollution in industrial and urban centres of both developed and developing countries has, of late, drawn the attention of a wide range of researchers. As early as 1971, the *Civic Affairs* journal carried a brief report of various studies relating to water and air pollution in the cities of Mumbai, Kanpur, Kolkata, Delhi and Agra. Other studies of Indian cities have also focussed on the problems of air and water pollution, inadequate supply of basic services, housing, population explosion, traffic congestion and the like and warned against the imminent danger of urban implosion (Pal 1972; Bulsara 1969;

Sivaramakrishnan 1971; Bonarjee 1973; Chatterjee and Ghosh 1973; Bladden and Karan 1977).

It may be noted here from the above brief survey of urban studies, that there have been very few attempts made to interrelate urban morphology, its social and economic structure and problems of environmental degradation in the cities. It is contended now that only when these factors are interrelated it will be possible to get a better idea of the urban social problems and the ecological crisis faced by several Indian cities.

Hence, the study seeks to concentrate on the backward and forward linkages that connect the city with its hinterland. The modern city while relying on energy and resource intensive technology affects the wider ecological system within which it is located. Therefore, an attempt is made in the subsequent sections to evolve a suitable model to properly grasp the social and ecological effects of modern industrialization and urbanization. This requires a proper understanding of the analyses of the current ecological crisis, which is attempted in the following section.

THEORETICAL ANALYSIS OF ENVIRONMENTAL CRISIS

The current debate on ecological crisis arising from large scale industrialization and urbanization is mainly based on two schools of thought. One school led by the Marxists says that the capitalist mode of production along with its distribution system and market leads to ecological crisis due to misutilization of natural resources and unequal distribution of goods and services. According to them, since the capitalist mode of production is based on profits and prosperity of the bourgeoisie and exploitation of the proletariat, the large scale manifestation of poverty and marginal settlements in terms of slums and squatter settlements adjacent to the factory areas and market followed by the inadequate provision of civic amenities, exacerbates environmental pollution of the region. The increasing profit motive of the capitalist class coupled with an expanding consumerism results in reckless exploitation of both renewable and nonrenewable resources ignoring their ecological effects in the long run (Fyodorov and Novik 1977; Kolbasov 1983; Ursul 1983; Gorizontov 1985).

Another variant of the Marxist approach views the contemporary environmental problems basically as a contradiction between inherently expansionist capitalist system and the finite resources of the earth. Economic expansion reflects the law of increasing firm size and the rise of big monopoly houses. Economic growth has historically permitted rising material standards for the working class and the consequent weakening of class conflict. It is therefore, anticipated that progressive environmental degradation will limit growth led solutions to class struggles. From this perspective, environmental problems are viewed as another emerging contradiction in an advanced capitalist society (Hardesty et al. 1971; England and Bluestone 1973; Salgo 1973; Enzenberger 1974).

By applying neo-Marxist theory to current ecological problems some of the scholars further add that despite low level of industrialization and urbanization the developing countries are becoming seats of acute environmental crisis because of their subordinate relationship with the developed capitalist countries of the world. According to them, the developed capitalist countries are exploiting cheap labour and natural resources of the developing countries and passing on their ecological crisis to them by taking advantage of their technological superiority and capital. In recent years many of the multinational corporations in the West, producing ecologically hazardous goods have shifted their venue of production to the developing countries, as there is strong protest from their more conscious citizens to ban and close down such factories, whose functioning affects the local environment adversely. For instance, DDT and BHC have been banned in the USA for over two decades, but continue to be produced, imported and used in India. Like this, as the production and use of asbestos declined sharply in the developed countries because of known health hazards like asbestosis, plants manufacturing asbestos were shifted to developing countries. Several American and European manufacturers have set up plants and collaborations in India to manufacture asbestos, asbestos cement, brake linings, etc. (Agarwal et al. 1985: 28). In contrast to this, the liberal non-Marxist school propagating the culture of free market economy for rapid economic growth and improving living standard, holds the view that the current ecological crisis is the effect of population explosion and use of wrong technology. Therefore, according to this school of thought, the emerging eco-crisis is mainly due to the use of obsolete technology, which is incapable of controlling the level of environmental pollution and unplanned utilization of scarce economic resources. They say that the current crisis can be averted by devising appropriate alternative technology that controls the rate of effluents and nondegradable biochemical wastes discharged into the atmosphere. Moreover, this alternative, environment-friendly technology will preserve the ecological balance and economize the use of scarce resources. According to Barry Commoner, the technologies that we have used for the last 75 years, to accelerate production and economic development are not eco-friendly and unfortunately they have been in use long before we were aware of their detrimental effects. He comments that the new technology is an economic success but because it is an ecological failure, he goes on to point out: 'We are concerned not with some fault in technology which is only coincident to its value, but with a failure that results from its basic success in industrial and agricultural production. If the ecological failure of modern technology is due to its success in accomplishing what it sets out to do, then the fault lies in its aims' (Commoner 1971: 186). However, Paul Ehrlich, Professor of Biology, with a particular interest in entomology, population dynamics and evolution, expresses his displeasure about the way Commoner has reduced population growth to a very small factor responsible for eco-crisis. He calls this one-dimensional ecology and argues that taking a base in 1900, and only treating the 75 years, which follow may have made the data more accessible and reliable. But it has hidden the fact that the impact of ecological crisis started since the time man moved into settled agriculture. According to him, the sheer pressure of numbers, the inertia of population growth, the social consequences of drought, famine and diseases are likely to be the significant fallout of our impending eco-catastrophe. The Ehrlichs, in their monumental work, *Population, Resources and Environment* (1972) highlight these aspects and also indict misguided technology. They frequently refer to the need to limit economic growth and also emphasize that population control is absolutely essential if the problems now facing human are to be solved.

The views mentioned above consider ecological crisis as the product of rapid economic growth and population explosion. What is missing is a sociological perspective, which locates ecological crisis firmly in the social structure and culture. Recent research by social scientists on environmental problems is found to be influenced by the early works of Emile Durkheim and Max Weber, to a great extent. A number of social scientists have adopted Durkheim's methodological posture of seeking to explain environmental problems in cultural terms. They say that the environmental degradation as noticed in modern urban-industrial society is a manifestation of 'inappropriately' shared social values. The modern values which facilitate structural differentiation of society, democracy, free market economy, universalistic achievement-oriented social order and other desirable elements also promote an over-aggressive individualism and an unbalanced view of economic development at the cost of exploitation of scarce resources, pollution of the biosphere resulting in ecological imbalances (Caldwell 1970; Klausner 1971; Wengert 1972). Ruff argues that a relatively high density of population and depletion of scarce natural resources are endemic in all industrial societies whether they are under capitalistic or socialistic form of government (Ruff 1972). Environmental externalities generated by the urban-industrial firms have social costs and benefits, which are not reflected in the balance sheets. For firms or individuals to 'internalize' these 'externalities', changes in shared values and positive attitude towards the need of a clean environment are necessary. These values will have to be institutionalized in the state and other organizations including the legal system. In any event, environmental problems are largely seen as the unanticipated consequence of industrialization, urbanization, structural differentiation and 'modernism'.

However, in the Weberian perspective environmental problems are viewed as another aspect of structure of power in the society. The Weberian scholars, argue that the elites of economic and political institutions make reckless exploitation of natural resources by legitimizing the ideology of economic expansionism. Although this philosophy has clearly indicated some economic benefits for the underprivileged, but the dominant strata of the society has reaped qualitatively larger benefits and power. Thus, Ridgeway writes that the 'value' of economic expansion or growth ignoring the ecology is the superordinate stratum's ideology imposed on subordinate strata through cultural institutions (Ridgeway 1971).

The above-mentioned sociological approaches including the Marxist approach to ecological crisis adopt mono-causal mode of explanation. Each of these approaches refers to critical factors like economic, social, cultural and political. But an adequate understanding of ecological crisis demands a different approach altogether. After all, it is now recognized that ecological crisis is the product of an interplay of social, cultural, political and economic factors with the natural environment. Even technology, which plays a critical role in shaping the environment, has to be seen as the product of interplay of such factors. Hence, in this study an attempt has been made to treat the ongoing ecological problems as the outcome of interactions between industry, ecology and society.

INTERRELATIONSHIPS BETWEEN INDUSTRY, ECOLOGY AND SOCIETY: TOWARDS A THEORETICAL FRAMEWORK

It has been found that there is a fundamental relationship existing between industry, ecology and the society. Industry here signifies the economic activity of factory based production of goods and services with the help of modern machinery and technology. Ecology here indicates the ecosystem or natural environment in which interactions between the living and nonliving organisms take place. Similarly, society here means the human settlements both rural and urban. Of all the living beings, man alone has the greatest adaptive capability to survive in different environmental surroundings, and he is the only creature endowed with a high intellectual capability to alter the environment according to his needs. It has been observed that human settlement patterns and the economic and social systems have evolved according to the natural resource base of the region. For example, the fertile land and favourable climatic conditions in the Indo-Gangetic plain have allowed the growth of densely populated urban and rural settlements with a predominantly agricultural economy. Similarly, the mineral-rich Chotanagpur plateau has encouraged the growth of many large industrial centres and new urban settlements in the recent past such as Bhilai, Rourkela, Bokaro, Ranchi, Jamshedpur, Durgapur and Chittaranjan; whereas in the desert areas of Rajasthan, due to adverse environmental conditions, human settlements are sparsely populated

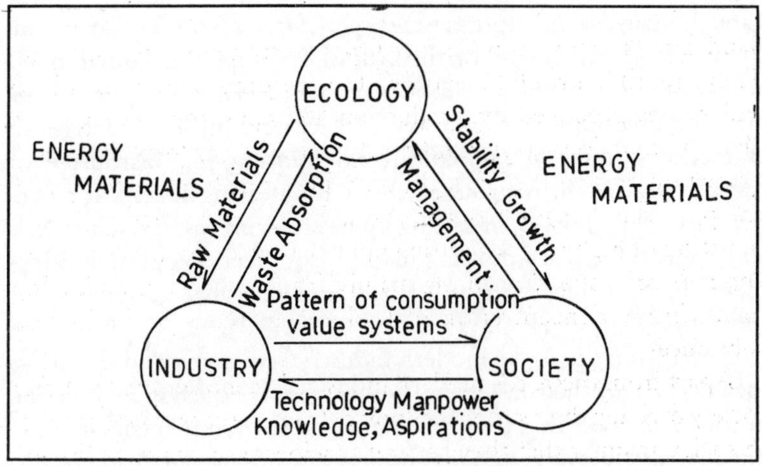

Fig. 2.1: Interrelations between Industry, Ecology and Society

and people are forced to lead a pastoral and nomadic life. It is, therefore, invention and innovation of science and technology that has enabled man to develop a new form of materialistic civilization by either controlling or altering the existing ecosystem commensurate with his personal needs (Mumford 1955).

However, there is a tolerance limit of an ecological region. Symbiotic relationships between living organisms and their environment are now being tampered by modern technology. It is now well known that industrialization is consuming renewable as well as nonrenewable resources so rapidly that the actual carrying and regenerating capacity of ecosphere is threatened. Effluents and wastes that are being discharged into the biosphere are exceeding the assimilating and recuperating capacity of the environment. Environmental degradation in turn poses problems for human survival. In their process of interaction, the ecology, the industry and the society affect one another in various ways. According to Dasgupta (1978), the ecosystem or the environment performs three basic functions with relation to man. They are (i) provision of amenities like enjoyable landscape for recreation, (ii) provision of natural resources, minerals, etc., (iii) absorption and assimilation of wastes produced by human beings; ranging from sewage disposal to carbon dioxide emitted by the respiration process. On the other hand, human action imposes four types of stresses on the ecosystem. They are: (i) 'eutrophic' or the task of decomposing human body and wastes produced by production and consumption activities, viz., the functioning of industry and society, (ii) 'exploitative' or extraction of minerals, agriculture and hunting, (iii) 'disruptive' or the physical changes brought about by clearing forests for construction of highways, or setting up new townships, (iv) 'chemicals and industrial stress' resulting mainly from technological development, heavy concentration of lead and mercury or radioactive substances.

Apart from these, the modern industrial economy and the urban society deriving their sustenance power from the ecosystem, function in such a manner that they generate socioeconomic inequality and unequal distribution of goods and services among the various strata of population. This leads to unhealthy development relationships in the society, where one section of people monopolize over a major portion of the goods and services, and the underprivileged sections are left with meagre resources. The lack of easy access to technology and basic services among the deprived groups exerts pressure on the environment, and sometimes exacerbates the rate of environmental pollution and ecological degradation due to misutilization and overexploitation of the available resources. The value systems and existing rules and regulations for the distribution of goods and services in the society also generate stress and crisis in the ecosystem if such patterns of distribution ignore the needs of the majority.

Some scholars such as Odum (1983) and Biplab Dasgupta (1978) have sought to analyse the deepening ecological crisis in terms of industry-ecology interrelationships. Odum develops the classification of life support systems in the following manner:

System	System attributes
1. Non-biological System (Urban industrial system)	Heterotopic city and industrial system dependent on large areas outside it for energy, fibre, water, etc. High energy consuming hot spots; larger and more poisonous output of waste products.

2. Mature Systems (Protective life support environment)	Old, grown forests, climax vegetation, oceans more protective than productive; stabilize substrata, buffer air and water cycles moderate, extremes in physical factors.
3. Dissipative Systems (Waste assimilative environment)	Natural or semi-natural ecosystems that bear the brunt of assimilating the wastes produced by urban- industrial and agricultural environments, e.g. inland and coastal waterways.
4. Growth Systems (Productive life support environment)	Early successional or growth type ecosystems such as croplands, pastures, tree plantations & intensively managed forests.

According to Odum, the non-biological system i.e. the urban-industrial system is supported by the other three systems. Ecological crisis for Odum therefore, is the runaway growth of the non-biological system, which weakens the capacity of the other systems sustaining it (Odum 1983). This analysis focuses attention on the dynamics of urban-industrial system as the major cause of ecological imbalance. It is important however, to recognize that the urban industrial system that Odum refers to implicates the society as well. Hence, it is important to grasp the social and economic forces that generate rapid industrialization. Further, while studying the implications of industrialization on ecology it is necessary to take into account the social consequences of industrialization, so that it is possible to evolve organizations and institutions which can sustain the balance between industry and society. Therefore in this research study, the ecological and social effects of industrialization will be assessed after analysing the role of social and economic forces that contribute to rapid industrialization. Thus our heuristic model, stresses more on the interrelationships between industry and society on the one hand, and industry and ecology on the other.

CHAPTER 3

Pre-Industrial Rourkela: An Analysis of Regional Ecology, Society and the Economy

Rourkela city, which is located in the erstwhile region of Gangpur State of the British era, owes its emergence to the Government of India's decision of locating the country's first public sector steel plant in the region. The construction of the steel plant began in the late 1950s in collaboration with Krupp Demag of the then West Germany. The city is located between 84° 50' east longitude and 22° 15' north latitude, at a distance of 413 km. from Kolkata. The main Howrah-Mumbai railway line passes through the city. The city is a part of Panposh subdivision of Sundergarh district in Orissa and the present Rourkela region covers an area of approximately 200 sq. km. The region previously consisted of 98 residential villages under the jurisdiction of three police stations namely Raghunathpali, Kalunga and Bisra. It is situated in a valley formed by the intersection of the Koel and Sankh rivers. The two rivers meet each other at Vedavyas near Rourkela and form the river Brahmani, a tributary of river Mahanadi. The valley is at an altitude of 150 to 300 mt. above sea level and is a fairly flat and open country interspersed with a few ridges. These ridges were once covered with green vegetation, which provided a picturesque backdrop surrounding the steel plant and township.

The climate of the region is hot and dry. During the months of December and January, it experiences a moderate winter. But the summers are severe with the maximum temperature reaching up to 45 °C. The rainy season lasts from June to September and the average rainfall of the region is around 150 cm.

The region that has become most industrialized and prosperous in Orissa after the location of the steel plant was once upon a time a green and hilly terrain. It was home for many tribals such as Oraons, Mundas, Kharias, Kisans, Bhuiyans, Bhumijs, etc. So, in order to know how and under what circumstances the present industrial city of Rourkela grew up, I make an effort in this chapter to highlight the ecological history of the region.

HISTORICAL BACKGROUND

With the Central Government's decision to locate a public sector steel plant at Rourkela, the Revenue Department of the Government of Orissa published a notification in the State Gazetteer on the 22 February 1954 specifying an area of about 200 sq. km. to be acquired for the development of industries, and establishment of a steel plant with allied and ancillary industries in an area around Rourkela comprising 92 revenue villages, which further consisted of 98 residential villages. The socioeconomic survey of the area conducted by the State Government under the supervision of S. Misra, revealed that these villages consisted of 5,363 households with a population of 33,041. Of the total population there was 26.6 per cent Hindus, 9.6 per cent scheduled castes, 45.3 per cent scheduled tribes and other religious groups such as Muslims and Christians were 18.5 per cent. Of the last category, Christian population formed 83.7 per cent; most of them being scheduled tribes (Misra 1958). Thus, the region was a predominantly tribal area just like the other parts of Sundergarh, in which it is located. As per the 1951 census, of the district's total population, 56.6 per cent belonged to scheduled tribes.

ECOLOGY OF THE REGION

Topography

Sundergarh district, in which Rourkela is situated, falls in the Chotanagpur plateau. It is not a compact region geographically. It consists of expansive and fairly open country dotted with tree-clad isolated hills, vast inaccessible forests, extensive river valleys and rugged terrain of different elevations broken up by torrential hill streams. The region is drained by the Ibb and Brahmani rivers.

The general slope of the land is from north to south (Senapati 1975: 5).

Two physically dissimilar tracts, one on the north and the other on the south has been clearly demarcated by the South-Eastern Railway line passing through the Panposh subdivision (Rourkela region), from east to west. The block to the north formed by the valley of the Sankh and the south by the Koel and Deo, although are interspersed with isolated hills and a series of small ridges striking east and west, is generally plain. The tract to the south is more hilly and wooded excepting the valley of the Brahmani, which extends to an appreciable distance south of Panposh. The region extending from south of Bisra to south of Chirobeda is much broken and hilly. It rises along the Singhbhum and Bonai boundaries to an elevation of 550 to 600 mt. The highest peak of the region is *Bhainsamunda Pahar* with an elevation of 680 mt. In the plains, the elevation is about 180 to 220 mt. The lowest elevation is only 175 mt. near Banki village in the Brahmani valley on the Bonai border. The land is highly denuded and stripped of its fertility and large tracts of ravines and rocky grounds are found. Before the setting up of the steel plant at Rourkela the area was fully covered by the Sal (*Shorea robusta*) forests (Senapati 1975: 5).

As far as the topography of the Rourkela industrial belt is concerned, there is a range of hillocks to the north of the railway track that runs east to west at Rourkela. The Brahmani river, which crosses the railway line from north to south has taken a sharp turn towards southeast on the southern side of the railway. The general slope of the area is from the hillocks on the northern boundary towards the river which forms the southern boundary of the Rourkela steel plant. The whole area comes under the laterite soil, which is highly suitable for heavy foundations and construction.

FOREST, FLORA AND FAUNA

Over 70 per cent of the total land area in Sundergarh district is classified under forest. The reserve forests cover 2,562 sq. km. and the protected forest 3,264 sq. km. The district is divided into two forest divisions, viz., Sundergarh division and Bonai division. The forests are of tropical dry deciduous type with a mixed variety of trees, Sal, being the dominant species here. Other varieties of trees found are Asan or Sahaj (*Terminalia tomantosa*), Kurum (*Adina cordifolia*), Bija or Piasal (*Pterocarpus marsupium*), Gambhari (*Gmelina arborea*), Kusum (*Scheleichera trijuga*), Aonla (*Phyllonthus emblica*), the Mahula or Mahua (*Bassia latifolia*), Karda (*Claistanthus colinus*), the fruit of Char (*Buchanania latifolia*), Sunari (*Casia fisiula*), Tendu or Kendu (*Diospyros melanxylon*), Khair (*Acacia catechu*), Shisham or Sisoo (*Dalbergia latifolia*), etc. The species of shrubs and grass mainly consists of Dhatuki (*Woodfordia fruiticosa*), Telai (*Wendlandia excerta*), Harsinghar (*Nyctanthes arbor-tristis*), Kurdu (*Gardenia summifera*), and Sabai or Panasi (*Eulaliopsis binata*) (Senapati 1975: 29-30).

In keeping with the nature of forests, Sundergarh district had a rich wildlife. Before the advent of industrialization and urbanization in the region, the forest had a fairly large population of elephants, tiger, panther, hyaena, wild dog, jackal, bison, wild buffalo, fox, deer, bear, *sambar*, boar, *langoor*, etc. Peacock, black and grey partridge, red spur fowl and painted spur fowl are the more common birds. The reptiles mainly consist of cobra, krait and python.

With the opening up of the region by modern transport and communications; and with industrialization and urbanization, the forested area of the district had shrunk. Cobden-Ramsay in his study of the Feudatory State, Gangpur in the early part of the twentieth century writes that the estate of Himgir and Nagra (Panposh subdivision comprising of Rourkela) and certain portions of the Khalsa or chief's own domain contained stretches of Sal forest, which was destroyed with the opening of the Bengal-Nagpur railway track through the State. The forests were recklessly exploited on all sides and little or no timber of any size was left except in the Khalsa, along the Ranchi plateau. The destruction of the vegetation has been enormous and large forest tracts of Himgir, Kinjir and Nagra were entirely wiped out. The advent of railways proved to be the death-knell of the wild buffalo, which was once quite plentiful in Gangpur State, along the valley of the river Brahmani (Cobden-Ramsay 1910). The primary jungle products such as lac, tusser silk, resin and catechu, which were a source of livelihood of the tribals and scheduled castes like *Gandas* and *Ghasis* are no longer available. In spite of the deforestation that started in the beginning of the twentieth century, it was revealed from the discussion held with an elderly *sanyasi* residing at Vedavyas near Rourkela, mentioned that the plant site and township area was full of forests and wild animals before the location of the steel plant. The adjacent villages were inaccessible because of thick forest cover. Although agriculture was the main occupation of the people, the yield was very low due to the use of primitive technology. Forest products were the main source of livelihood of the tribals and they had hardly known the use of clothes. They were mostly clad in barks and even some of them were moving about naked. The economy of the region was based on food-gathering.

ECONOMY AND SOCIETY

Land and the People

Sundergarh region was inhabited by man since the early palaeolithic age as evidenced from the findings of early stone age tools in various parts of the district (Senapati 1975). It may be mentioned here that the present Sundergarh district consists of two ex-feudal States of Gangpur and Bonai. The area was mainly inhabited by the Bhuiyans. During his tour in 1863-4, Colonel T Dalton found Bonai 'for the most part a mass of uninhabited hills, only of the whole one, 1/12th being under cultivation'. He observed 83 deserted villages in the State. People were emigrating to neighbouring States because of the oppressive land revenue system. However, during the last quarter of the nineteenth century, the new ruler Dayanidhi Deo granted various concessions to people. He even encouraged Mundas, Oraon and other people from Ranchi and Singhbhum to come into his State and occupy jungle areas on easy terms. According to Dalton's accounts, there were 217 inhabited villages in Bonai State in the nineteenth century, with an estimated population of roughly 15,600. Of this, about half of the agricultural population were the Bhuiyans. He further mentioned that the Bonai hills sheltered some thousands of tribals, commonly called Coles, who at some period of time emigrated from Singhbhum in the Chotanagpur plateau. They had not benefited in any way by the change although their brethren in the Chotanagpur region were better off. These emigrants to the Bonai hills found the old country becoming too civilized for them and so, they fled from their original homes they had been, to hide themselves in the hill forests and gradually their condition worsened.

The State of Gangpur was twice the size of Bonai State, with an area of about 7,680 sq. km., as per Dalton's account in the late nineteenth century. Of its total land area only one-tenth was under cultivation. Like in the Bonai State the Bhuiyans formed the majority of the population in Gangpur State. They were the first settlers and all the Zamindars under the Rajah belonged to that race, says Dalton. The Oraons, Mundas and Kharias generally called Coles, were emigrants from the Chotanagpur plateau of Bihar. As most of the land in Gangpur State was lying uninhabited and the region was malaria prone, the Rajah and Zamindars had encouraged the tribals from Ranchi and Singhbhum to settle in their territories by clearing forests and making the land habitable. Dalton mentions that the new settlers were given three years of absolute immunity from revenue of every kind and in the fourth year they were called on to pay a light assessment. According to Dalton the Coles, who had migrated from the Ranchi-Singhbhum belt were evidently a good pioneering race, fond of new clearings and the luxuriant and easily raised crops of the virgin soil and had constitutions that thrived on malaria (Senapati 1975).

Although the present district of Sundergarh is still one of the sparsely populated districts of Orissa, between 1901 and 1951 its population almost doubled. Laying of railway tracks through this district was an important factor in the opening up of certain areas. During the period 1911 to 1921, dolomite and limestone deposits were found in Rajgangpur and Raghunathpali (modern Rourkela region). Reclamation of waste lands was taken up and cultivable area was extended. In 1922, railway line was extended upto Biramitrapur, and the limestone and manganese quarries were developed further. By the year 1951, the district had been through with certain amount of industrialization. A cement factory was started at Rajgangpur. There was considerable expansion of work in limestone quarries and because of these factors, a good deal of immigration of people into this district occurred particularly from Chotanagpur region. However, the volume of migration in the district was very low upto 1951. From 1961 onwards the region started registering a high population growth, due to rapid industrialization and urbanization occurring from the multiple benefits of the steel plant at Rourkela. At the time of 1961 census, the district had a fairly large number of migrants, who constituted 16 per cent of the total population. Of these, 10 per cent were born outside the State of Orissa.

OCCUPATIONAL STRUCTURE AND ECONOMIC ACTIVITIES

Orissa is primarily an agricultural State. According to the State Economic Survey of 1954, 82.9 per cent of the families in rural Orissa were solely dependent on agriculture. As compared to this 82.3 per cent of the families in rural areas of Sundergarh district, and 84.8 per cent of the families in Rourkela region[1] comprising 98 villages had adopted agriculture as their principal means of livelihood (Misra 1958: 31). The district had a high density of tribal population, accounting for 58.1 per cent of its total population as per the 1961 census. Of the 62 tribes distinguished as scheduled tribes for Orissa, as many as 40 tribes are found in this district alone. The numerically important tribes are Oraon, Munda, Kharia, Kisan, Bhuiyan and Gond. Prior to the exposure of the district to the outsiders, the tribals led a simple and primitive way of life. They were restricted to the remote and less accessible areas of the district. The Oraons, who had migrated from Chotanagpur and Singhbhum, were mostly serving as agricultural labourers. For a long time they did not attempt to procure land for themselves for cultivation, although land was available in plenty. The Mundas, the *Pahari* or hill Kharias and the *Paharia* or hill Bhuiyans were basically living in dense forests. They were mainly food gatherers, collecting honey, silk cocoon, lac, edible herbs and tubers and other minor forest produces.

However, as the region opened up, the tribals also gradually resorted to settled agricultural activity by clearing forests. As mentioned earlier, the Kings and Zamindars of erstwhile States of Bonai and Gangpur also encouraged the immigrant tribals to clear jungles and develop agricultural lands on easy terms and conditions (Senapati 1975).

The Orissa economic survey of 1954 revealed that though the Rourkela region was highly agricultural, the techniques used were very primitive. The region had 84.8 per cent agricultural families and 15.2 per cent non-agricultural families as compared to 82.3 per cent agricultural and 17.7 per cent non-agricultural families, in the case of the rural areas of Sundergarh district, and 82.9 per cent agricultural and 17.1 per cent non-agricultural families respectively, in the case of rural Orissa as a whole. The landowners in the Rourkela region constituted 78.7 per cent of the total number of households, whereas for the district of Sundergarh and the entire rural Orissa the figures were 70.3 per cent and 56.4 per cent respectively. Likewise, while 21.6 per cent of the total number of families in Orissa came under the category of landless agricultural labourers, they constituted only 9.9 per cent and 4.6 per cent respectively in the district of Sundergarh and Rourkela region. Non-owner cultivators were only 1.1 per cent and land owning families, which did not cultivate at all were only three in a thousand. This clearly shows that owner cultivators formed a more influential section of the agricultural population in the Rourkela region. The tribal families of Rourkela were agricultural to even a greater extent. The survey of the region revealed that while 84.3 per cent of the tribal families had adopted agriculture as their main occupation, among the general caste Hindus it was 76.1 per cent and among the scheduled castes, 72.6 per cent (Misra 1958: 32-4).

Of the remaining 15.2 per cent families in the non-agricultural Rourkela region, 5.9 per cent were working as labourers in the forests, mines and quarries, etc., 3.9 per cent were in trade and transport, 3.6 per cent in production other than cultivation and the remaining 1.8 per cent were professionals in service. In comparison to this, the non-agricultural families in rural Orissa and rural Sundergarh, respectively formed 17.1 per cent and 17.7 per cent of the total (Misra 1958: 32-4).

Besides these principal occupations many families in the Rourkela region, were following subsidiary occupations as their earning was insufficient and effective employment of the adult members in the household was highly inadequate. About 73.5 per cent of the total agricultural families had subsidiary occupations to supplement their earnings. Similarly, 45.5 per cent of the non-agricultural families were having subsidiary occupations. Thus agriculture in the Rourkela region was mostly of subsistence nature and it was not in a position to provide adequate employment and earning to the majority of the families.

In his description of the economy of ex-Gangpur State Cobden-Ramsay, also confirms that the principal occupation of the people was agriculture (84.5%), followed by industry (10.8%), trade (1.1%) and other professions (0.4%). There were no indigenous manufacturers in the State. The village weaver made the cloth required by people, but eked out only a precarious livelihood owing to the competition from mill-made goods. Although there were a few lime and manganese quarries, and forest-based industries such as two timber companies at Rourkela and Kalunga, and one factory to compress *sabai* grass at Bisra, these could hardly generate enough employment for the people of the region (Cobden-Ramsay 1910).

The main crops grown in the State were jowar, millet, rice, sugar-cane, oilseeds and tobacco mainly on a subsistence basis. The inferior grades of cereals were grown, not because they were preferred but because they were cheaper to cultivate and could be harvested conveniently.

The northern portions of the State (modern Rourkela and Biramitrapur region) occupied mainly by the tribal people was less fertile and the cultivators were at a disadvantage owing to the ravages of wild animals, ignorance and poverty. But the area resided by the Agrias in the Ibb valley in southern part of the State was fertile. The Agrias are a sturdy agriculturist caste. They constructed reservoirs to irrigate large areas and displayed con-siderable engineering skill. The condition of these cultivators was, on the whole, prosperous. General living conditions of the tenant cultivators was good; prices were low and rent assessment was very light. No rent was required to be paid for the vast tracts of upland cultivation and in return *begari* or free labour was rendered to the State and certain *Panchas* or contributions in kind were made (Senapati op. cit.).

LAND AND REVENUE SYSTEM

There was no regular settlement system of land in Gangpur State. The rent for land was paid to the ruler according to the seed capacity, e.g. land which required 4 maunds (150 kgs) of paddy for sowing paid Rs. 3-14-6 in cash, 30 seers of rice and 3 seers of *birhi* in kind (Cobden-Ramsay 1910: 182). Sir W. Hunter, in his statistical account of the Chotanagpur States, has described that villages in the Gangpur State were classified as *kut* and *akut* villages (Cobden-Ramsay 1910: 182). The *kut* villages were those where a rough estimate by the eye had been made of the cultivated lands and were practically entirely held by the *gaontias* or village headmen. They held the land under a simple household tenure for a period of three to five years. This was not hereditary and it was usually not held by any of the indigenous tribes. The *gaontia* paid a stated annual rent and was remunerated by the surplus collections from the tenants on account of new lands brought into cultivation and by certain *bhogra* or service lands held rent-free. On the other hand, the *Akut* villages were those in which no eye estimate had been made and the heads of these villages were known as *ganjhus*. The *ganjhu* was usually the original clearer of the soil or a direct descendant. He was superior in position to that of a *gaontia* and he paid nothing in case of inheritance during the currency of his lease, whereas the latter had to pay regular fees for mutation. In the Nagra Zamindari area (modern Panposh subdivision) the *ganjhus* were very powerful. Many of them had actually asserted claims to the forest in their villages and tried for years to style themselves *shikmi zamindars* (under).

PATTERNS OF LAND HOLDING AND DISTRIBUTION

According to the findings of the Economic Survey of Orissa, 1954, man-land ratio was the highest in Sundergarh district. The per capita availability of agricultural land in the year of survey was only 0.82 acre in Orissa as a whole, whereas the per capita supply of agricultural land in Sundergarh district and Rourkela region respectively were of 1.27 acres and 1.17 acres (Misra 1958: 48). The land-man ratio in Sundergarh district also started declining with the advent of railways resulting in significant immigration of tribals from Chotanagpur. The census report of 1951 pointed out that the per capita cultivated area in Sundergarh had declined by about 30 per cent since 1921. Notwithstanding this in 1954, the average size of land holding in the district of Sundergarh and Rourkela region respectively was 7.9 acres and 8 acres, as compared to only 5.1 acres in the State as a whole. Added to this, it was found that land distribution in Sundergarh district and Rourkela region was more equitable and economic than in the State as a whole. As mentioned earlier, the percentage of owner cultivators in the district of Sundergarh and Rourkela region were much higher than in the State. The percentage of small holdings, i.e. below six acres in Rourkela region and Sundergarh district was 51.4 and 56.4 respectively, and the percentage of cultivable land available in this category was 21.1 and 23.1 respectively. Contrary to this, in case of the State as a whole, the percentage of holdings and land under the above category was 76.4 and 36.4 respectively (Misra 1958: 53).

MINERALS

The region being a part of Chotanagpur Plateau was rich in several mineral deposits. However, they had remained unexplored because the dense forests were inaccessible. The important minerals found in the district are iron ore, manganese, limestone, dolomite and fire clay. Besides, the region was also rich in mica, bauxite, quartz, lead, copper, zinc, etc. Commercial exploitation of limestone and dolomite was first started in 12 acres of land at Panposh, Rourkela in 1898. Manganese deposits were first found in 1907. Iron ore was first exploited in the district in early 1950s and the first lease was granted in 1955. The huge deposits of iron ore in Bonai region that remained unexploited in the past were also being tapped.

INDUSTRIES

Before the location of the steel plant at Rourkela, the whole of Sundergarh district was industrially backward despite being rich in mineral resources. Mining and allied activities during British rule were mainly extractive in nature. The older industries in the region was timber located at Rourkela and Kalunga which were set up after the Howrah-Nagpur railway tracks were laid. The local blacksmiths were smelting iron ore, picked up from the surface and producing excellent iron. All the domestic and agricultural implements used throughout the district were made of indigenous iron. Hand spinning and weaving of cotton was one of the oldest industries in the district since cotton was being grown extensively specially in Bonai subdivision. However, with the proliferation of mill-made yarn from Calcutta, in the beginning of the twentieth century, the locally produced articles were ousted. Cotton cultivation was almost stopped and the weavers were reduced to mere wage-earners or petty cultivators. The scheduled castes and tribes like Turi, Dom and Khond made bamboo mats and wicker baskets, etc. The Bhumijs of Bonai were manufacturing soapstone items or *khadi* for domestic use.

Modern industry in the region started with the establishment of the private sector unit, Orissa Cement Co. Ltd. at Rajgangpur in 1948. The huge deposits of limestone and dolomite at Raiboga, Birmitrapur, Hatibari, Lanjiberna and Kiringsera of Panposh region provided large quantities of raw material needed for the growth of this industry.

GENERAL LIVING CONDITIONS

The tribal people of Sundergarh district hardly practised any kind of cultivation. Poultry, dairy farming and piggery were found at the domestic level. The important source of livelihood of these people were hand-pounding of rice, pottery, basket weaving, rope making and stitching '*siali*' leaves. The people were dependent upon the forests to a great extent. They searched the forests for edible roots, leaves, fruits and flowers for their living. Collecting minor forest products like *myrobalans*, *mahua* flowers and seeds, *dhatuki* flowers, resins, etc., was an important subsidiary source of income. Till the 1960s these forest products were sold or exchanged in the weekly markets to procure salt, rice, and other household items.

The economy of the region was highly unstable in nature. It is reported that during the early twentieth century the economic condition of the people was good. There was ample room for agricultural expansion, which encouraged immigration from the neighbouring areas of Chotanagpur Plateau. The construction of Bengal-Nagpur railway line through Panposh subdivision opened up the region and contact with other states increased. However, between 1911-20, the district suffered from poor harvests. Epidemics like influenza, cholera and smallpox ravaged the entire region (Senapati 1975: 263-4).

Later the extension of the railway line to Biramitrapur in 1922, coupled with the development of manganese and limestone quarries brought prosperity to the region. But, unfortunately again during the Second World War, the district further suffered from more economic and health crisis. Forests were destroyed in order to supply timber for the war and prosperity in any form was not reflected upon the poor *raiyat* and labourers. Every year there was a large exodus to Jamshedpur and Assam in search of better opportunities.

The economic survey of the Rourkela region comprising 98 villages, conducted by the Government of Orissa, on the eve of the establishment of the steel plant at Rourkela in 1954, revealed that the average living condition of the people was very poor. The per capita income of the people in this region of the Sundergarh district worked out to be around Rs. 144. This was about half of the per capita income for the whole of India. Only those families pursuing trade, services and other profession as their main source of livelihood had a relatively higher level of earning. But they formed only three per cent of the total number of households residing in the region. Agriculture which was the mainstay of the people was in a primitive state and the per capita income of the household engaged in this sector was only Rs. 142.47 per annum, and for the agricultural labour, this was as low as Rs. 117.50 (Misra 1958: 75).

ESTABLISHMENT OF THE STEEL PLANT

However, the socioeconomic condition of the region took an interesting turn just before setting the steel plant. Rourkela Steel Plant was the first to be constructed of the three steel plants proposed during Second Five Year Plan of India. In December 1953, the Government of India signed an agreement with Krupp-Demag of Germany for establishing a half-a-million tonne plant in the public sector. As a follow up, a company named Hindustan Steel Limited (HSL) with an authorized capital of Rs. 100 crore was also formed. However, anticipating an increase in requirements of steel in the future, the government decided to double the capacity of the projected steel plant to one million tonnes. Hence, a supplementary agreement was signed with Krupp-Demag in July 1955, and the revised project report for the enlarged plant was received in November of the same year, with a provision for subsequent expansion of capacity to 1.6 million tonnes at a later stage.

SITE SELECTION

Following the decision to set up the steel plant, a team of experts was assigned the job for selecting a suitable site for the plant. After inspecting many sites, the team finally selected Rourkela for its advantages. The region was rich in good quality iron ore deposits within a radius of 80 km. Limestone and dolomite, the two essential fluxing materials were available within a distance of about 30 km. Manganese was also available in plenty in the nearby mines of Bonai-Keonjhar. Abundant power and water supply was available from Hirakud dam on the Mahanadi river situated at a distance of 150 km. Water supply during the lean season was ensured and an earthen dam was proposed to be constructed on river Sankh at Mandira.

DISPLACEMENT, AGITATIONS AND REHABILITATION

When the Master Plan for the proposed steel plant at Rourkela was drawn up, it became obvious that for the location of the steel plant and ancillary industries and also the various conveniences and servicing institutions, vast stretches of land had to be acquired. In January 1955, the HSL submitted its blue print to the Government of India, indicating the area required for the township, steel plant and other buildings needed at Rourkela. The requirements were drastically changed and by December 1962, the Government of Orissa had handed over to the HSL 19,557 acres land, of which 4,882 acres were government land and the rest was private. Altogether, 30 villages inhabited by around 2,500 households were affected by the acquisition of private land. All these affected villages were mostly inhabited by the tribal people which was about 67.73 per cent of the total population of the region. It can be seen from Table 3.1 that out of 2,467 households, the tribal households in these villages consisted of 67.23 per cent of which the Munda

TABLE 3.1: ETHNIC COMPOSITION OF DISPLACED HOUSEHOLDS OF 30 VILLAGES BEFORE THEIR ACQUISITION BY THE ROURKELA STEEL PLANT

Sl. No.	Ethnic Group	No. of Households	Percentage of Households
1.	Scheduled Tribes	1,671	67.73
	a. Bhumij	315	12.77
	b. Kharia	155	6.28
	c. Kisan	145	5.88
	d. Munda	558	22.62
	e. Oraon	498	20.19
2.	Scheduled Castes	195	7.90
	a. Behera	5	0.30
	b. Ghasi	2	0.08
	c. Keota	8	0.32
	d. Mahali	2	0.08
	e. Muchi	4	0.16
	f. Pana	5	0.20
	g. Puran	40	1.62
	h. Dhobi	13	0.53
	i. Tanti	116	4.70
3.	Upper Castes	85	3.44
	a. Brahmin	77	3.12
	b. Karana	8	0.32
4.	Middle Castes	151	6.12
	a. Gaud	86	3.49
	b. Khandait	44	1.78
	c. Rautia	21	0.85
5.	Lower Castes	266	10.78
	a. Kumhar	47	1.90
	b. Kurmi	82	3.32
	c. Lohar	97	3.93
	d. Mali	1	0.04
	e. Nai	23	0.93
	f. Teli	16	0.65
6.	Muslims	42	1.70
7.	Others	57	2.31
Total		2,467	99.98

SOURCES: B.K. Roy Burman (1968), *Social Processes in the Industrialization of Rourkela*; Census of India (1961), Vol. 1, *Monograph Series*, Monograph No. 1, Part XI E.

households were the largest single majority (22.62%), followed by the Oraon households (20.19%). The scheduled caste households in these villages constituted 7.90 per cent of the total households and among them the Panatanti were the largest group. The lower caste households like Kumhar, Kurmi, Lohar, etc., constituted 10.78 per cent of the households and the upper caste and middle caste households respectively consisted of 3.44 per cent and 6.12 per cent of the total. Besides this, the Muslims and other groups of households constituted 1.70 per cent and 2.31 per cent respectively. The main occupation of the people in these villages was agriculture and collection of forest produce. The people were mostly simple and illiterate. In 1951 when the government took the first step for the acquisition of private land for the project and the survey officers began to visit the locality they showed little interest. However, by the end of 1952, the village people began to show their resentment. To pacify them the Government of Orissa issued a Press Note taking responsibility for the rehabilitation of displaced people. It is also said that the influence of German Lutheran Church, on the local tribal people had partly prevented the agitation in the locality of the steel plant as it was being constructed with German collaboration.

Notwithstanding this, resentment among the locals was simmering. Towards the end of 1951, the *ganjhus* of several villages convened a public meeting in which 200 people participated. They passed a resolution that the people of the locality did not want a steel plant by sacrificing their hearth and home. The locals had started organizing themselves from around 1953 and an organization called 'Steel Plant Site People's Federation' was formed with Dhanurjay Mohanty as its president. A delegation of the Federation had made a representation before the District Collector at Sundergarh, to protect their interests. The collector assured them that their interest in land would be taken up and they would be given preference when employment in the steel plant was concerned.

At the initial stage the people were ignorant about the effects of the steel plant on their livelihood and hence had adopted an ambivalent attitude towards it. But, in course of time, most of the villagers had overcome their initial hesitation and tried to come together to protect their interests. Within a short time the agitation of the locals increased in magnitude and the leadership passed into the hands of politicians. In the beginning of 1953, a meeting was called at Vedavyas, which was addressed by Shri Nabakrushna Choudhury, the then Chief Minister of Orissa. He assured the displaced people that their interest would be looked after as far as land and employment was concerned. This calmed down the situation and thereby removing opposition from the local people.

Nevertheless, people's attention was then diverted to the issue of compensation. In mid-1953 a movement began demanding increased rate of compensation. By and large the leadership of this agitation rested with the village headmen and local leaders. Almost daily people began to assemble in small groups at the construction sites. This required a second intervention by the Orissa Chief Minister and though a totally acceptable formula was not worked out, the situation slightly recovered. By 1955, the HSL had submitted their layout design for the steel plant. The Government of Orissa was still in a quandary and did not know how to satisfy both the steel plant authorities and the local people who were to be displaced. When the work started the people's leaders persuaded the locals not to work as labourers in the HSL project. As a result, it was often difficult for the HSL to procure cheap labour locally, particularly when agricultural lands belonging to them were involved. Apparently, all this happened because of social pressure at the village level rather than the instigations of outside political parties (Roy Burman 1968: 3).

However, by the end of 1955, there was an interesting development. Till then, the local leaders both tribals and non-tribals were united. Suddenly around this time, some of the local leaders, especially the non-tribals decided to go by the advice of the Chief Minister of Orissa. But the tribal leaders, particularly belonging to the villages under the influence of the Catholic Church continued to oppose the project. Joakim Sahu of Hamirpur (Rourkela) was their spokesman. He expressed discontentment with the working of the Steel Plant Site People's Federation, and asked the people neither to vacate their land nor to cooperate with the authorities, till the issue of compensation was addressed to their satisfaction. This section later came in contact with the tribal leaders from Ranchi. They pleaded that in the matter of rehabilitation the tribals should receive special consideration, otherwise they would be lagging behind the other communities because of the inherent weakness in their social structure. Soon the demand began to gain popularity and spread to other tribal communities and did not remain confined to the catholic section alone.

At this time, the State's political parties joined the fray. In March 1955, it was quite a common sight to witness groups of people attempting to stop work at the construction site and the excavation of channels for *Guradinala.*[2] The agitations were originally started by the District Congress Committee, under the leadership of Dhanurjay Mohanty, who was also the President of the 'Steel Plant Site People's Federation'. Later on when he withdrew, the State Ganatantra Parishad and Socialists took up the case and the situation steadily worsened. Even then, the plant was coming up. As different demands of the locals began to be conceded, the direction of the movement gradually changed. First, it was opposition to construction of the plant itself. Next was the question of better compensation and rehabilitation. The HSL paid adequate money to the displaced people according to the standardized gradation of their land and the houses. The company also promised to employ at least one member in the steel plant from each displaced household. The Government of Orissa took the responsibility of rehabilitation of the displaced people. Under the rehabilitation scheme, the government laid out three colonies at Jalda, Jhirpani and Bandomunda and allotted housing plots (18.29 mt. × 12.19 mt.) to the head of the displaced families. Besides, 15 reclamation areas were demarcated within a radius of 100 km. of Rourkela by clearing forests. In these reclamation sites the displaced persons were allowed to reclaim land for which a subsidy of Rs. 100 per acre had to be paid. However, as the region didn't have a proper revenue system since the British days, the tribals were verbally allowed by the king of Gangpur State to settle in the region and most of them did not possess official records of rights over the land. As a result, many of them failed to get any displacement benefits. On the other hand, the *ganjhus* took away the maximum amount of compensation taking advantage of the tribal's ignorance and illiteracy. Thus, the compensation never really reached the tribal people, who needed the most.

To sum up, this was the sorry picture of society and economy of Rourkela region and Sundergarh district before industrialization and urbanization of the region.

In the subsequent chapters an attempt has been made to analyse the present state of society and economy and assess their impact on the ecology of the region. It is believed that such an analysis of Rourkela region will throw light on the socio-economic changes and their impact on the ecosystem.

NOTES

1. Rourkela region, here, refers to the former 98 villages encircling the steel plant, covered by the economic survey of the Government of Orissa, in early 1950s.
2. *Guradinala* is a drain in which the effluents of the steel plant are discharged and after sedimentation flows into river Brahmani.

CHAPTER 4

Industrialization and the Patterns of Industrial Growth

Sundergarh district had no manufacturing industry worth mentioning in the past. The villages of the district were self-contained with their own blacksmiths, potters, carpenters, weavers, etc. Iron-smelting, gold-washing and making vessels out of soapstone for domestic use were some of the important old time industries of the district. Besides, large quantities of wild *tussar* silkworms were bred to obtain cocoons, which were exported from Bonai State in the early twentieth century. Before independence industrial activity in Sundergarh was confined only to Biramitrapur near Rourkela, where a limestone quarry was located. A private sector cement factory was set up by the Dalmia group at Rajgangpur in 1951. However, the district had poor infrastructure and despite its rich mineral deposits the region could hardly attract investors from large private sector industrial houses. In the early forties only Sundergarh town had a small diesel-run powerhouse of 130 KW, which provided street lighting and supplied electricity to a limited number of affluent households. In 1950, a thermal power station of 3,000 KW capacity was installed at Rajgangpur for the exclusive use of the newly established cement factory.

With the commissioning of the steel plant at Rourkela in the late 1950s, the landscape of the region soon began to change. The industrial town of Rourkela was connected with all major towns and cities of India by rail and road. An airstrip was also constructed. Roadways and branch railway lines were developed to exploit iron ores and other mineral resources needed by the steel plant. Telecommunication networks were rapidly developed to connect the area with other principal towns and cities of India. To meet the requirements of water the Steel Plant Authority constructed a water reservoir on river Sankh at Mandira, near Rourkela. In the late 1950s, the Hirakud hydroelectric power project started supplying electricity to the steel plant and the growing township. The fulfledged functioning of the integrated steel plant in the early 1960s and its subsequent expansion generated forward and backward linkage effects, stimulating the growth of industries in the region. Rapid urbanization followed which further provided incentives to many consumer goods industries. According to the Annual Survey of Industries in Orissa 1984-5 (organized factory sector), because of the giant steel plant at Rourkela, the district of Sundergarh is the most industrialized district in the State. Although the district shares only 12.8 per cent of the reporting factories in the State, its share of productive capital is 48.1 per cent, factory employment 29.1 per cent and output 58.4 per cent. The contribution of the district to the value-added by manufacture is 49.8 per cent (Government of Orissa 1991: 24).

THE STEEL PLANT AND ITS CONSTRUCTION

Soon after independence in 1948, the Government of India appointed three consultants to survey and study the problems connected with setting up a public sector steel plant. As late as 1950, the country's steel output was only 1.01 million tonnes. This was not sufficient to meet the growing demand of iron and steel in the country. The import value of iron and steel to meet the additional requirement was more than Rs. 100 crore per annum, which constituted one-sixth of total exports earnings of the country. Therefore, when the country's First Five Year Plan was formulated, the government decided to set up a public sector steel plant with an annual installed capacity of half a million tonnes of ingot steel. As a follow up in 1953, it signed an agreement with Messers Fried Krupp Essen and Messers Demag AG of Duisberg (the then West Germany) the known world leaders in iron and steel technology. Later the government floated a new company called Hindustan Steel Limited (HSL), with an authorized capital of Rs. 100 crore, of which Rs. 5 lakh was issued and paid up. A technical survey of the sites for the location of the plant was made in 1953-4. After inspecting many sites in the country the experts found that the area around Rourkela village in Sundergarh district of Orissa could be one of the best sites for setting up of a steel plant from the techno-economic point of view. This would also help in attaining balanced regional growth. Good quality iron ore deposits were found in abundant quantity, within a distance of 80 km. from Rourkela. Limestone and dolomite were available within a distance of 30 km. Manganese was also available in abundance from the nearby mines. Hirakud Dam situated at a distance of 150 km. was in a position to supply 55 MW of electricity for running the steel plant and water requirements could be met from river Brahmani.

Orissa being an industrially and economically backward state, the need for a steel plant was felt, which would substantially benefit the people by providing employment directly as well as indirectly. So, the State Government took keen interest in the project. It provided more than 20,000 acres of land to the HSL by uprooting around 2,500 families in 30 villages to construct the steel plant and the residential quarters for its employees.

Although the original Indo-German Agreement was signed in December 1953, it was only in January 1955 that Krupp-Demag submitted to the Government of India, for their perusal and approval, the final project report for half a million tonne steel plant. However, in anticipation of the growing requirements of steel in the future, the government set a target production of six million tonnes of steel by the end of the Second Five Year Plan in 1960-1. Hence, it was decided to double the capacity of the projected Rourkela plant to a million tonne and a supplementary agreement was signed with Krupp-Demag on 21 July 1955. The revised Project Report, for the enlarged plant was received in November 1955. The report recommended among other things, the design of the plant and the master plan of the township. The adoption of a new process of steel making known as the LD (Linzer Dusenstahl) process reduced the production cost of low carbon steels. Provisions were also made for increasing production capacity of the plant to 1.6 million tonnes of steel at a later stage. The plant was designed to manufacture mainly flat products like hot and cold rolled plates, sheets, etc., required by industries like ship building and automobile manufacturing (Government of India 1959).

The construction work of the steel plant and its township was started in 1955 on a war-footing, according to the revised blueprint of the project. In the second half of the 1950s about 59,000 skilled and unskilled people, brought from various parts of the country by the many contractors and subcontractors worked day and night to complete the construction works of the plant and its township at an early date. By the beginning of the year 1959, the project provided direct employment in construction to 3,366 technical and non-technical staff. In addition 9,292 work-charged staff and 45,873 contract labourers were working regularly for completing the work at the earliest (Government of India 1959: 14).

On 3 February 1959, the then President of India, Dr Rajendra Prasad inaugurated the first blast furnace of the Rourkela Steel Plant. The steel township initially consisted of 7,500 houses to cater to an estimated population of 75,000. The township had plans to construct further 20,000 houses to accommodate an ultimate population of one lakh (Bose 1960).

In the initial stage the steel plant was to have a planned capacity of one million tonne of steel ingots per annum. However, during the Third Five Year Plan, the annual installed capacity of the plant was raised to 1.8 million tonnes, and a provision was made for setting up three new plants, as a part of the integrated steel plant such as an electrolyting tin plant, continuous galvanizing plant and a plant for steel sheets. By the end of the Fourth Five Year Plan, the capacity was further raised to 2.3 million tonnes. Plans for the starting of a number of auxiliary industries such as pipe plant, grey iron foundry and fertilizer plant were also prepared.

At present the main plant at Rourkela consists of the following units:

(i) Coke oven: 5 batteries of 370 ovens.
(ii) Three blast furnaces of 1,000 thm (tonnes of hot metal)/day and one of 1,500 thm/day.
(iii) Steel melting shop (SMS) consisting of three mixers of 1,100 tonnes capacity each, four open hearth furnaces of 80 to 90 tonnes per heat, three LD converters of 40 to 50 tonnes per blow and two LD converters of 60 to 66 tonnes per blow.

(iv) Hot rolling mills comprising of soaking pits, blooming and slabbing mill, hot strip mill, plate mill, electrical sheet mill and reheating furnaces.

(v) Cold rolling mills comprising of two pickling lines, two cold rolling reversing mills, one five stand tandem mill, hood annealing furnace section, continuous annealing line, three skin pass mills, facilities for sheet shearing, one electrolytic tinning line, two continuous galvanizing lines with corrugating machines.

(vi) Slag granulation plant of 0.6 mt/yr (metric tonne per year).

(vii) Fertilizer plant of 0.46 mt/yr CAN (Calcium, Ammonium, Nitrate) with 25 per cent nitrogen.

(viii) By-products plant.

There are several support systems in the steel plant. Two captive power plants of 128 MW and 120 MW, to meet the plant's daily power requirement of 140 MW have been provided. However, due to ageing of equipments, the first captive plant is at present producing about 25 MW of power and the second one generates around 60 MW of power only. The remaining requirement is obtained from Orissa State Electricity Board (OSEB). The other support systems include medium pressure boilers for steam generation, an oxygen plant to cater to the LD unit, tar bonded dolomite brick manufacturing plant, steel foundries, grey iron and non-ferrous castings, 350 million-gallon water circulating system, railway network for inward and outward traffic, loco repair shop and mechanical and electrical repair shops.

Besides the above, there are centralized services like Production Planning and Control, Perspective Planning, Energy Management, Research and Control Laboratory, Research and Development, Design and Project Engineering, Safety Engineering, Statistical Quality Control, Electrical Data Processing, Training and Development Centre to integrate the total system of functioning of the steel plant to its optimum.

Over the years the steel township has grown enormously. The Plant has taken adequate steps to provide housing and other facilities in the township to its all employees. There are now 245 registered small scale industrial (SSI) units working in and around Rourkela, to supply various engineering spare parts and consumables to the steel plant. The units are being encouraged by way of providing technical guidance, material assistance and preference in order placement. According to the information provided by the sub-contracting department of the steel plant during the year 1986-7, the plant made a purchase of Rs. 15.39 crore, from these small scale units. Since the commissioning of the steel plant in the early sixties some expansion programmes have been going on. The sintering plant was commissioned in 1965. Expansion of LD converters and blast furnace were completed in 1966 and 1967 respectively. The tandem mill, electrolytic tinning line and electrical sheet mills were commissioned in 1968. The SW (Spirally Welded) pipe plant was commissioned in 1976. In the second half of the 1980s, a 110 crore rupees silicon steel project was set up with American collaboration. Apart from this in the 1980s the plant added a new battery to the coke ovens, constructed a new power plant and a slag cement plant. Also to increase the annual production capacity of the plant to 2.5 million tonnes, the Steel Authority of India Limited (SAIL) had sanctioned Rs. 1,650 crore under a modernization programme.

STEPS FOR INDUSTRIALIZATION

The establishment of the steel plant paved the way for growth of several industries in the region. Employment for more than 20,000 workers were generated by the steel plant after its fulfledged operation started in the early 1960s. As a result the influx of considerable number of migrant construction workers helped to convert the tiny village of Rourkela into a big industrial town. With stability and increasing security of jobs in the steel plant, the workers brought their families, further raising the population of the town. Thus the steel plant generated multiple and propulsive effects on the regional economy which accelerated the growth of a wide variety of industries including consumer goods industries.

At the time of independence, Orissa was one of the least industrialized states in the country. With the Central Government's decision to locate its first public sector steel plant at Rourkela, the Government of Orissa also made special efforts to promote small-scale industrial units in the state. In order to regulate the growth of these units and to provide them infrastructural facilities, the Second

Five Year Plan of the State initiated the setting up of industrial estates and growth centres in various districts. Industrial estates facilitated with a large number of sheds, proper transport and communication networks, adequate water supply and electricity connections were built. The government also set up the Orissa State Financial Corporation (OSFC) in 1956 with branch offices in several district headquarters and towns including Rourkela to assist entrepreneurs in setting up small scale industrial units.

As a follow up of this policy, the Government of Orissa in the early 1960s also set up an industrial estate near Panposh locality of Rourkela. Many entrepreneurs from other states were offered attractive terms and conditions to set up their industrial units here. The steel plant assured supply of raw materials on a priority basis to these feeder units. In the seventies, the government set up a commercial estate in Area Nos. 7 and 8 of Rourkela and developed another industrial estate, adjacent to the Panposh industrial estate to encourage several new medium and small industries. Further, to disperse industrial growth and ease the pressure of population in the city, the government in the 1970s and 1980s developed several growth centres in Sundergarh district, such as Sundergarh town centre, Rajgangpur, Biramitrapur, Bonai and Kalunga, Vedavyas, Kuanrmunda, Kanshbahal, Bandomunda and Lathikata near Rourkela. To promote a large number of labour intensive small scale industrial units throughout the country, the Janata Government at the Centre in 1978, opened District Industries Centre (DIC) in all districts of the country. Followed by this in 1980, the Congress (I) Government in the State formulated its new industrial policy to accelerate the pace of industrialization, as Orissa had a very narrow industrial base compared to other major industrial States of the country. The Industrial Promotion and Investment Corporation of Orissa Limited (IPICOL) and DICs were projected as the major institutions to promote the growth of large, medium and small scale industries in the State. As per this new industrial policy, the State Government provided a package of incentives to the entrepreneurs, which included 15 per cent investment subsidy on fixed capital subject to a limit of Rs. 15 lakh, in all the districts of the State. Subsidy on outright purchase or hire purchase of industrial sheds in the industrial estates, exemption of octroi duty, concessions in water and electricity supply rates and sales tax relief to small scale units on the sale of their finished goods was also allowed. Consequently Rourkela, which had become an industrially advanced region, further attracted more industries in the 1980s.

DEVELOPMENT OF MINES

With the onset of the industrialization process in Rourkela, mining activities in the region were also intensified. They became more mechanized and mining activity itself became an industry. In the pre-independence days and before the location of the steel plant, the exploitation of mineral resources of the district was mainly confined to limestone, dolomite and manganese ores and that too in an unorganized way to cater to the needs of industries located outside the region. The location of the steel plant at Rourkela led to extensive exploration of iron ore, dolomite, limestone, fire clay, manganese, lead, etc., which are extensively found in Sundergarh region. The steel plant developed its captive iron ore mines at Kalta and Barsuan, limestone and dolomite quarries at Purunapani, Hathibari and Biramitrapur, manganese ore at Bonai-Keonjhar border and lead in the Sargipali mines of Sundergarh. Besides catering to the needs of the steel plant at Rourkela, the mineral and metal resources of the region serve many other large industries such as cement factory at Rajgangpur, iron and steel industry at Bhilai, Bokaro and Jamshedpur. According to the latest available data from the District Statistical Office in the year 1983, there were 56 working mines in the district with area coverage of 19,566 hectares. The main minerals presently extracted in the district are iron ore, manganese, fireclay, limestone, dolomite, quartz and lead. The total mineral output of the district during 1983 was 5.77 million metric tonnes with a total production value of Rs. 3,586.65 million. The total number of people employed in these mines was 17,370.

PATTERN AND GROWTH OF INDUSTRIES

As mentioned earlier, before the establishment of the steel plant at Rourkela, the region[1] had only one industrial unit in the form of a large cement factory set up in 1951 at Rajgangpur, under the management of a private sector company namely, the Orissa Cement Limited, Rajgangpur. After the steel plant started operating many large and medium industrial units started growing. In 1956, the Orissa Cement Limited, further diversified its range of production and set up a refractory plant with technical aid from a firm in West Germany, to meet the needs of special refractories by the three public sector steel plants at Rourkela, Bhilai and Durgapur. Followed by this the Utkal Machinery Limited was established at Kanshabahal, to manufacture equipment for steel plants, pulp and paper plants, chemical plants, crushing and screening machinery and hydraulic equipments as well. This unit with an investment of Rs. 3.35 crore, provided employment to about 1,230 people. In 1963, the Orissa Industries Limited, Lathikata came up in the vicinity of Rourkela, with a capital investment of Rs. 52 lakh. The plant produces all types of refractory materials and provides employment to around 650 people. In 1969, the Indian Detonator Limited with a capital investment of Rs. 150 lakh and employment capacity of 234 persons, was set up at Rourkela to produce powerful explosives. Added to this, in the early seventies two new medium scale industries namely Asiatic Gases Limited and Orissa Fertilizers and Chemicals Limited came up. These two units respectively manufacture compressed oxygen gas and phosphatic fertilizer and provided employment to around 328 people. In the 1980s another new medium scale unit, Kalinga Cement Limited started its production and provided employment to another 120 people.

Consequent to such rapid industrialization of the region, the district of Sundergarh acquired a well-developed and organized industrial sector. According to Table 4.1, the district with 5.07 per cent share of population of the State in 1981 possessed 12.39 per cent of operating organized factories in the State during 1982-3. Moreover, these factories employed 29.38 per cent of the people in the organized factory sector of Orissa. It is evident from this table that in the organized factory sector, Orissa has a high location quotient of forest and wood-based industries (29.55%), followed by food and allied industries (23.19%), engineering and metal-based industries (13.18%), repairing and servicing industries (8.10%), non-metallic mineral based industries (7.94%) and so on. The low location quotient industries in the organized factory sector of the state are livestock and leather-based units (0.24%) followed by electricals and electronics goods units (1.03%) and rubber and plastic goods units

TABLE 4.1: CATEGORYWISE NUMBER OF OPERATING ORGANIZED FACTORIES AND EMPLOYMENT IN ORISSA AND SUNDERGARH DISTRICT DURING 1982-3 AND THE PERCENTAGE SHARE OF SUNDERGARH IN FACTORIES AND EMPLOYMENT IN ORISSA

Sl. No.	Category	Orissa		Sundergarh		Sundergarh's share of factories in Orissa	Sundergarh's share of factory employment in Orissa
		No. of factories	No. of persons employed	No. of factories	No. of persons employed		
1.	Food and Allied	292 (23.19)	10,689 (7.55)	0 (0.00)	0 (0.00)	0.00	0.00
2.	Chemicals and Allied	61 (4.84)	4.601 (3.25)	10 (6.41)	1,633 (3.92)	16.39	35.49
3.	Electricals and Electronics	13 (1.03)	969 (0.68)	0 (0.00)	0 (0.00)	0.00	0.00
4.	Engineering and Metal Based	166 (13.18)	44,194 (31.20)	73 (46.79)	33,195 (79.76)	43.98	75.11
5.	Forest and Wood Based	372 (29.55)	4,836 (3.41)	30 (19.23)	392 (0.94)	8.06	8.11
6.	Non-metallic Minerals	100 (7.94)	13,996 (9.88)	9 (5.77)	3,934 (9.45)	9.00	28.11
7.	Livestock and Leather	3 (0.24)	89 (0.06)	0 (0.00)	0 (0.00)	0.00	0.00
8.	Paper and Paper Products	40 (3.18)	13,809 (9.75)	0 (0.00)	0 (0.00)	0.00	0.00
9.	Rubber and Plastics	14 (1.11)	336 (0.24)	0 (0.00)	0 (0.00)	0.00	0.00
10.	Textiles and Allied	40 (3.18)	8,459 (5.97)	0 (0.00)	0 (0.00)	0.00	0.00

(contd.)

TABLE 4.1 (contd.)

11. Misc. Manu-facturing	56	4,478	30	2,358	53.57	52.66
	(4.45)	(3.16)	(19.23)	(5.67)		
12. Repairing and Servicing*	102	35,194	4	106	3.92	0.30
	(8.10)	(24.85)	(2.56)	(0.25)		
Total	1,259	1,41,650	156	41,618	12.39	29.38
	(99.99)	(100.00)	(99.99)	(99.99)		

NOTES: 1. Figures in bracket indicate percentage.
2. Directorate of Industries in Orissa have made 12 broad categories of industries. Hence, to reconcile with their classification of industries, some of the major industrial groups in manufacturing division of NSIC classification have been merged together.
* Includes electricity generating and transmitting units.

SOURCE: Government of Orissa, *A Report on Annual Survey of Industries in Orissa (Organized Factory Sector) 1979-80 to 1982-83*, Directorate of Economics and Statistics, Bhubaneswar.

(1.11%). However, in terms of employment in the organized factory sector, engineering and metal based units provided the highest percentage of employment (31.20), followed by repairing and servicing units (24.85), non-metallic mineral based units (9.88), paper and paper product units (9.75), food and allied groups (7.55) and so on.

When we look at the industrial scenario of Sundergarh district in Table 4.1, it is noticed that out of 12 broad categories of industries as found in Orissa, the district has only six categories of functioning industries in the organized factory sector. These include:

(i) chemicals and allied group (6.41%),
(ii) engineering and metal-based industries (46.79%),
(iii) forest and wood-based industries (19.23%),
(iv) nonmetallic mineral-based group of industries (5.77%),
(v) miscellaneous manufacturing industries (19.23%), and
(vi) repairing and servicing industries (2.56%).

Because of the linkage effects of the Rourkela Steel Plant, units in engineering and metal-based group not only have the highest location quotient of the organized factory sector in Sundergarh district but also they constitute 43.98 per cent of the total engineering and metal-based organized industries in the state, with an employment share of 75.11 per cent. The other categories of industries in which the district has a relatively higher percentage of share in terms of both units and employment respectively are:

(i) chemicals and allied group of industries (16.39% and 35.49%), (ii) non-metallic minerals (9.00% and 28.11%) and (iii) miscellaneous manufacturing group (53.37% and 52.66%). Since most of the items produced by these units are mainly required by the steel plant and its well-paid employees, we may say that the high location quotient of the aforesaid industries in the district is also mainly due to the propulsive and multiplier effects of the Rourkela Steel Plant.

The growth of industries in the small scale sector (SSI) has also followed the same pattern like the growth of organized factory sector units in the district. It is seen from Table 4.2 that by the end of 1987-8, Sundergarh district had in total 2,827 SSI units with a capital investment of Rs. 4,593 lakh and providing employment to 31,555 persons. In the same year, the total number of SSI units in Orissa was 31,724, with a total capital investment of Rs. 33,661 lakh and employing 2,37,320 persons. This implies that the district of Sundergarh has a share of 8.91 per cent SSI units, 13.64 per cent of capital investment and 13.30 per cent employment in the SSI sector of Orissa, which is higher than the population share of the district in the State, i.e. 5.07 per cent. It can also be observed from the table that the average capital investment per unit and the average employment generated per unit are relatively higher than the corresponding figures for the state as a whole. This implies that Sundergarh district has a fairly large number of modern sophisticated SSI units in the State of Orissa. As in the case of the organized factory sector, the SSI sector of the district is also dominated by higher concentration of engineering and metallurgical industries with 26.21 per cent of units, 46.46 per cent of capital investment and 39.59 per cent of the total employment. In terms of capital investment and employment generation, this is followed by nonmetallic mineral-based industries. Although food and allied group of industries and miscellaneous manufacturing industries have fairly high percentage of SSI units in

TABLE 4.2 CATEGORYWISE SSI UNITS, INVESTMENT AND EMPLOYMENT IN ORISSA AND SUNDERGARH DISTRICT BY THE END OF 1987-8

Sl. No.	Category	Orissa					Sundergarh				
		No. of units	Investment (Rs. in lakh)	Employment	Av. Inv. per unit (Rs. in lakh)	Av. Emp. per unit	No. of units	Investment Rs. in lakh	Employment	Av. Inv. per unit (Rs. in lakh)	Av. Emp. per unit
1.	Food & Allied	7429 (23.42)	7551 (22.43)	40679 (17.14)	1.02	5.48	436 (15.42)	368 (8.01)	2369 (7.51)	0.84	5.43
2.	Chemicals & Allied	1501 (4.73)	2206 (6.55)	11076 (4.68)	1.47	7.38	144 (5.09)	398 (8.66)	1575 (4.99)	2.76	10.94
3.	Electricals & Electronics	356 (1.12)	887 (2.63)	2619 (1.10)	2.49	7.36	62 (2.19)	105 (2.29)	416 (1.32)	1.69	6.71
4.	Engineering & Metal Based	3702 (11.67)	7007 (20.82)	35177 (14.82)	1.89	9.50	741 (26.21)	2134 (46.46)	12492 (39.59)	2.88	16.86
5.	Forest & Wood Based	3222 (10.16)	1424 (4.23)	20528 (8.65)	0.44	6.37	184 (6.51)	146 (3.18)	1357 (4.30)	0.79	7.37
6.	Non-metallic Minerals	3235 (10.20)	3626 (10.77)	63488 (26.75)	1.12	19.62	284 (10.05)	562 (12.24)	8355 (26.48)	1.98	29.42

(contd.)

TABLE 4.2 (contd.)

Sl. No.	Category	Orissa					Sundergarh				
		No. of units	Investment (Rs. in lakh)	Employ-ment	Av. Inv. per unit (Rs. in lakh)	Av. Emp. per unit	No. of units	Investment Rs. in lakh	Employ-ment	Av. Inv. per unit (Rs. in lakh)	Av. Emp. per unit
7.	Livestock and Leather	263 (0.83)	267 (0.79)	1617 (0.68)	1.01	6.15	17 (0.60)	5 (0.11)	80 (0.25)	0.29	4.71
8.	Paper and Paper Products	1082 (3.41)	1418 (4.21)	6833 (2.88)	1.31	6.31	98 (3.47)	134 (2.92)	664 (2.10)	1.37	6.78
9.	Rubber and Plastics	692 (2.18)	1574 (4.68)	3575 (1.51)	2.27	5.17	82 (2.90)	125 (2.72)	454 (1.44)	1.52	5.54
10.	Taxtiles and Allied	4049 (12.89)	1899 (5.64)	24258 (10.22)	0.46	5.93	144 (5.09)	44 (0.96)	609 (1.93)	0.31	4.23
11.	Misc. Manu-facturing	2049 (6.46)	4469 (13.28)	12588 (5.30)	2.18	6.14	207 (7.32)	483 (10.52)	1803 (5.71)	2.33	8.71
12.	Repairing & Servicing	4103 (12.93)	1333 (3.96)	14882 (6.27)	0.32	3.63	428 (15.14)	89 (1.94)	1381 (4.38)	0.22	3.23
Total		31727 (100.00)	33661 (99.99)	237320 (100.00)	1.06	7.48	2817 (99.99)	4593 (100.00)	31555 (100.00)	1.62	11.16

NOTE: Figures in brackets indicate percentage share.
SOURCE: Govt. of Orissa, *Statistical Hand Book 1987-88*, Directorate of Industries, Cuttack.

the district, their shares in capital investment and employment generation are relatively less than the aforesaid percentage of SSI units. This clearly shows that the pattern of growth of small industrial units in the district has also been significantly influenced by the forward and backward linkage effects of the steel plant. It was further confirmed from the officials of District Industry Department, that the Rourkela-Rajgangpur industrial belt, which can broadly be called Rourkela region, contains most of the large, medium and small scale industrial units of the district. The other two subdivisions, viz., Sundergarh Sadar and Bonai have only a few of the small scale industrial units.

It has been found that with the expansion of production capacity in Rourkela Steel Plant many large, medium and small scale industries have grown up in and around the city over the years. Within a span of about 30 years of its operation, the steel plant at Rourkela has been successful in converting the region into the most advanced industrial belt in Orissa. The city's population has grown by leaps and bounds and it seems the region is emerging as one of the advanced centres of engineering and metal-based industries in Orissa.

It should not however, be imagined that the linkage effects of the steel plant at Rourkela were all realized at any one point of time. The linked industrial units came up in phases, with the growth of the township and with the periodic expansion in the production capacity of the steel plant. From the list of growth of SSI units at Rourkela (with investment on plant and machinery worth more than Rs. 2 lakh), it can be observed that the growth of number of industrial units in the steel city is increasing every year and the region is still in its expanding phase of industrial growth.

It can be seen from Table 4.3 that by the end of March 1988, there were 154 SSI units in the Rourkela urban agglomeration. It can be also seen that till the end of 1960, when the steel plant was in its initial stage of production, there was not a single SSI unit at Rourkela. During 1961-5 period, five SSI units came up followed by six more new units during 1966-70. It means by the end of the 1960s there were only 11 SSI units at Rourkela. However in the early 1970s, 32 new SSI units were set up and the second half of 1970s saw the coming up of another 23 new SSI units. It seems that as the production in the steel plant picked up, the city grew and the scope

TABLE 4.3: PERIODWISE ESTABLISHMENT OF NEW SSI UNITS AND TOTAL NUMBER OF SSI UNITS WITH INVESTMENT ON PLANT AND MACHINERY OF MORE THAN RS. 2 LAKH AT ROURKELA

Sl. No.	Period	No. of new units established	Total no. of units (cumulated)
1.	1951-5	0	0
2.	1956-60	0	0
3.	1961-5	5	5
4.	1966-70	6	11
5.	1971-5	32	43
6.	1976-80	23	66
7.	1981-5	65	131
8.	1986-8	23	154

SOURCE: District Industries Centre, Rourkela, Orissa.

for SSI units also increased. Hence, the first half of 1980s facilitated the setting up of 65 additional SSI units followed by another 23 units during 1986-8.

The categorywise location quotient of these SSI units in Rourkela city shows that the steel plant has a profound influence in the categorywise increase of SSI units. As is evident from Table 4.4, the units in engineering and metal-based group have a very high location quotient at Rourkela, i.e. 62.34 per cent of the total SSI units and 63.5 per cent of the total capital investment. Next to this, the units in chemicals and allied group of industries have a location quotient of 11.69 per cent of the total units and 10.35 per cent of total capital investment. The other groups of SSI units with significant percentage share of units and capital investment are nonmetallic minerals-based industries with a share of 4.54 per cent of units and 9.59 per cent of capital, paper and paper products group with a share of 5.19 per cent units and 3.59 per cent of capital, food and allied group with a share of 3.25 per cent of units and 3.39 per cent of capital and repairing and servicing group with units share of 4.54 per cent and capital share of 4.44 per cent.

Thus from the high location quotient of particular groups of industries and an increase in the number of units in Rourkela region as well as in Sundergarh district, especially after the steel plant has

TABLE 4.4: CATEGORYWISE SSI UNITS WITH INVESTMENT ON PLANT AND MACHINERY OF MORE THAN RS. 2 LAKH AT ROURKELA DURING 1987-8

Sl. No.	Category	No. of Units		Total Investment (Rs. in lakh)	
1.	Food and Allied	5	(3.25)	69.5	(3.39)
2.	Chemicals and Allied	18	(11.69)	212.0	(10.35)
3.	Electricals and Electronics	2	(1.30)	10.0	(0.49)
4.	Engineering and Metal-based	96	(62.34)	1300.7	(63.50)
5.	Forest and Wood-based	2	(1.30)	16.0	(0.78)
6.	Nonmetallic Minerals	7	(4.54)	196.0	(9.59)
7.	Livestock and Leather	1	(0.65)	4.0	(0.19)
8.	Paper and Paper Products	8	(5.19)	73.5	(3.59)
9.	Rubber and Plastics	4	(2.60)	28.0	(1.37)
10.	Textiles and Allied	2	(1.30)	18.0	(0.88)
11.	Misc. Manufacturing	2	(1.30)	29.0	(1.42)
12.	Repairing and Servicing	7	(4.54)	91.0	(4.44)
Total		154	(100.0)	2048.2	(99.99)

NOTE: Figures in brackets indicate percentage.
SOURCE: District Industries Centre, Rourkela, Orissa.

been set up, we may undisputably say that the region has achieved a high degree of industrialization. This has made Sundergarh industrially the most advanced among all the old undivided 13 districts of Orissa, although it has a very high percentage of tribal population.

It can be seen from Table 4.5 that because of the steel plant the district has the highest share in all the selected industrial characteristics except the share of reporting organized factories and employment. With a share of 12.77 per cent of organized factories in Orissa during 1984-5, the district had a productive capital share of 48.12 per cent, employment share of 29.12 per cent, inputs share of 61.54 per cent, output share of 58.36 per cent and value-added by manufacturing industries share of 49.80 per cent. It thus surpasses other districts of the State in its degree and extent of industrial activities. Moreover, it may be pointed out that although the district of Puri comes next to Sundergarh, with respect to certain industrial characteristics, the actual position is different. In the industry group 'generation and transmission of electric energy', the then Orissa State

TABLE 4.5: DISTRICTWISE RELATIVE SHARE OF FACTORIES, CAPITAL, EMPLOYMENT, INPUT, OUTPUT AND VALUE-ADDED IN THE ORGANIZED FACTORY SECTOR OF ORISSA, 1984-5

Sl. No.	District	No. of reporting factories	Productive Capital	No. of emplo-yees	Input (Rs.)	Output (Rs.)	Value-added (Rs.)
1.	Balasore	88	5458	2981	4110	4780	241
		(6.93)	(2.72)	(2.15)	(3.14)	(2.80)	(0.73)
2.	Bolangir	41	167	712	271	334	60
		(3.23)(1.88)	(0.91)	(0.77)	(-0.01)		
5.	Ganjam	116	1870	3533	1543	1980	299
		(9.14)	(0.93)	(2.55)	(1.18)	(1.16)	(0.91)
6.	Kalahandi	32	350	880	639	704	54
		(2.52)	(0.17)	(0.64)	(0.49)	(0.41)	(0.16)
7.	Keonjhar	23	8013	1514	2055	2829	742
		(1.81)	(4.00)	(1.09)	(1.57)	(1.65)	(2.25)
8.	Koraput	81	5149	6713	5542	7794	1818
		(6.38)	(2.57)	(4.85)	(4.24)	(4.56)	(5.52)
9.	Mayurbhanj	48	874	1459	1331	1567	101
		(3.78)	(0.44)	(1.05)	(1.02)	(0.92)	(0.31)
10.	Phulbani	4	20	141	36	33	6
		(0.31)	(0.01)	(0.10)	(0.03)	(0.02)	(0.02)
11.	Puri	234	65832	44238	8468	16087	5634
		(18.44)	(32.86)	(31.95)	(6.47)	(9.41)	(17.10)
12.	Sambalpur	171	9473	15260	17269	22113	4358
		(13.47)	(4.73)	(11.02)	(13.20)	(12.94)	(13.23)
13.	Sundergarh	162	96405	40319	80490	99767	16396
		(12.77)	(48.12)	(29.12)	(61.54)	(58.36)	(49.80)
	Orissa	1269	200334	138470	130794	170949	32938
		(100.00)	(99.98)	(99.99)	(100.00)	(100.00)	(100.00)

NOTE: Figures in bracket indicate percentage.
SOURCE: Government of Orissa (1991), *Annual Survey of Industries (Organized Factory Sector), Orissa, 1983-84 and 1984-85*, Directorate of Economics and Statistics, Bhubaneswar, p. 24.

Electricity Board (OSEB), used to furnish a consolidated return from all its 38 units located in various places besides Puri. As the OSEB headquarter was located at Bhubaneswar of the undivided Puri district, the data pertaining to electricity generation has been unavoidably shown against Puri, in the absence of annual returns of individual units of OSEB located in other districts of the State. This in fact, has inflated the value of different industrial indicators of the undivided Puri district (Government of Orissa 1991: 25).

ROURKELA: THE MAIN INDUSTRIAL CENTRE

It has already been mentioned in the previous chapter that before the setting up of the Rourkela Steel Plant, the two ex-feudatory States of Gangpur and Bonai comprising the present Sundergarh district were one of the most backward regions of Orissa. Despite its rich mineral deposits the district had a very low industrial base and the hilly terrains with its tropical climate and predominance of tribal population provided only limited opportunity for the development of mechanized agriculture with high productivity. The district was sparsely populated and a majority of the people had a subsistence level of living. The present Rourkela region was forested and resided mainly by the tribals in only about 30 small villages in a primitive socioeconomic set up. However, after the steel plant at Rourkela came into existence the economy of the region had a new look. Over the years Sundergarh has emerged as the leading industrial district of the State, and within the district the Rourkela-Rajgangpur belt is found to be most industrialized. The Rourkela urban agglomeration alone seems to be contributing a major share of industrial income to the district and as seen from Table 4.5, because of Rourkela Steel Plant, Sundergarh contributes the lion's share in the form of output, and employment generation to the organized manufacturing sector of the State economy. It can be observed from Table 4.6 that although according to 1981 census, the district had 5.07 per cent share of the State population, it contributed 12.69 per cent of the State's secondary sector workers, 6.96 per cent of the tertiary sector workers and only 3.88 per cent of the primary sector workers. Moreover, the district alone contributed 21.78 per cent of the non-household industrial workers. This clearly proves that the economy of Sundergarh district now has a high industrial base.

Apart from that it can be seen from Table 4.6 that within the district, Rourkela urban agglomeration alone contributes the lion's share to this achievement. In 1981 the city alone constituted 24.11 per cent of the total district's population and its share in urban population of the district was 78.81 per cent. Within this setup of

TABLE 4.6: INDICATORS OF INDUSTRIAL DEVELOPMENT IN SUNDERGARH DISTRICT AND ROURKELA CITY

Sl. No.	Indicators	% share of Sundergarh district in Orissa during 1981 census	% share of Rourkela city in Sundergarh district during 1981 census
1.	Population	5.07	24.11
2.	Primary sector workers	3.88	1.37
3.	Secondary sector workers	12.69	53.58
4.	Nonhousehold industry workers	21.78	59.00
5.	Tertiary sector workers	6.96	53.81

SOURCE: Census of India, 1981, *General Economics Tables*, Series 16, Part III A & B (i), Orissa.

population distribution, the city alone shared 53.58 per cent of the secondary sector workers and 53.81 per cent of the tertiary sector workers employed in the district. Of the total number of non-household industry workers employed in various large, medium and small scale industries of the district, the share of Rourkela city alone was 59 per cent.

It is an established fact that after the setting up of the steel plant, the township at Rourkela began to grow and over the years because of the propulsive and multiplier effects of the steel plant, it could achieve the status of a large class-I town. The steel plant alone provides a large portion of direct employment in the industrial sector of the city. In the year 1987-8, the steel plant alone had a total regular employment strength of 37,783 persons.[2] If all the employees of the steel plant are considered as belonging to the category of non-household industry workers then the share of the steel plant alone in the generation of direct employment in the non-household industry sector of the city is 93.81 per cent according to 1981 census. However, according to the census classification, quite a few employees of the plant may be classified under the tertiary sector workers also. So, if we add the total number of secondary and tertiary sector workers of the city, it will come to 92,585 according to 1981 census, and on the basis of this data we can say that the steel plant alone has directly generated 40.81 per cent of the employment in the city of Rourkela, since there is little variation in the employment strength of the plant in between 1980 and 1988.[3]

Thus, the analysis of the process of industrialization and urbanization in Rourkela region and as well as in Sundergarh district proves that the location of the public sector steel plant at Rourkela in the late 1950s is the prime factor behind the spurt industrial development of the district. However, industrialization has also become the prime mover of radical changes in polity, society and the ecosystem. Clark Kerr et al. say that the common characteristic of industrialization in every society regardless of its historic back-ground and political orientation is the use of new technology. This is the common denominator of new and diverse skills, large scale productive endeavours, large cities and much else (Kerr et al. 1970). However, the application of modern science and technology should take into consideration not only the intended positive effects of industrialization but also the unintended negative social and environmental consequences as well. In the subsequent chapters an attempt has been made to explore such effects of industrialization in Rourkela.

NOTES

1. The region here refers to Rourkela-Rajgangpur industrial belt whose radius is around 30 to 40 km. from the steel plant at Rourkela.
2. According to the *Annual Statistics, 1987-88* published by the Rourkela Steel Plant in the year ending 31.3.1988 there were 2,959 executives and 34,783 non-executives working in the plant. Excluding this, the plant had 139 trainee workers and 92 temporary workers.
3. It is found out from the Personnel Department of Rourkela Steel Plant that since 1980 the Plant has stopped making any major recruitment of workers at the non-executives level. Hence, since 1980 till date the total employment strength of the plant is reported to have remained at around 35,000.

CHAPTER 5

Birth of a Town: City Ecology and the Urban Social Structure

Before the location of the public sector steel plant, Rourkela was not a very well known place in Sundergarh district. It gained some importance after the opening of Rourkela-Biramitrapur (29 km.) railway line in 1927 and a small railway station was also constructed in Rourkela. Even then the region was sparsely populated and the population of Rourkela village including the bustee was only 2,533 in 1951.[1] As discussed earlier, the HSL in January 1955 submitted a blue-print to the government indicating the layout of Rourkela township, the steel plant and other industries to be built over an area of 207.37 sq. km. Later on the plan was drastically revised and the State Government agreed to transfer 5,181.86 acres of government land to HSL. It also promised to acquire 15,305.92 acres of private land for the project. Altogether 30 villages inhabited by around 2,500 households were affected and displaced by the acquisition of land by the government for setting up of the steel plant and its township.

After the acquisition of land and approval of the project's blue print, construction work of the steel plant and the township was taken up in the mid-1950s on a war footing. When in the early 1960s the plant went into operation, Rourkela occupied a prominent place in the industrial map of India. On account of large scale immigration of people to the project site from various parts of the country for employment in the steel plant, the total population of the area, which was around 15,000 in 1951 sprang up to 90,287 in 1961. In the 1961 census for the first time Rourkela was recorded as a town and that too as the largest one in Sundergarh district. Over the years, the rate of population growth has increased considerably. Today it is recognised as one of the largest towns in Orissa, with a total population of 3.99 lakh at the time of 1991 census.

PLANNING OF THE TOWNSHIP

The Master Plan of the steel township envisaged that when the industrialization of Rourkela would be in full swing, the population of the township is expected to be around one lakh including the employees of the steel project as well as that of the ancillary industries, servicing institutions and commercial enterprises. An industrial township with 19 sectors was planned, and provision was made for the construction of 14,000 well-appointed houses to provide residential facilities to the employees of the steel plant. To provide quality education to the employees' children and to develop educated and technically qualified manpower, the Master Plan had provisions for a number of primary and secondary schools in various sectors of the town. In addition to this, provision was also made for setting up a Science College and an Engineering College, which was later on known as Regional Engineering College. For building up technically superior manpower at the non-executive level, for the future expansion of the steel plant, the plan envisaged the setting up of a full-fledged training institute. To provide adequate medical facilities to the plant employees and their family members, provisions were made for a well-equipped modern hospital, several health centres and small dispensaries distributed in various sectors. Besides all these, the Master Plan of the township contained provisions for shopping centres, recreation centres and various conveniences and servicing institutions, necessary for the residents of the township.

Consequent upon the location of the steel plant the original village of Rourkela also began to grow as a town adjacent to the steel township. The population of the civil town, which was less than 4,000 in 1951, suddenly increased to 35,000 by the year 1961. The civil township of Rourkela, thus, started growing in a narrow wedge of land between the steel plant and the steel township. In order to prevent haphazard and sporadic growth in the immediate vicinity of the steel township and to remove the existing congestion, the Town Planning Organization of the Government of Orissa drew up another Master Plan in 1965, for a more systematic growth of the civil town. The projected population for the civil town after the development of different areas in the Civil Township Master Plan by about 1975 was estimated to be 80,000.

To accommodate the growing population of the civil town and

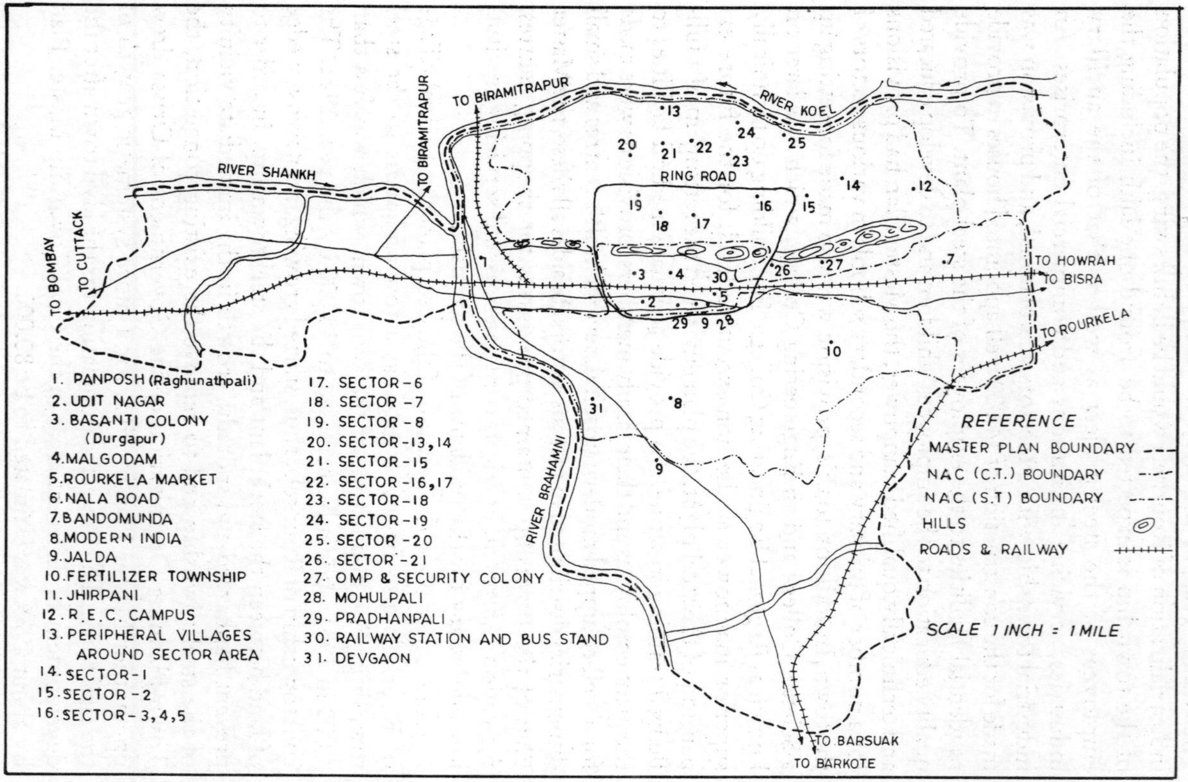

Fig. 5.1: Master Plan and the Selected Localities of Rourkela

to reduce congestion and spatial concentration of population in pockets in the east of the Udit Nagar Court area and west of the railway station, the Master Plan made adequate provision of housing and civic amenities, by developing residential plots according to the needs of the different classes of people, in the covered area of Pradhanpali, Mohulpali, Durgapur, Raghunathpali, Bandomunda Marshalling Yard, etc. (Fig 5.1). Adequate provisions were also made for the location of educational institutions, government offices, green belts, small parks, play grounds, shopping and community centres etc., in various zones.

ZONING REGULATIONS

As the civil township of Rourkela came up rather haphazardly, there was no zoning regulation. The small industrial and commercial establishments were interspersed with the residential areas and no definite demarcation had been maintained. The commercial areas of the city, at present, predominate Bisra-Panposh road. The small scale industries were located on the Panposh road before the preparation of the Master Plan, and some of them are still found in this locality. These are mostly saw mills, flour mills, light engineering works and the like. A preliminary survey conducted in 1959, had enlisted nearly 50 industrial establishments with a total employment potential of 300 workers in this area. So, to ease the pressure of small industrial units near the residential localities, the government set up an industrial estate with 32 units in 1960 near Panposh. In the Master Plan, land was also provided for service industries towards the west of the newly set up Rourkela railway station and Bisra-Panposh road east of Udit Nagar Court area. Similar strip of land in Area Nos. 7 and 8, west of the ring road connecting the steel plant, civil township and the steel township was also earmarked for industries. The plan made zoning regulations and declared that only light industries may be located in areas adjacent to all residential sectors.

In order to provide healthy living to the inhabitants of the civil town in a pollution free environment, the township was divided into three zones, viz., (i) residential zone, (ii) commercial zone and (iii) light industry zone. The Master Plan provided for certain regulations in utilization of space in these regions also (Fig. 5.2). In the residential zone, utilization of space was permitted for residential

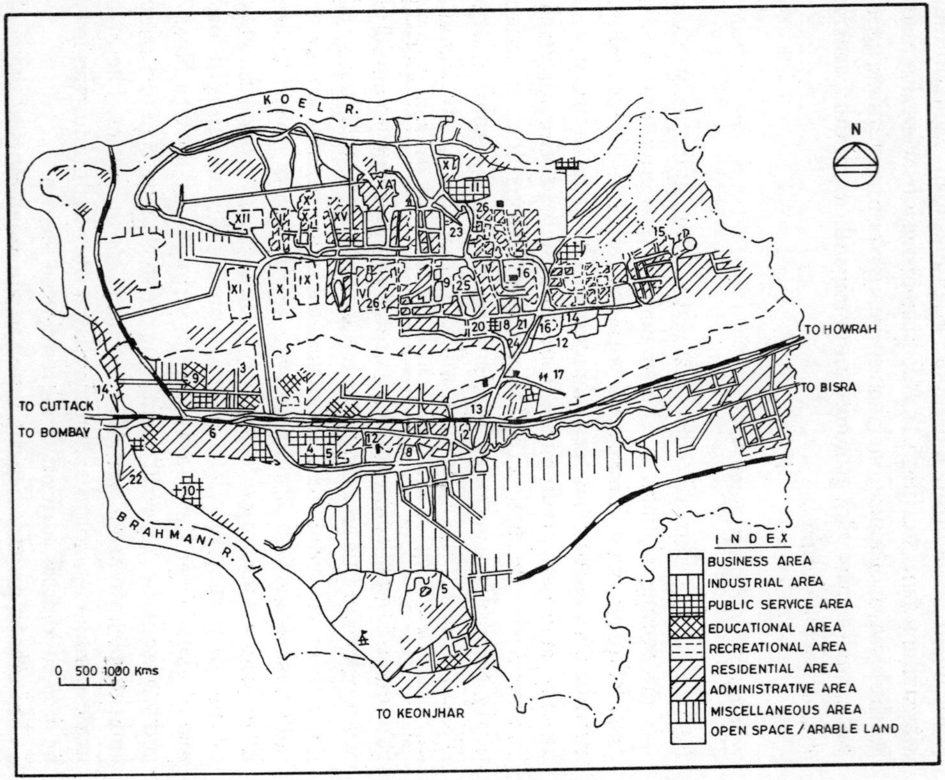

Fig. 5.2: Rourkela Urban Land Use, 1981

houses, hotels, places of worship, schools, libraries, gardens, nurseries, recreational centres of non-profit type, customary home occupations and the like. The plan also provided for the restricted use of space in residential zone for certain other purposes on appeal to the special planning authority such as municipal, state and central government offices, public utilities, cemeteries, hospitals (except mental hospitals), convalescent homes, sanatoria, philanthropic purposes, removal of gravel, clay, sand or stone from the premises and keeping dairy and poultry animals for domestic use. Barring these, other uses of space in the residential zone was totally prohibited.

The commercial zone of the Master Plan contained provisions for offices, shops, hotels, printing presses, banks, community halls and auditoriums, restaurants, advertising kiosks, temples and other religious places, schools and such other institutions, libraries, Municipal, State or Central Government offices and above all wholesale or retail business establishments and other services. In addition to this, on appeal to the relevant authority, commercial zones permitted restricted use of space for petrol and diesel filling stations, garages and manufacturing establishments, employing not more than ten workers. Residential quarters were also allowed on floors other than the ground floor, in retail shopping and general business area but not in wholesale and warehousing area. However, use of space for storage of building materials, warehouses and any use detrimental to the neighbourhood by reason of emission of smoke, noise, odour, vibration, dust or fumes and all other uses not specifically mentioned above were strictly prohibited in the commercial zone of the city.

In the light industry zone, the Master Plan permitted uses of space for warehousing, timber storage, yard building, materials storage, any use permitted or permissible on appeal in the commercial zone and above all manufacturing and processing establishments using power and employing not more than 30 workers or 60 workers without using power. But this zone strictly prohibited the use of space for residential houses, hostels, trade, industry or other use detrimental to the neighbourhood. Restriction was imposed on hazardous industries such as manufacture or refining of ammonia, bleaching powder, chlorine, asphalt, brick, terracotta, gypsum, lime, plaster of paris, coke, creosote, dextrin, glucose, starch, dye and explosives or fireworks.

POTABLE WATER SUPPLY

As Rourkela is located in a hilly region and the Brahmani river goes dry during summer, the region experienced acute shortage of water needed by a large number of people, who came there after the construction of the steel plant. In order to facilitate water supply to the steel plant and to the township all around the year, the HSL constructed the Mandira dam, on the river Sankh and a pick up dam at Tarkera near Panposh.

To meet the water requirements of the civil town, the HSL in 1965, was making available 80,000 gallons of water per day through its water works at Tarkera. A pumping station at Panposh was also built to further regularize water supply. However, the approximate existing capacity in 1965 was only 3 million gallons of potable water per day. As the population in the town was growing, the Master Plan proposed to increase filtered water supply to 6 million gallons at the rate of 40 gallons per head per day.

DRAINAGE AND SEWERAGE

The Master Plan of Rourkela steel township was laid out before the birth of the town. So, there were adequate arrangements for drainage and sewerage and the effluents of the township were discharged into the river Koel after treatment. Similarly, the discharge of industrial wastes from the steel plant was effected through the *Guradinala* near Deogaon after neutralization. However, for the civil township of Rourkela there was no proper drainage and sewerage system because of its haphazard growth and conversion of sparse rural settlements into urban settlements in the wake of industrialization and large scale immigration of people. Hence, the newly prepared Master Plan made necessary provisions to develop drainage and sewerage system in the civil town. It proposed to discharge the sewerage of the civil town near the village Deogaon, so that the vast agricultural land available there would be utilized for sewage farming.

TRANSPORT AND COMMUNICATION

The forms and content of man's collective life is a function of his means of transportation and communication (Hawley 1972). Without the development of modern transport and communication system, the aggregation of human population in large urban centres is next to impossible. Hence, the Master Plan of the city made necessary provisions for the development of transportation and communication networks of the new town. The blue print of the steel plant and township laid out a limited access ring road for high speed traffic, connecting the steel township in the north to the steel plant in the south. The Master Plan of the civil town took into account the problem of the main railway line and the state highway running almost parallel to each other, and dividing the township into north and south blocks and devised the main access roads and branch roads accordingly. It proposed to lay out a number of branch roads with some points of access to the ring road to eliminate the bottlenecks. The Bisra-Panposh road was proposed to be re-constructed to terminate on the approach road leading from the railway station to the ring road. The above road was proposed to continue further east to Bisra, beyond the ring road junction. According to the Master Plan, this road starting from the ring road to the west, to the railway station approach road to the east and passing through the congested market places of the civil town, was proposed to be widened to 44 feet with a stipulation of 8 feet of open space in front of all buildings on both sides. The Bisra-Panposh road west of the ring road right to Panposh was also proposed to be widened to 100 feet. It was planned that the traffic coming from the Panposh side would have access to the ring road east of Area Nos. 7 and 8, and only the essential traffic schedule for Udit Nagar area would use the 44 feet wide-road beyond the ring road. The Plan also proposed to construct an over-bridge across the railway line con-necting Udit Nagar and Area No. 17 of the Master Plan or the present Basanti Colony area of the Civil Town (Fig. 5.1).

Thus, from the very beginning the State Government and the Plant Management Authority took all possible steps for the planned growth of the newly emerging industrial town at Rourkela.

GROWTH OF POPULATION AND EXPANSION OF THE CITY

The growth of population in both the steel and the civil townships has exceeded the earlier Master Plan projection of 2 lakh people when Rourkela region was fully developed. When the construction work for the steel plant and the township were begun in the mid-1950s, more than 50 thousand workers from different parts of the country were brought to the project site by various contractors and sub-contractors. With the completion of construction works and commissioning of plants and machineries, the HSL started recruiting a large number of skilled and unskilled labour in the project site, besides recruiting managerial executives at the all India level through a strict selection process. While recruiting workers for the steel plant; besides the local people, those workers who were associated with the construction activities of the plant and its township were given preference. A Muster Roll of the construction workers was initially prepared to absorb them subsequently on regular jobs. As a result, most of the construction workers instead of returning to their native place after the completion of construction, continued to reside in Rourkela in the hope of getting regular jobs in the steel plant and in its ancillary industries. Those who got regular jobs in the steel plant brought their family members as well. Thus, within a span of five or six years, the population in the project site started growing enormously. With the growth of population in the newly born township of Rourkela, the demand for goods and services produced in the informal manufacturing and tertiary sector picked up. Many poor and illiterate people from various parts of the state as well as from the neighbouring states such as Bihar and Madhya Pradesh, started moving to Rourkela with the hope of finding jobs. As only a few of them could be absorbed on a regular basis in the steel plant, others joined the informal sector factories at minimum wages. Since there was hardly any provision for housing and other basic amenities of these people, slums and squatter settlements in vacant public and private lands located near work sites sprang up. This resulted in haphazard growth of the city, except the sector areas of the steel township. Even vacant lands in the steel township area are found to have been occupied by poor slum dwellers. It has been observed that many slums and squatters have come up around the boundary of the steel plant, industrial estates and the main market area of the city. The growth pattern of the city shows that it is expanding in a west and south-east direction (Fig. 5.3).

According to 1951 census, the total population of acquired villages including Rourkela was 15,562. The population of Rourkela village including its slum population was 2,533. However, with the commissioning of the steel plant in 1960, it registered an enormous increase in its population. The erstwhile villages lost their identity and the new industrial town came to be known as Rourkela. At the time of 1961 census, the new industrial town was recorded for the first time as a big class-II town, with a total population of 90,287 within an urban boundary of 94.21 sq. km. This town all of a sudden became the largest town of Sundergarh district, surpassing the population figure of the oldest and the former largest town, Sundergarh, by more than three times. It is seen from Table 5.1 that since the birth of Rourkela as an industrial town in the early 1960s, the city has registered a steady increase in its area and population. During 1961-71 and 1971-81, the growth of population in the city was 91.06 per cent and 87.02 per cent respectively. The boundary of the city also increased from 94.21 sq. km. to 121.73 sq. km., in 1971 to 139.04 sq. km. in 1981 and further to 157.17 sq. km. in 1991. However, it seems from the findings of the 1991 census as well as 2001 census that the city now has stabilized in its growth for

TABLE 5.1: GROWTH OF POPULATION IN ROURKELA 1951-91

Sl. No.	Census Year	Area in sq. kms.	Total Population	% of Growth of Population
1.	1951	-	15,562	-
2.	1961	94.21	90,287	480.18
3.	1971	121.73	1,72,502	91.06
4.	1981	139.04	3,22,610	87.02
5.	1991	157.17	3,98,692	23.58
6.	2001	-	4,84,292	21.47

SOURCES: (i) *District Census Hand Book–Sundergarh* (different years), Directorate of Census Operations, Bhubaneswar.
(ii) Census of India (2001), *Provisional Population Totals,* Paper 2 of 2001, Registrar General and Census Commissioner, New Delhi.

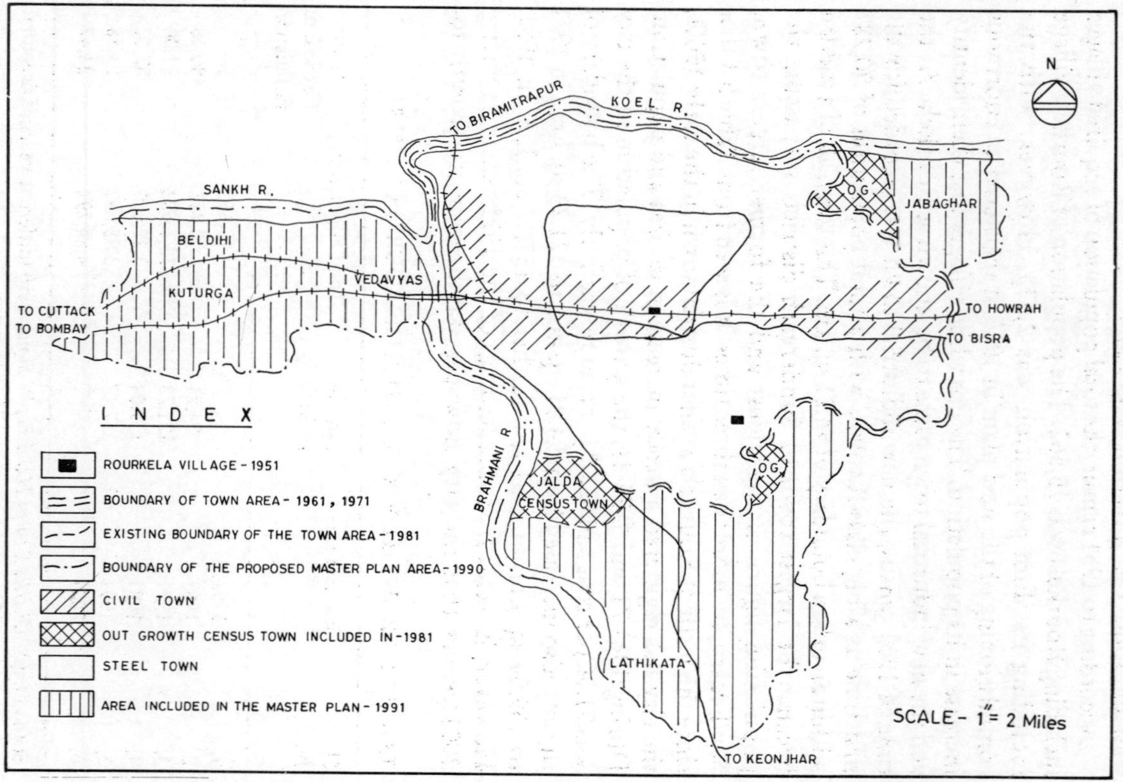

Fig. 5.3: Rourkela Phasewise Growth

unknown reasons, unlike other growing industrial towns of the country. During 1981-91 the city registered a population increase of only 23.58 per cent and during 1991-2001 this further slid down to 21.47 per cent. The total population of the city including urban agglomeration area according to the latest 2001 census is 4,84,292 persons only.

PATTERN OF IMMIGRATION

Rourkela belongs to the category of new industrial towns like Jamshedpur, Bokaro, Bhilai, Durgapur and Chittaranjan. There is a positive relation between industrialization and urbanization (Sovani 1981). The new urban centres grow by utilizing human and material resources of the hinterland, migration of people from different areas of the country and the aggregation of economic activities generated by the forces of modern industrialization. The modern pattern of industrialization coupled with the development of rapid transport and communication systems enabled people from diverse sociocultural, linguistic and geographical regions to migrate to Rourkela and settle down.

To expedite construction work of the steel plant, the project authority off-loaded work to many reputed construction companies and contractors hailing from different parts of the country. These companies further subdivided the work and distributed job works to many small companies and sub-contractors. As a large number of workers in skilled, semi-skilled and unskilled category were required for the construction work, and there was shortage of labour in the immediate hinterland, these companies and contractors either brought workers from their own regions or they took the help of middlemen to recruit the required number of workers. As these middlemen mainly relied on their local networks in their own villages and towns, quite a significant number of workers were drawn from particular regions, castes and communities. Subsequently, with the functioning of the steel plant, some of the construction workers decided to stay back at Rourkela, to work either as Muster Roll workers in the steel plant or to engage in the secondary and tertiary sectors of the newly growing town. Further, the scarcity of skilled and technically qualified personnel in Orissa during the 1950s and

1960s encouraged people from far-off places to come and work in Rourkela due to easy availability of jobs and lack of severe competition. As a result, the new industrial town of Rourkela got a cosmopolitan character, with its fairly large migrant population from various parts of the country and also from foreign countries who came to work in the giant public sector steel plant.

As discussed earlier, from a small little known village in the 1950s, Rourkela suddenly gained the status of a big class-II town by the time the 1961 census was out because of the presence of the steel plant. It is seen from Table 5.2 that as compared to other class-I category towns in Orissa, the city of Rourkela had a fairly high percentage of migrant population at the time of 1971 census. The percentage of non-migrant population in Rourkela during 1971 was only 29.14; whereas in case of other class-I category towns such as Bhubaneswar, Berhampur, Cuttack and Sambalpur it was between

TABLE 5.2: MIGRANT AND NON-MIGRANT POPULATION IN THE CLASS-I TOWNS OF ORISSA DURING 1971

Sl. No.	City/Urban Agglomeration	Total Population	Non-Migrant Population	Intrastate Migrant Population	Inter-Dist. Migrant Pop.	Inter-State Migrant Pop.
1.	Berhampur	1,17,065	72,575 (62.00)	27,860 (23.80)	8,680 (7.41)	7,950 (6.79)
2.	Bhubaneswar	1,04,745	34,695 (33.12)	19,990 (19.08)	41,555 (39.67)	8,505 (8.12)
3.	Cuttack	2,03,905	1,21,450 (59.56)	33,855 (16.60)	31,475 (15.44)	17,125 (8.40)
4.	Rourkela	1,70,000	49,540 (29.14)	13,160 (7.74)	44,955 (26.44)	62,345 (36.67)
5.	Sambalpur	1,03,855	49,775 (47.93)	19,690 (18.96)	22,400 (21.57)	11,990 (11.54)
	All cities	6,99,570	3,28,035 (46.89)	1,14,555 (27.85)	1,49,065 (21.31)	1,07,915 (15.43)

NOTE: Figures in bracket indicate percentage.

SOURCE: Census of India, 1971, *Migration Tables*, Series 16, Part II D, Orissa, pp. 334-5.

33 per cent to 62 per cent and for all class-I towns population put together it was 46.89 per cent. Similarly, the percentage of inter-district migrant population hailing from Orissa was 26.44, which was higher than other class-I towns of Orissa except Bhubaneswar. The percentage of inter-state migrant population in the city was quite high (36.67%), as compared to any other city in Orissa. The percentage of migrant population in other class-I towns of Orissa such as Berhampur, Bhubaneswar, Cuttack and Sambalpur varied between 6.79 to 11.54. This shows that by 1971, Rourkela had already gained the status of a national town by virtue of its representation of a fairly high percentage of inter-district and inter-state migrant population.

The 1981 census data reveals that the city of Rourkela alone had a share of 78 per cent of the total urban population in the district of Sundergarh. It is seen from Table 5.3 that in 1981, among the urban male population of the district more than 50 per cent were those

TABLE 5.3: PERCENTAGE OF MALES BORN IN OTHER STATES OF INDIA AND OTHER DISTRICTS OF ORISSA BUT WERE ENUMERATED IN THE URBAN AREAS OF SUNDERGARH DISTRICT IN 1981

Sl. No.	State of Birth	Percentage	District of Birth	Percentage
1.	Andhra Pradesh	1.21	Sambalpur	2.20
2.	Bihar	14.06	Kendujhar	0.27
3.	Haryana	0.50	Mayurbhanj	2.00
4.	Kerala	0.98	Baleswar	1.92
5.	Madhya Pradesh	1.66	Cuttack	8.16
6.	Maharashtra	0.18	Dhenkanal	1.23
7.	Punjab	0.63	Phulbani	0.07
8.	Rajasthan	0.43	Bolangir	0.85
9.	Tamil Nadu	0.37	Kalahandi	0.22
10.	Uttar Pradesh	2.26	Koraput	0.06
11.	West Bengal	3.69	Ganjam	4.98
12.	Other States and Union Territories	0.67	Puri	1.93
Total		26.64		23.90

SOURCE: Census of India, 1981, *Migration Tables*, Series 16, Part V A & B, Orissa.

whose native place was other than the district of Sundergarh. Unlike in the case of female population, the presence and reporting of male population in places other than their place of birth, at the time of the census reveals their migratory status. Hence, it may be assumed that the urban areas of Sundergarh district had a fairly high percentage of migrant population and Rourkela being the major urban centre of the district with a cosmopolitan composition, it might be inferred that more than 50 per cent of the population in Rourkela at the time of 1981 Census comprised of migrants from other districts of Orissa, and other states of India as well. It is seen from Table 5.3 that in the urban areas of Sundergarh district, the percentage of male population hailing from other states of the country excluding Orissa was 26.64 in 1981 and from the other districts of Orissa it was 23.90. Among these inter-State migrants, the highest number came from Bihar (14.06%), followed by West Bengal (3.69%), Uttar Pradesh (2.26%), Madhya Pradesh (1.66%), Andhra Pradesh (1.21%), Kerala (0.98%), Punjab (0.63%), Haryana (0.50%), and the remaining states put together constituted 1.65 per cent of the inter-State migrant male population. Similarly in the category of migrants from other districts of the State of Orissa to the urban areas of Sundergarh district, the coastal districts of Cuttack (9.16%), Puri (1.93%), Baleswar (1.92%), and Ganjam (4.98%) had a larger share as compared to the adjacent districts of Sambalpur (2.02%), Kendujhar (0.27%), Dhenkanal (1.23%) and Mayurbhanj (2.00%).

Cityward migration in India reveals an interesting aspect of population movement in the wake of industrialization. As mentioned earlier, although many scholars have analysed cityward migration in terms of either push factors such as the pressure of population on land, large scale unemployment in rural areas, deterioration of the village economy, or the pull factors such as employment opportunities, better civic amenities, scope of higher education for children and the like, it is necessary to supplement it with a deeper analysis of the social linkages involved in the process of migration to understand the social characteristics of urban complexes in India. It is noticed that among the people placed in similar socio-economic conditions, there are some who tend to move, whereas others do not. Very rarely people move without prior information and linkage of some kind or the other. In his studies of migration, Rao found that social network like kinship, caste, village and language was the most effective channel of information system which favours decision making in migration (Rao 1974 and 1976).

So, in order to find out how the migrants from the other districts of Orissa and from other states of the country came to Rourkela and what is their representation of population in the city, a section on migrational behaviour was incorporated in the questionnaire. From a sample of 316 households, it is seen from Table 5.4 that there are 127 (40.19%) migrant households whose place of origin is other than the State of Orissa. Among these inter-State migrant households, 77 (24.37%) have come from Bihar, 15 (4.75%) from West Bengal, 13 (4.11%) from Uttar Pradesh, 8 (2.53%) from Madhya Pradesh, 5 (1.58%) from Punjab, 4 (1.27%) from Andhra Pradesh and the remaining 5 (1.58%) from the States like Haryana, Maharashtra, Kerala and the neighbouring country Nepal. Of the remaining 189 (59.81%) households belonging to the State of Orissa, only 64 (20.25%) households in the city reported their place of origin

TABLE 5.4: PLACE OF BIRTH OF THE HEAD OF THE SAMPLE HOUSEHOLDS RESIDING IN THE CITY OF ROURKELA DURING 1988-9

Sl. No.	Place of Birth	No. of Households	Percentage
A.	*Orissa*	198	59.81
1.	Sundergarh	64	20.25
2.	Ganjam	50	15.82
3.	Cuttack	43	13.61
4.	Puri	05	1.58
5.	Balasore	06	1.58
6.	Sambalpur	05	1.58
7.	Bolangir	05	1.58
8.	Mayurbhanj	04	1.27
9.	Dhenkanal	03	0.95
10.	Kendujhar	02	0.63
11.	Kalahandi	02	0.63
B.	*Bihar*	77	24.37
1.	Gaya	21	6.65
2.	Singhbhum	15	4.75
3.	Jamshedpur	12	3.80
4.	Ranchi	09	2.85
5.	Mungher	06	1.90
6.	Patna	03	0.95

(contd.)

TABLE 5.4 (contd.)

7.	Chhapra	03	0.95
8.	Darbhanga	02	0.63
9.	Siwan	01	0.32
10.	Gopalganj	01	0.32
11.	Giridih	01	0.32
12.	Ghatsila	01	0.32
13.	Rohtas	01	0.32
14.	Muzaffarpur	01	0.32
C.	*West Bengal*	15	4.75
1.	Purulia	04	1.27
2.	Kolkata	04	1.27
3.	Murshidabad	03	0.63
4.	Jhargram	01	0.32
5.	Howrah	01	0.32
6.	Midnapore	02	0.63
7.	Darjeeling	01	0.32
D.	*Uttar Pradesh*	13	4.11
1.	Kanpur	06	1.90
2.	Gorakhpur	02	0.63
3.	Varanasi	02	0.63
4.	Meerut	01	0.32
5.	Ghazipur	01	0.32
6.	Fatehpur	01	0.32
E.	*Madhya Pradesh*	08	2.53
1.	Bilaspur	05	1.58
2.	Durg	02	0.63
3.	Raipur	01	0.32
F.	*Punjab*	05	1.58
1.	Hoshiarpur	02	0.63
2.	Amritsar	01	0.32
3.	Faridkot	01	0.32
4.	Sangrur	01	0.32
G.	*Andhra Pradesh*	04	1.27
1.	Srikakulam	04	1.27
H.	*Haryana*	02	0.63
1.	Rohtak	02	0.63
I.	*Maharashtra*	01	0.32
1.	Nagpur	01	0.32
J.	*Kerala*	01	0.32
1.	Allepy	01	0.32
K.	*Nepal*	01	0.32
	Total	316	100.00

SOURCE: Field Data, 1988-9.

TABLE 5.5: YEARS OF RESIDENCE OF THE SAMPLE HOUSEHOLDS AT ROURKELA

Sl. No.	Years	No. of Households	Percentage
1.	Residing since birth	27	8.54
2.	30 years and above	90	28.48
3.	20 to 30 years	100	31.65
4.	10 to 20 years	64	20.25
5.	0 to 10 years	35	11.08
	Total	316	100.00

SOURCE: Field Data, 1988-9.

as Sundergarh district, and the remaining 125 (39.56%) households have come from the other districts of Orissa. More so, among these inter-district migrant households 43 (13.61%) are from Cuttack district, 50 (15.82%) from Ganjam district, 5 (1.58%) each from the districts of Baleśwar, Bolangir, Puri and Sambalpur and the rest 11 (3.48%) are from other districts of Orissa.

It is in fact revealed from Table 5.5 that the heads of only 27 (8.54%) households were born in the city, whereas the remaining 289 (91.46%) heads of households came and settled down in Rourkela after the establishment of the steel plant. Among these immigrant households, the heads of as many as 90 (28.48%) households have been residing in the city for the past 30 years or so, and they came to Rourkela to work at the construction sites of the steel plant and the township. The numbers of heads of households reported to be residing in the city for the last 20 to 30 years are 100 (31.65%) in the sample, whereas 99 (31.33%) have come to the city during the past 20 years.

From the reporting of the respondents in the sample, it is found that kinship, caste, regional and linguistic ties have played an important role in the migration of immigrant households to the city of Rourkela. It is found from Table 5.6 that out of 289 immigrant households, only the heads of 105 (36.33%) households reported that they had come to the city on their own to work in the steel plant. From the informal discussion with such people it was observed that quite a few of them were skilled workers, who had completed

TABLE 5.6: PERSONS WHO HELPED HEADS OF THE SAMPLE HOUSEHOLDS (MIGRANTS) IN COMING TO ROURKELA

Sl. No.	Persons	No. of Households	Percentage
1.	Relatives	95	32.87
2.	Friends	7	2.42
3.	Native people	73	25.26
4.	Contractor	9	3.11
5.	Self	105	36.33
	Total	289	99.99

SOURCE: Field Data, 1988-9.

diploma and certificate courses in various technical schools and initially joined the plant as trainees. But in case of the remaining immigrant households it was revealed that the heads of 95 (32.87%) households had come to Rourkela because some of their relatives were either working in the plant or township and they helped them in securing jobs in Rourkela. The heads of another 73 (25.26%) households reported that they came in groups along with the local people of the region they originate from, when the construction work at the steel plant was started. Their source of information regarding availability of jobs in the project site was the '*jamadars*' or middlemen under whose guidance they moved to the project site. Of the remaining 16 households, 9 (13.11%) mentioned that they were brought directly by the contractors to work under them, and 7 (2.42%) said that their friends, who were working in Rourkela helped them in coming to the city, provided them shelter and also arranged jobs for them through their local contacts and influences. This finding supports the observations made by urban studies that the cityward migration of people in urban India and other third world countries, is not merely due to the push and pull factors. The social and personal network of the migrants and also their contacts in urban areas determine to a great extent the destination and their means of livelihood in the city (Patel 1963; ILO 1972; Rao 1974 and 1976).

SOCIAL ECOLOGY OF THE CITY AND RESIDENTIAL SEGREGATION OF THE ETHNIC GROUPS

Owing to the growth of many industries and the large size of industrial workforce, the tertiary sector activity in the city has also registered a noticeable increase, thereby adding further to the population and pushing further outward the boundary of the city. As mentioned earlier, the population of Rourkela village including the bustee was only 2,533 at the time of 1951 census and the 30 villages acquired for the purpose of steel plant and its township had a total population of 15,562 in the 1950s. The ethnic composition of population in these displaced villages revealed that there were 67.73 per cent tribal households, 7.90 per cent scheduled caste households, 3.44 per cent upper caste households, 6.12 per cent middle caste households, 10.78 per cent lower caste households, 1.70 per cent Muslim households and 2.31 per cent of other minority group households residing during 1950s. The physical boundary of the new town was only 94.21 sq. km. at the time of 1961 census. However, this increased to 121.73 sq. km. in 1971 and 139.04 sq. km. in 1981 registering thereby an increase in area of 29.21 per cent during 1961-71 and 14.22 per cent during 1971-81 (Fig. 5.3). With the growth of the township, the ethnic composition of population in the city also started registering a remarkable change over the years. It is found from the census data that in 1961 when Rourkela suddenly gained the status of a big class-II town, the composition of scheduled castes and scheduled tribes in the town all of a sudden came down to 5.20 per cent and 22.07 per cent respectively. This was due to large scale immigration of Hindus and other minority groups to this industrial town from various parts of the country. Although the percentage of scheduled castes population in the city registered a slight increase in the subsequent decades (6.02 per cent in 1971 and 8.15 per cent in 1981), the percentage share of scheduled tribe population further came down to 12.20 per cent in 1971 and registered only a marginal increase in 1981, i.e. to 16.40 per cent. Thus, with the growth of the township and increase in population over the years, the social characteristics of the households residing in the city also began to change. The existing tribal subsistence agricultural socioeconomic set up in the region, during the 1950s gradually made way for the growth of a modern industrial urban economy. Urbanization and industrialization also resulted in detribalization on a large scale.

RESIDENTIAL AREAS AND DISTRIBUTION OF CASTES AND OTHER ETHNIC GROUPS

After the 1931 census, the Indian Population Census in subsequent decades stopped collecting details of information on caste composition of the population. So, it is not possible to get detail information on caste and ethnic composition of population and households residing at Rourkela city by relying on census data. However, from the 1984 voters' list of Rourkela Assembly Constituency, which covers a total of 59,661 households and works out to 85.94 per cent of the total number of 69,423 households recorded to be residing in the city at the time of 1981 census, I have broadly delimited the caste and ethnic composition of the households and presented them in Table 5.7.

Since the voters' list contains the name and surname of voters in various households residing in various localities of the city constituency, I have identified the caste and ethnic background of the households from my knowledge of surnames of voters. In case of confusion and doubts I have consulted the people residing in the locality. Hence, although the method adopted by me is not entirely scientific to give an accurate picture of caste and ethnic composition of the households residing in various localities of Rourkela city, nevertheless, it gives approximate configuration of the caste and ethnic groups living in the city.

It is seen from Table 5.7 that in the Rourkela Assembly Constituency the higher caste households such as Brahmins, Kayasthas (Karans in Oriya) and Kshatriyas comprise 25.50 per cent, middle caste household consisting of Khandayat, Chasa, Bania, Marwari, Agaria, etc., constitute 26.62 per cent and the lower caste households consisting of blacksmiths (*luharas*), potters (*kumbhara*), weavers (*tantis*), milk-men (*gaudas*), goldsmiths (*sunaris*), gardeners (*malis*) and the like constitute 11.15 per cent. This means Hindu households constitute more than 60 per cent of the total voter households in the constituency. The share of Scheduled Caste

TABLE 5.7: CASTE, RELIGION AND LINGUISTIC DISTRIBUTION OF HOUSEHOLDS IN ROURKELA ASSEMBLY CONSTITUENCY ACCORDING TO 1984 VOTERS' LIST

Sl. No.	Name of Locality	No. of Households	Higher Castes	Middle Castes	Lower Castes	S.C.	S.T.	Muslims	Christians	Sikhs	Non-Oriya (excluding Muslims)
1	2	3	4	5	6	7	8	9	10	11	12
1.	Panposh area	3866	901	1071	433	400	904	119	216	25	626
			(23.31)	(27.70)	(11.20)	(10.35)	(23.38)	(3.08)	(5.59)	(0.65)	(16.19)
2.	Uditnagar area	2422	603	685	282	282	531	35	76	51	454
			(24.90)	(28.23)	(11.64)	(11.64)	(21.92)	(1.44)	(3.14)	(2.11)	(18.74)
3.	Basanti colony	1595	575	521	117	81	244	19	57	34	292
			(36.95)	(32.66)	(7.33)	(5.08)	(15.30)	(1.14)	(3.37)	(2.13)	(18.31)
4.	Malgodam area	4678	779	1079	739	1094	831	133	163	20	978
			(16.65)	(23.06)	(15.80)	(23.39)	(17.76)	(2.84)	(3.48)	(0.43)	(20.91)
5.	Rourkela market area	3173	681	1169	340	308	164	251	21	260	1279
			(21.46)	(36.84)	(10.71)	(9.71)	(5.17)	(7.91)	(0.66)	(8.19)	(40.31)
6.	Nala road area	1298	42	78	37	39	13	1088	1	1	–
			(3.24)	(6.01)	(2.85)	(3.00)	(1.00)	(83.88)	(0.08)	(0.08)	–
7.	Bandomunda area	5596	1293	1129	631	912	1489	89	141	48	1826
			(23.11)	(20.17)	(11.28)	(16.30)	(26.61)	(1.59)	(2.52)	(0.86)	(32.63)

(contd.)

TABLE 5.7 (contd.)

Sl. No.	Name of Locality	No. of Households	Higher Castes	Middle Castes	Lower Castes	S.C.	S.T.	Muslims	Christians	Sikhs	Non-Oriya (excluding Muslims)
1	2	3	4	5	6	7	8	9	10	11	12
8.	Modern India area	4198	739 (17.60)	1312 (31.25)	442 (10.53)	594 (14.15)	1051 (25.04)	34 (0.81)	120 (2.86)	24 (0.57)	394 (9.38)
9.	Jalda area	4120	168 (4.08)	375 (9.10)	509 (12.35)	495 (12.01)	2425 (58.86)	13 (0.32)	492 (11.94)	3 (0.07)	136 (3.30)
10.	Fertilizer town area	1206	487 (40.38)	348 (28.86)	115 (9.54)	108 (8.95)	91 (7.55)	26 (2.16)	52 (4.31)	28 (2.32)	442 (36.65)
11.	Jhirpani resettlement area	1158	111 (9.58)	94 (8.12)	101 (8.72)	196 (16.93)	651 (56.22)	5 (0.43)	175 (15.11)	– –	24 (2.07)
12.	REC Campus area	686	290 (42.27)	177 (25.80)	51 (7.43)	49 (7.14)	106 (15.45)	10 (1.46)	20 (2.91)	1 (0.15)	64 (9.33)
13.	Peripheral villages around steel township (Luakera, Tumkela, Hamirpur, Bhawanipur)	1175	63 (5.36)	130 (11.06)	202 (17.19)	232 (19.74)	517 (44.00)	31 (2.64)	102 (8.68)	– (2.89)	34

14. Sector 1	2482	791	857	232	232	305	33	38	25	359
		(31.87)	(34.53)	(9.35)	(9.35)	(12.29)	(1.33)	(1.53)	(1.01)	(14.46)
15. Sector 2	2032	555	554	230	320	318	40	25	15	357
		(27.31)	(27.26)	(11.32)	(15.75)	(15.65)	(1.97)	(1.23)	(0.74)	(17.57)
16. Sectors 3, 4 & 5	2149	909	634	248	201	71	43	29	36	577
		(42.30)	(29.50)	(11.54)	(9.35)	(3.30)	(2.00)	(1.35)	(1.67)	(26.85)
17. Sector 6	2798	1006	910	327	356	133	19	43	38	658
		(35.95)	(32.52)	(11.69)	(12.72)	(4.75)	(0.68)	(4.54)	(1.36)	(23.52)
18. Sector 7	1294	596	454	127	54	35	5	27	23	507
		(46.06)	(35.08)	(9.81)	(4.71)	(2.70)	(0.39)	(2.09)	(1.78)	(39.18)
19. Sector 8	1575	615	568	153	95	107	11	34	26	505
		(39.05)	(36.06)	(9.71)	(6.03)	(6.79)	(0.70)	(2.16)	(1.65)	(32.06)
20. Sectors 13 & 14	1569	664	485	166	100	115	8	53	31	767
		(42.32)	(30.91)	(10.58)	(6.37)	(7.33)	(0.51)	(3.38)	(1.98)	(48.88)
21. Sector 15	2162	454	637	176	117	186	572	44	20	368
		(21.00)	(29.46)	(8.14)	(5.41)	(8.60)	(26.46)	(2.03)	(0.93)	(17.02)
22. Sectors 16 & 17	2189	674	742	271	226	195	21	61	60	524
		(30.79)	(33.90)	(12.38)	(10.32)	(8.91)	(0.96)	(2.79)	(2.74)	(23.94)
23. Sector 18	1576	556	471	215	169	77	64	29	19	445
		(35.28)	(29.89)	(13.64)	(10.72)	(4.89)	(4.06)	(1.84)	(1.21)	(28.24)
24. Sector 19	1127	454	327	100	126	87	17	41	2	259
		(40.28)	(29.01)	(8.87)	(11.18)	(7.72)	(1.51)	(3.64)	(0.18)	(22.99)

(contd.)

TABLE 5.7 (contd.)

Sl. No.	Name of Locality	No. of Households	Higher Castes	Middle Castes	Lower Castes	S.C.	S.T.	Muslims	Christians	Sikhs	Non-Oriya (excluding Muslims)
1	2	3	4	5	6	7	8	9	10	11	12
25.	Sector 20	1800	701 (38.94)	511 (28.39)	215 (11.94)	226 (12.56)	89 (4.94)	22 (1.22)	48 (2.67)	32 (1.78)	550 (30.56)
26.	Sector 21	363	148 (40.78)	108 (29.75)	47 (12.95)	30 (8.26)	15 (4.13)	8 (2.20)	8 (2.20)	7 (1.93)	126 (34.71)
27.	OMP Colony and Security Colony area (Near Sector 21)	1374	358 (26.05)	457 (33.26)	146 (10.63)	166 (12.08)	218 (15.87)	24 (1.75)	12 (0.87)	5 (0.36)	176 (12.81)
Total		59661	15213 (25.50)	15883 (26.62)	6652 (11.15)	7208 (12.08)	10968 (18.38)	2740 (4.59)	2128 (3.57)	834 (1.40)	12727 (21.33)

SOURCE: Government of Orissa (1984), *Voters' List of Rourkela Assembly Constituency*, Office of the Sub-Collector, Panposh Subdivision, Rourkela.

households in the constituency is only 12.08 per cent and despite their numerical majority of population in Sundergarh district, the share of tribal households in the city constituency is merely 18.38 per cent. Besides this, Muslim households in the constituency comprise 4.59 per cent, Christians including converted tribals 3.57 per cent and the Sikhs constitute 1.40 per cent of total number of voter households. It is further observed that excluding Muslim households, the percentage of non-Oriya households in the constituency comes approximately to 21.33. In the delimitation process of the non-Oriya voter households we have deliberately excluded the Muslim households, because it is not possible to know the provincial origin of the households from family surnames.

Apart from this, it is observed from the broad classification of the City Constituency into 27 localities, presented in Table 5.7, that there are some localities and pockets in the city where there is a concentration of certain castes and ethnic groups. Although Rourkela is a modern industrial town belonging to post independent India, there are certain localities like Regional Engineering College (REC) campus area, fertilizer township area and Sectors 3, 4, 5, 7, 13, 14, 19 and 21 of the steel township, where the concentration of higher caste households is more than 40 per cent. Interestingly these localities are mainly resided by highly paid professionals such as educationists, executives and supervisory staff of the steel plant and a few 'blue-collar' plant workers. The localities like Jalda Resettlement Colony, Jhirpani Resettlement Colony and the peripheral villages around the steel township such as Luakera, Tumkela, Hamirpur and Bhawanipur, mainly consists of tribal households and the earning members mostly belong to informal sector with very low levels of income. The Nala Road area mainly consists of Muslims of both high and low income groups. Similarly, certain localities such as Rourkela market area, Bandomunda area, fertilizer township area, Sectors 7, 8, 13, 14, 20 and 21 of the steel township, have a fairly high percentage of non-Oriya households, than their average percentage (21.33 per cent) of representation in the constituency. Here the main earning members of the households are mainly executives and supervisory staff belonging to the steel plant, railways or are big traders and merchant community of the city. Bandomunda is mainly resided by the railway employees of different grades. The Rourkela market area is mainly resided by the trading castes and communities; whereas the sectored area of the steel township and fertilizer township are mainly resided by the senior employees of the steel plant. Moreover, it is to be noted that the broad classification of the city localities in the table conceals many facts regarding caste, communities, ethnic and regional concentration of households in different sublocalities and 'mohallas' of the industrial city. Although the higher, middle and lower caste groups continue to live together without any discrimination, it has been observed that the scheduled castes and scheduled tribes in various localities continue to live in isolated clusters. The minority groups like the Muslims, Christians and Sikhs have also preferred to retain their identity by living in large numbers in localities like Nala Road and Mahatma Gandhi Road and Gurudwara Road of Rourkela market area. Even in the planned sector area of the steel township the Muslim workers of the steel plant have preferred to stay in large numbers in certain blocks of Sector 15 which are adjacent to one another. Hence, it is evident that the sociocultural factors like caste, religion, language and regional affiliation have mostly determined the choice of living in different localities of the city, although some of them might have given equal weightage to their place of employment and income, while selecting their residential area.

In order to know, whether there is a significant variation in the distribution of various castes and minority households in different localities of Rourkela city, we have used ANOVA (Analysis of Variance) test by classifying the various localities presented in Table 5.7, into ten broad regions in Table 5.8. It is to be noted that these ten regions are formed and named so (R_1, R_2......R_{10}) for our convenience, by taking into consideration the geographical location and homogeneity of various sub-regions in the city. From our ANOVA test it is found that the variation in distribution of households between castes and other community groups and also between localities is significant at 1 per cent level of significance (Table 5.9). Therefore it can be deduced that there is a wide variation in the distribution of various castes and minority households in different localities of Rourkela. The variance ratio or 'F' value of variation between castes and other community groups is $4.29 > 3.07$ and between regions, it is $5.43 > 2.67$.

TABLE 5.8: DISTRIBUTION OF VARIOUS CASTES AND MINORITY HOUSEHOLDS IN DIFFERENT REGIONS OF ROURKELA ASSEMBLY CONSTITUENCY

Sl. No.	Region	Total no. of Households	No. of Higher Caste HHs	No. of Middle Caste HHs	No. of Lower Caste HHs	No. of S.C. HHs	No. of S.T. HHs	No. of Muslim HHs	No. of other Category HHs
1	2	3	4	5	6	7	8	9	10
1.	Panposh area (R^1)	3866	901 (23.31)	1071 (27.70)	433 (11.20)	400 (10.35)	904 (23.38)	119 (3.08)	38 (0.98)
2.	Uditnagar area (R^2)	4017	1178 (29.33)	1206 (30.02)	399 (9.93)	363 (9.04)	775 (19.29)	54 (1.34)	42 (1.05)
3.	Malgodam area (R^3)	4678	779 (16.65)	1079 (23.07)	739 (15.80)	1094 (23.39)	831 (17.76)	133 (2.84)	23 (0.49)
4.	Rourkela Market area (R^4)	4471	723 (16.17)	1247 (27.89)	377 (8.43)	347 (7.76)	177 (3.96)	1339 (29.95)	261 (5.84)
5.	Bandomunda area (R^5)	5596	1293 (23.10)	1129 (20.17)	631 (11.28)	912 (16.30)	1489 (26.61)	89 (1.59)	53 (0.95)
6.	Modern India & Fertilizer								

(contd.)

TABLE 5.8 (contd.)

township (R^{6})	5404	1226 (22.69)	1660 (30.72)	557 (10.31)	702 (12.99)	1142 (21.13)	60 (1.11)	57 (1.05)
7. Jalda Resettle-ment area (R^{7})	4120	168 (4.08)	375 (9.10)	509 (12.35)	495 (12.01)	2425 (58.86)	13 (0.32)	135 (3.28)
8. Peripheral villages & Jhirpani (R^{8})	2333	174 (7.46)	324 (9.60)	303 (12.99)	428 (18.35)	1168 (50.06)	36 (1.54)	0 (0.00)
9. Sectors 3, 4, 5, 19 & REC Campus (R^{9})	3962	1653 (41.72)	1138 (28.72)	399 (10.07)	376 (9.49)	264 (6.66)	70 (1.77)	62 (1.57)
10. Other Sector area of steel township (R^{10})	21214	7118 (33.55)	6754 (31.84)	2305 (10.87)	2091 (9.36)	1793 (8.45)	287 (3.90)	326 (1.54)
Total	59661	15213 (25.50)	15883 (26.62)	6652 (11.15)	7208 (12.08)	10968 (18.38)	2740 (4.59)	997 (1.68)

NOTE.: Figures in brackets indicate percentage.

TABLE 5.9: ANOVA SUMMARY TABLE: DISTRIBUTION OF VARIOUS CASTES AND MINORITY HOUSEHOLDS IN DIFFERENT REGIONS OF ROURKELA ASSEMBLY CONSTITUENCY

Sl. No.	Sources of Variation	Sums of Squares (SS)	Degrees of Freedom (df)	Mean Squares (MS)	Variance Ratio or 'F' value
1.	Between castes and other community groups	2002.1736	6	333.6956	4.29*
2.	Between localities	3795.4177	9	421.7131	5.43*
3.	Error	4195.3139	54	77.6986	–
	Total (TSS)	9993.3139	69	–	–

NOTE: *Significant at 1 per cent level of significance.

Further, in order to know, which of these ten regions have statistically significant level of differences, in the distribution of various castes and other minority households in comparison to the aggregate level of distribution of castes and other ethnic groups in the city, the X^2 test has been used. It is seen from Table 5.10 that the regions R_3, R_4, R_7, R_8 and R_9 have very high X^2 values, i.e. greater than 12.59 at 5 per cent significant level. This means the five regions, viz, (i) Malgodam area, (ii) Rourkela market area, (iii) Jalda Resettlement Colony area, (iv) Peripheral villages and Jhirpani Resettlement Colony area and (v) Sectors 3, 4, 5, 19 and Regional Engineering College campus area of the steel township, have wide variation in the distribution of various castes and other minority households as compared to their aggregate/percentage level distribution in the city of Rourkela Assembly Constituency as a whole. In fact, these regions consist of various sub-regions or localities like Malgodam slum, Gualapara, Madhusudanpalli and Gopabandhupalli in R_3, Nala Road, Mahulpali, Plantsite, Gandhi Road, Gurudwara Road and Rourkela main market area in R_4, Deogaon village and Jalda 'A', 'B' and 'C' blocks of Jalda Resettlement Colony in R_7; peripheral villages like Luakera, Tumkela, Hamirpur and Jhirpani Resettlement Colony in R_8; and above all Sectors 3, 4, 5, 19 and Regional Engineering College campus of the steel township in R_9. Thus, according to the findings of our

TABLE 5.10: TEST OF DIFFERENCES IN THE CASTES AND OTHER MINORITY HOUSEHOLDS DISTRIBUTION IN DIFFERENT REGIONS OF ROURKELA ASSEMBLY CONSTITUENCY

Sl. No.	Caste/ Community	R_1	R_2	R_3	R_4	R_5	R_6	R_7	R_8	R_9	R_{10}	Aggregate
1.	Higher Castes	23.31	29.33	16.65	16.17	23.10	22.69	4.08	7.46	41.72	33.55	25.50
2.	Middle Castes	27.70	30.02	23.07	27.89	20.17	30.72	9.10	9.60	28.72	31.84	26.62
3.	Lower Castes	11.20	9.93	15.80	8.43	11.28	10.31	12.35	12.99	10.07	10.87	11.15
4.	Scheduled Castes	10.35	9.04	23.39	7.76	16.30	12.99	12.01	18.35	9.49	19.86	12.08
5.	Scheduled Tribes	23.38	19.29	17.76	3.96	26.61	21.13	58.86	50.06	6.66	8.45	18.38
6.	Muslims	3.08	1.34	2.84	29.95	1.59	1.11	0.32	1.54	1.77	3.90	4.59
7.	Others	0.98	1.05	0.49	5.84	0.95	1.05	3.28	0.00	1.57	1.54	1.68
	X^2 Value	(2.63)	(4.49)	(17.60)	(167.41)	(9.23)	(4.36)	(124.30)	(85.51)	(20.25)	(9.46)	-

ANOVA and X^2 tests, we can firmly conclude that notwithstanding partial planning and modern industrial dominance of the Rourkela city, localities are formed and developed on the basis of high concentration of certain caste and ethnic groups deliberately. As a result, the whole population of the city is divided along caste, region, language and ethnic lines, with the dominance of certain castes and ethnic groups in certain pockets.

THE CITY ECOLOGY

It is observed from the city maps (Figs. 5.1 to 5.4 and 1.1) that the location of the public sector steel plant has determined the growth and expansion of spatial structure at Rourkela, although various cultural forces such as caste, community, region, language and linguistic origin of the population have broadly affected the formation of neighbourhoods in the city. In the north adjacent to the steel plant the main market area of the city, railway station and the bus stand are located. This region broadly may be called the central business district of the city. The second ring of the zone in transition consists of localities like Nala Road, Mahulpali, Oraon-para, Plantsite Police Station area, Kumbharpara, Malgodam, Madhusudanpalli, Gopabandhupalli in the north of the steel plant; Modern India area comprising localities like Tarapur, Laltanki, Construction Colony, Modern India Labour Colony, etc., in the south-east and Captive Power Plant area, Phulbari, Champagarh Labour Colony, etc., in the north-east. It is noticed that this zone has a cheek-by-jowl mixture of land uses; industry, commerce and business intermingle with high-density, highly subdivided residential accommodation and sub-standard quarters in which mostly poor informal sector workers reside. The main slum and squatter areas of the city such as Malgodam, Madhusudanpalli, Gopabandhupalli, Kumbharpara, Nala Road, Mohulpali on the north side of the plant's main gate, Laltanki, Tarapur, Construction Colony, Modern India Labour Colony in the south-east side; Captive Power Plant Jhonpri, Champagarh Labour Colony, Phulbari, etc., in the north-east are found in this zone. These slums occupied by low income groups are located within a distance of 3 km. from the boundary of the steel plant and the main market area of the city. However, there is no clear demarcation between the third zone housing of the working class and the fourth zone—the zone of better residences providing accommodation for the white collar employees and the professionals. The steel township, which is located on the opposite side of the Durgapur hills, towards the north of the steel plant consists of 17 sectors with composite and mixed housing patterns. Nevertheless, it is observed that Sectors 1 and 2 are mainly resided by the low income group workers, Sectors 6, 7, 8 and 18 by the middle level non-executive workers and Sectors 3, 4, 5 and 19 by the senior executives. Similarly, in the civil township area it is observed that the Udit Nagar and Basanti Colony area meet the residential requirements of low, middle and high income groups of the State Government employees and self-employed people. The fertilizer township located adjacent to the Modern India area towards the south-east of the plant is also a mixed residential area, providing accommodation to all categories of workers and executives employed in the fertilizer plant, attached to the Rourkela Steel Plant. The affluent and posh colonies like Area Nos. 7 and 8 in the civil township located in between Panposh and Udit Nagar on the west side of the plant and the Koel Nagar and Shakti Nagar near Sector 20 of steel township in the north side may be considered as the fifth zone or the suburban area, where many distinguished bungalows have come up in recent years in order to accommodate the richer section in a relatively spacious and clean environment.

However, although this gives us a broad picture of city's social ecology and growth and formation of different functional areas, there is some deviation from the Master Plan, because of several unanticipated effects of urbanization. This is how the industrial estate accommodating small and ancillary industries have come up in the northwest side of the steel plant, in the vicinity of Area Nos. 7 and 8 and Panposh and Raghunathpali village. Beyond Panposh in the west, another big industrial estate, i.e. Kalunga has also come up across the river Brahmani. In the south too the city has expanded upto Lathikata beyond Jalda resettlement colony in Rourkela-Bonai road. The growth of Lathikata is mainly due to two large scale units—the refractory plant and Suidihi distillery. Similarly in the east it has expanded upto Bandomunda, the site of the diesel locomotive workshop of the Indian Railways. But as these localities are still growing, it is very difficult to say, what kind of impact and change they will bring about in the social ecology and urban social structure of the city in the long run.

GROWTH OF SLUMS

The Town Planning Department of Rourkela did not foresee that the propulsive and multiple effects of the public sector steel plant would lead to the growth of numerous small and informal manufacturing and servicing industries in the city, besides the growth of a few large and medium industries. Easy availability of jobs for the semi-skilled and underqualified people in the formative years of the steel plant, and its associated establishments attracted many poor and distressed people from the countryside towards Rourkela. Since the steel plant and a few other big and medium size industries could only absorb a limited number of early migrants to the city, the latecomers joined the growing informal manufacturing and servicing sector in order to earn their livelihood. The policy of the government was to promote labour intensive ancillary and small scale industries in the vicinity of the key larger industries, so that they can get enough small job works from the big concerns through backward and forward linkage effects. This encouraged the growth of segmented labour market and informal secondary and tertiary sector economy in the city. Moreover, the growth of an enclave type township of highly paid public sector workers and their families generated a wide demand for large variety of consumer goods and services. As a result, informal sector manufacturing and servicing activities (carpentry, masonry, plumbing, electric wiring and servicing, pottery, manufacture of metal utensils and shoes, tailoring, retailing, vegetable vending, scavenging and sweeping, load lifting and rickshaw pulling) started flourishing. The scarcity of capital, low level of technological development and above all abundance of underqualified manpower and country artisans, further necessitated the growth of dualistic economy and segmented labour market in this city like in all other growing cities in the developing countries (Gilbert and Gugler 1987).

However, the increasing supply of labour and easy availability of goods and services from the informal sector economy of the city, keeps the level of earning of poor workers at a minimal subsistence level. Further, the inapplicability of labour laws and low bargaining strength of the workers vis-a-vis their employers brings down their wages. So, in order to survive in the city they adopt various methods to meet their basic necessities. As a bulk of their earnings is spent on food and clothing, proper housing becomes prohibitive for them because of the high cost of accommodation in city. Hence, they live in temporary hutments in illegal settlements by encroaching on vacant public or private land close to their work places. They do not bother much about the availability of basic civic amenities such as proper toilets, supply of potable water, electricity and so on. With the proliferation of informal sector economy and large scale exodus of unskilled workers from the countryside, at a later stage the urban residential growth of Rourkela also got infested with numerous slums and squatter localities around the steel plant and main market areas of the city including sector areas of the steel township (Fig. 5.4).

There is no proper official record with regard to the growth of slums in the city. The survey made by the Town Planning Unit, Rourkela during 1986 recorded that the city had 40 slum localities harbouring around 1.11 lakh people, with a total number of 21,500 independent households. This reveals that the average family size of slum households is 5.17 persons as against 4.65 persons for the city as a whole according to 1981 population census. As shown earlier in Table 5.1 during the decade 1981-91, the city of Rourkela (urban agglomeration) has registered a total population growth of 23.58 per cent only or 2.36 per cent per annum. On this basis, if we estimate the city's population in 1986 taking 1981 as the base year, it comes to 3,60,878 or 3.61 lakh approximately. Hence, we may say that according to the survey of Town Planning Unit, Rourkela, the city had 30.75 per cent slum population during 1986.

However, from the Survey Report, 1988 of Town Planning Unit, Rourkela, it was found that among the list of 40 localities classified as slums, there are quite a few localities like Tangarpali, Luakera, Tumkela and Hamirpur, which are actually peripheral villages resided by the tribals. On the other hand, the report has not mentioned anything about quite a few slum areas of the city such as Construction Colony, Modern India Labour Colony, Kalinga Auto Colony, Champagarh Labour Colony, Captive Power Plant Area Jhonpri, Phulbari and Bricks Labour Colony, Hatibandha Labour

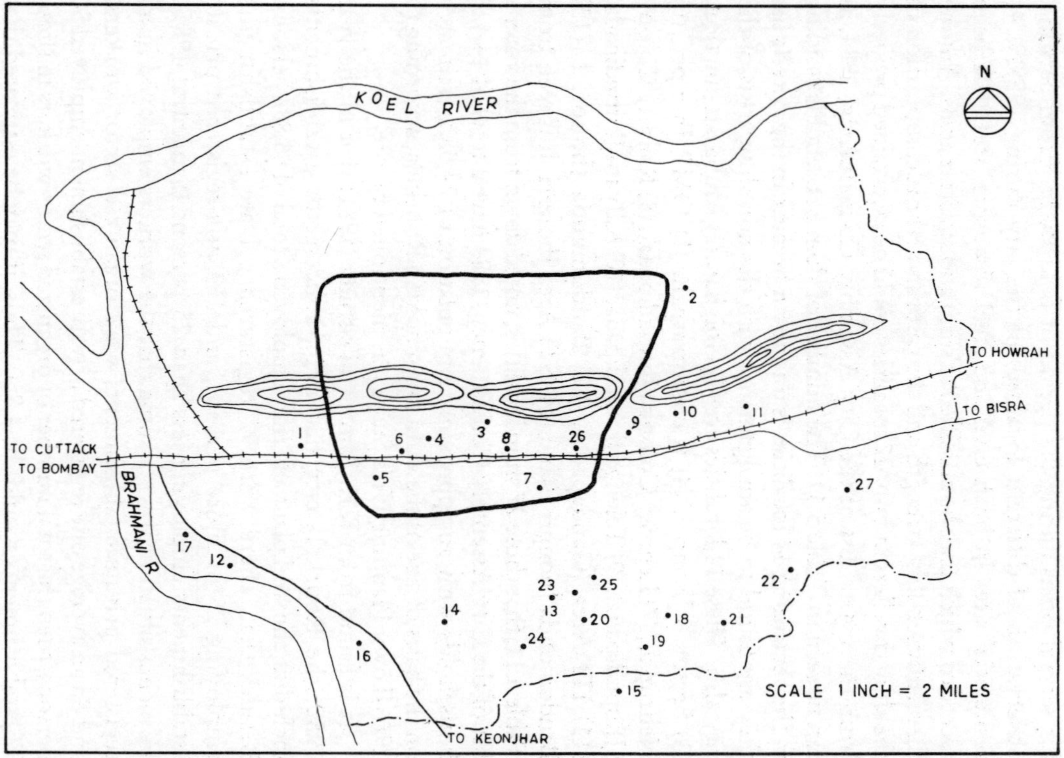

Fig. 5.4: Location of Selected Slums in Rourkela

Colony, Kansar, Bijubandha Jhonpri and the like. So, it was decided to detect slum localities in both the civil township and steel township of Rourkela, while going round the whole city covering all localities for several times during the period of field study. From personal observation of different localities of the city during 1988-9, 41 residential sites in both civil and steel township areas has been recorded which may be classified as slum and squatter areas. Among these, households' strength and the caste and ethnic composition of the slum dwellers in only 27 localities could be ascertained properly from the voters' list of the City Assembly Constituency, 1984, as can be seen in Table 5.11. The number of slum households residing in the remaining 14 localities is unknown because in the voter's list they are found to be amalgamated with the non-slum areas of the city also. These 14 localities are (1) Golghar, (2) Ambagan junction, (3) Sector 6 Jhonpri, (4) Kavisamratpali, (5) OMP Jhonpri, (6) Nehrupali, (7) Leprosy Colony (Jhupudipada), (8) Railway Colony (Jhupudipada), (9) Telenga Jhupudipada, (10) Kalyani Jhupudipada, (11) ITI Area (Gaudapada), (12) Bandomunda Jhonpri I, (13) Bandomunda Jhonpri II and (14) STI Area Jhonpri. It is seen from Table 5.11, that those 27 slum localities, noted down from the voter's list of the City Assembly Constituency, 1984 have a total of 14,426 households with an approximate population of 74,582, estimated on the basis of size of the slum household in Rourkela, according to 1986 Town Planning Unit Survey as mentioned before.

It is found from R.K. Samantrai's study (1981) that in the year 1980, the Rourkela city had 291 public sector establishments including the steel plant and they employed a total of 66,884 persons. Besides that, there were 97 registered private establishments employing 25 or more persons, and 163 non-registered private establishments employing less than 25 persons (Samantrai 1981). In such a situation if we assume that the workers employed in all registered private establishments were organized sector workers, and on an average one registered private establishment employed 50 persons, then the total number of organized sector workers in those 97 establishments would be 4,850. Thus, it may be estimated that the total number of organized sector workers in 1980 was 71,734. According to 1981 census the city had 96,172 main workers. This means 24,438 (25.41%) persons in the city of Rourkela were

TABLE 5.11: CASTE AND COMMUNITYWISE TOTAL NUMBER OF SQUATTER HOUSEHOLDS AND THEIR ESTIMATED POPULATION IN VARIOUS SLUM AND SQUATTER LOCALITIES OF ROURKELA

Sl. No.	Name of Locality	Total no. of HHs	No. of S.C. HHs	No. of S.T. HHs	No. of other Back-ward Caste HHs	No. of Higher Caste HHs	No. of Minority HHs	Estimated Population
1	2	3	4	5	6	7	8	9
1.	ITI & Industrial Estate Jhonpri	701	93 (13.27)	161 (22.97)	87 (12.41)	340 (48.50)	91 (12.98)	3260
2.	Sector-2 Labour Colony (Khariabahal)	576	134 (23.26)	135 (23.44)	74 (12.85)	222 (38.54)	16 (2.78)	2678
3.	Gopabandhu-palli	1449	286 (19.74)	254 (17.53)	257 (17.74)	596 (41.13)	123 (8.49)	6738
4.	Madhusudan-palli	1218	302 (24.80)	259 (21.26)	269 (22.08)	351 (28.81)	55 (4.51)	5664
5.	Gualapara	280	14 (5.00)	123 (43.93)	31 (11.07)	104 (37.14)	37 (13.21)	1574

(contd.)

TABLE 5.11 (contd.)

Sl. No.	Name of Locality	Total no. of HHs	No. of S.C. HHs	No. of S.T. HHs	No. of other Back-ward Caste HHs	No. of Higher Caste HHs	No. of Minority HHs	Estimated Population
1	2	3	4	5	6	7	8	9
6.	Malgodam	1311	406 (30.97)	318 (24.26)	193 (14.72)	353 (25.93)	84 (6.41)	6096
7.	Nala Road	1298	39 (3.00)	13 (1.00)	37 (2.85)	120 (9.24)	1090 (83.97)	6036
8.	Old Labour Colony	247 (15.79)	39 (43.32)	107 (10.12)	25 (22.67)	56 (10.12)	25	1149
9.	Captive Power Plant Area	190 (7.37)	14 (78.48)	149 (7.89)	15 (6.32)	12 (0.53)	1	883
10.	Champagarh Labour Colony	292 (7.88)	23 (47.26)	138 (12.33)	36 (31.85)	93 (0.68)	2	1358
11.	Phulbari & Bricks Labour Colony	737 (13.70)	101 (52.10)	384 (9.50)	70 (23.61)	174 (3.53)	26	3427

12.	Balijodi	567	42	247	57	220	69	2637
		(7.41)	(43.56)	(10.05)	(38.80)	(12.17)		
13.	Tarapur	762	131	189	87	348	40	3543
		(17.19)	(24.80)	(11.42)	(45.67)	(5.25)		
14.	Hatibandha Labour Colony	768	10	697	38	23	37	3571
		(1.30)	(90.75)	(4.95)	(2.99)	(4.82)		
15.	Kansar	141	24	102	10	5	5	656
		(17.02)	(72.34)	(7.09)	(3.55)	(3.55)		
16.	Old Jalda	265	36	164	35	23	40	1232
		(13.58)	(61.89)	(13.21)	(8.68)	(15.09)		
17.	Deogaon & Quarry Area	486	112	95	70	195	33	
		(23.04)	(19.55)	(14.40)	(40.12)	(6.79)	2260	
18.	Kalinga Auto Colony	121	6	15	20	78	5	563
			(4.96)	(12.39)	(16.53)	(64.46)	(4.13)	
19.	Jharmunda	159	13	66	21	57	8	739
			(8.18)	(41.51)	(13.21)	(35.85)	(5.03)	
20.	Construction Colony	872	126	50	108	581	16	4055
			(14.45)	(5.73)	(12.38)	(66.63)	(1.83)	
21.	Kaintabasa	107	12	79	5	11	1	498
			(11.21)	(73.83)	(4.67)	(10.28)	(0.93)	

(contd.)

TABLE 5.11 (contd.)

Sl. No.	Name of Locality	Total no. of HHs	No. of S.C. HHs	No. of S.T. HHs	No. of other Backward Caste HHs	No. of Higher Caste HHs	No. of Minority HHs	Estimated Population
1	2	3	4	5	6	7	8	9
22.	Langrabasa	79	12 (15.19)	39 (49.37)	12 (15.19)	16 (20.25)	0 (0.00)	367
23.	Laltanki	351	73 (20.80)	81 (23.08)	52 (14.81)	137 (39.03)	34 (9.69)	1632
24.	Balipoda	87	11 (12.64)	19 (21.84)	5 (5.75)	52 (59.77)	0 (0.00)	405
25.	Modern India Labour Colony	721	107 (14.84)	85 (11.79)	66 (9.15)	440 (61.02)	24 (3.33)	3353
26.	Old Rourkela Labour Colony	279	35 (12.54)	34 (12.19)	28 (10.04)	172 (61.65)	17 (6.09)	1297
27.	Bijubandha Jhonpri	362	39 (10.77)	308 (85.08)	9 (2.49)	6 (1.66)	30 (8.29)	1683
	Total	14,426	2240 (15.53)	4311 (29.88)	1717 (11.90)	4785 (33.17)	1909 (13.23)	67,354

SOURCE: Voters' List of Rourkela Assembly Constituency, 1984.

employed in the informal sector during 1981, and therefore they might be the permanent slum dwellers of the city.

From the scenario of caste and ethnic distribution of households in the slum localities, it is observed that quite a high proportion of the slum households consists of the minorities and vulnerable section of Indian society, viz., the scheduled castes and the scheduled tribes, the backward castes, the Muslims and the converted tribal Christians. Out of a total number of 14,426 slum households residing in these 27 localities, the upper caste households constitute 33.17 per cent only, whereas, the number of scheduled caste and scheduled tribe households residing in slums, comes to 15.33 per cent and 29.88 per cent respectively. Their respective shares of population in the city at the time of 1981 census are found to be 8.15 per cent and 16.40 per cent. From the distribution pattern of castes and religious groups in these 27 slum localities of Rourkela, it is observed that the aggregation of residential locality even in the slums is determined to a great extent by the sociocultural identities of the poor migrants. Localities like Gualapara, Old Labour Colony, Captive Power Plant Area, Champagarh Labour Colony, Phulbari and Bricks Labour Colony, Balijodi, Hatibandha Labour Colony, Kansar, Old Jalda, Jharmunda, Kaintabasa, Langrabasa and Bijubandha Jhonpri, are mainly resided by tribal households. Here, the tribal households constitute more than 40 per cent of all the households. Similarly, in localities like ITI and Industrial Estate Jhonpri, Gopabandhupalli, Tarapur, Deongaon and Quarry Area, Kalinga Auto Colony, Construction Colony, Balipoda, Modern India Labour Colony and Old Rourkela Labour Colony, the concentration of upper caste households is more than 40 per cent of the total number of households. Besides this the Nala Road locality is found to be resided exclusively by the Muslim families where their concentration is 84.16 per cent. However, the scheduled castes and the backward classes living in slums are not found to be predominant in any of these localities, in comparison to their total percentage share of the households respectively of 15.53 per cent for the scheduled caste and 11.90 per cent for the backward classes. Malgodam (30.97%), Madhusudanpalli (24.80%), and Sector 2 Labour Colony (23.26%) have relatively high percentage of scheduled caste households and Gopabandhupalli (17.74%) and Madhusudanpalli (22.08%) have relatively high percentage of backward caste households.

Thus, from the distribution pattern of the various types of households in different localities of Rourkela Assembly Constituency including the slum and squatter areas, it may be inferred that the social ecology and the formation of various residential zones in the city have been influenced by the sociocultural factors. This is found to be true mostly in case of the minority households. For example, although Nala Road is a degenerated slum area of the city (civil town), the rich Muslim households have preferred to build palatial houses in this locality instead of moving into the Area Nos. 7 and 8, located in the outer zone of the city in the west, which is regarded as the posh locality of Rourkela. Like this, irrespective of their economic status the Sikh households are found to be highly concentrated in Gurudwara Road and Gandhi Road near the Rourkela railway station. However, among the Hindus in the upper income level there are some exceptions. Nevertheless, it is observed that given an opportunity they would feel comfortable if they reside together with people belonging to the same culture, religion, caste, region and language and of course, within the same income group. This clearly shows that urban India is yet to reach the modern secular form where things are governed more by the economic factors rather than the social and cultural factors. We get a clearer picture of this, when we analyse the social structure of Rourkela.

URBAN SOCIAL STRUCTURE

It is found from the survey of selected sample households as well as from informal discussions with the people working in the steel plant and other industries and service establishments of the city, that many unskilled and semi-skilled workers have come to Rourkela from distant provinces of the country like Punjab, Haryana, Rajasthan, Kerala, Andhra Pradesh, Madhya Pradesh, Uttar Pradesh, Bihar and West Bengal, although these categories of jobs normally should have been cornered by the surplus and disguised unemployed workforce available locally in the project site. The local tribals, apart from the fortunate few who were displaced, work either as contract labourers in the steel plant or as casual labourers in the construction sites and small scale industries of the city. On the growth of industrial townships in India, in the late 1950s, Vithal Babu mentions that there is a spectacular example of displacement without absorption that occured in Rourkela and Durgapur, with the construction of new steel plants. In the context of Rourkela he writes that out of 5,973 able-bodied displaced persons in the late fifties, only 161 were provided with regular employment, 223 as the work-charged and 630 as the muster roll workers; whereas the others were idle or unemployed, living day to day on the money paid by way of compensation by the steel project authorities. According to him, it was reported that skilled, semi-skilled and even unskilled workers were brought by the contractors from different parts of the country, mainly from outside the province (Babu 1959: 237).

It is further noticed that most of the unskilled and semi-skilled jobs in the steel plant including subsequently created new vacancies with the expansion of production capacity, which in normal circumstances should have been made available for the local people living in the periphery, in fact, got monopolized by the high and middle caste people belonging to Brahmins, Karanas and Khandayats hailing from the relatively advanced districts of coastal Orissa, viz., Cuttack, Puri, Baleswar and Ganjam. Although, the backward castes including the scheduled castes and the scheduled tribes constitute more than 70 per cent of the State's population, only a few of them could get regular jobs in the steel plant, because they did not have education and necessary social and political support. Despite appalling economic conditions they were less mobile than the higher and middle caste people because in the mid-1950s and 1960s, neither the State had a good transport and communication system nor these people had wide social networks and contacts to help them in their migration to distant places. It is found that a fairly substantial number of people from particular villages of the coastal districts are found to be working in the steel plant and also in other establishments of the city. This is mainly because the contractors associated with the construction work in Rourkela mostly hailed from coastal districts and they brought their relatives and friends to work in the plant site. There are certain villages like Polosara, Netinga, Gahama, Origad in Ganjam district, Editala in Baleswar district and Beruna in Cuttack district from where many people have got employment in the steel plant. From my informal conversations with the workers of the steel plant, I found that more than 500 workers hail from

Editala and its nearby villages in Baleswar district. Thirty to forty workers have come from Origad, 30 to 40 from village Polosora and another 30 to 40 workers from village Beruna. It seems the people of the peripheral villages have got very little benefit of plant's direct employment. Brahmanitarang, a small village located in the west at a distance of 8 km. from the Rourkela steel plant has hardly 10 regular plant employees. The tribals and low caste inmigrants from the nearby areas namely Ranchi, Gumla and Singhbhum districts in Jharkhand and Mayurbhanj, Kendujhar, Sambalpur, Bolangir and Kalahandi districts in Orissa mostly earn their livelihood in the informal sector of the city by working as rickshaw pullers, coolies, construction workers, street peddlers, vegetable vendors, sweepers and the like. Even quite a high percentage of people from the home district presently depend on informal sector economy for their employment, as they are late inmigrants to the city.

It is observed that people hailing from certain regions, castes and religions have acquired a near monopoly position in certain trades or occupations over the years because of the strong articulation of social networks based on kinship, caste, religion, region, language and the neighbourhood ties. The moulders in the Foundry Workshops of Rourkela invariably hail either from Pipli area of Puri district in Orissa or from Chakulia area of West Bengal as the people of these areas are well-acquainted with moulding and casting works since time immemorial. Among the workers in the informal sector, a large section of construction workers and handcart pullers hail from the Chhattisgarh region of Madhya Pradesh (present Chhattisgarh State), contract labour of the steel plant from the tribal belt of Sundergarh, Kendujhar, Mayurbhanj, and from the adjacent districts of southern Bihar (present Jharkhand State) such as Ranchi, Gumla and Singhbhum, rickshaw pullers from the low caste manpower pool of Sambalpur, Bolangir and Kalahandi districts of western Orissa, coolies from Parlakhemundi region of Ganjam district, vegetable vendors from Jajpur region of Cuttack district, betel shop owners from Baleswar and Cuttack districts of Orissa and the like.[2] Similarly, the organized trade and commerce and the entrepreneurship of small scale industries in the city are dominated by the trading and business communities of Gujarat, Rajasthan, Haryana, Punjab and West Bengal and the unorganized trade and commerce by the Muslim Community of Gaya, Ranchi and Mungher districts of Bihar.

On account of the prevalence of this system in urban industrial centres, the urban settlement pattern in India over the years reflects more or less the aggregation of people on the basis of caste, kin, language and ethnic affinity and the modern industrial city of Rourkela has been affected by this sort of population congregation to a large extent. Besides, the old residential localities of the city such as Raghunathpali, Panposh, Oraonpara, Kumbharpara, etc., where the clustering of houses on the basis of caste, kin, language, religion are more prominent, the other parts of the civil town and the steel township also reflect that the various ethnic groups with similarities either in caste, language, culture, religion or income have preferred to reside in one neighbourhood. The high concentration of Bengali households in Sectors 13 and 14, the south Indian and Bengali workers' households in Sectors 7 and 18, Hindi speaking employee households in Sectors 5, 16 and 20, the Muslim workers in Sector 15 and above all the aggregation of Oriya worker households in Sectors 1 and 2 of the steel township shows that despite its national characteristics the neighbourhood areas in various sectors have been formed more or less on the basis of ethnic and linguistic affinity of the population. The squatter areas of Rourkela also reflect the aggregation of migrant families on the basis of division of caste, language, region and religion.

The Modern India Labour Colony, one of the big squatter localities of the city, was set up by the HSL in the 1950s to accommodate the construction workers. This colony is surrounded by the steel plant boundary on the one end and fertilizer township boundary on the other. It is mainly resided by the people of Bhanjanagar area and other parts of Ganjam district in Orissa belonging to Khandayat and other cultivating castes in one neighbourhood with their own close community life. Another portion of the colony on the other side of the road connecting the colony to the fertilizer township is being resided by the tribal people, mostly Mundas of South Bihar (present Jharkhand). Most of the people residing in this locality mainly work as contract labour in the steel plant and some of them are regular employees of the steel plant hailing from Ganjam district. The latter have preferred to stay in this locality with their kith and kin or caste members working as contract labour notwithstanding the unhealthy surroundings of the locality with inadequate civic amenities such as water, electricity and sanitation facilities. The other adjacent squatter localities such as Construction Colony, Gajalakshmi Market, Laltanki, Tarapur, Filter Colony, etc., are also found to be resided by the contract workers and low-graded unskilled workers of the steel plant hailing mostly from Ganjam and Cuttack districts of Orissa. Similarly, in Mahulpali squatter area, which is located beside the ring road in between the daily market and the main gate of the steel plant, a majority of the migrant households are Veniyata by caste and most of them have come from a particular village in Parlakhemundi region of undivided Ganjam district. They are all casual and contract labourers earning their bread in the informal tertiary sector of the city or as contract labour of the steel plant. The biggest squatter localities of the city such as Malgodam, Madhusudanpalli and Gopabandhupalli located beside the railway line in between Basanti Colony and Rourkela railway station also give a picture of spatial distribution of migrant households on the basis of their region, language and caste affiliation. The goalas from Bihar reside in a separate mohalla, the Bilaspuri workers in a separate cluster, the tribals of Chotanagpur belt in another and the migrant families of coastal districts and western belt of Orissa such as Sambalpur, Bolangir, Kalahandi and Sundergrh districts in distinctly separate and isolated mohallas. Like this, the migrant Muslim families to the city have preferred to stay in Nala Road area adjacent to the main city market despite congestion, suffocation and unhealthy ambience of the locality. The slums that have come up in the steel township area also give the same picture of spatial distribution of population on the basis of caste, kin and other ethnic ties. The Khariabahal Jhonpri located in between Sectors 1 and 2, near the OSRTC (Orissa State Road Transport Corporation) bus stand is mainly resided by the migrant scheduled castes and backward castes families of Sambalpur, Bolangir, Kalahandi and Sundergarh districts of western Orissa. The earners in these families mainly work as contract labourers inside the steel plant or as rickshaw pullers, coolies and unskilled construction workers in the poverty induced informal sector of the city economy.

Thus, the pattern of rural-urban migration to the city and the spatial organization of residential localities, while not duplicating the complete social structure of a few villages and the towns from which the inhabitants are drawn, they have retained enough of their native bases to serve as a link for the future migrants. The migrants continue to maintain their regional and rural ties. There is continuity between the rural and urban social structures and the institutions and social structures of the migrant population are more or less replicated in the city of Rourkela.

These types of partial monopolization of jobs by people of certain castes, religions, regions or linguistic groups is a widespread urban phenomenon in a job scarce, labour surplus economy such as that of India and a few Third World countries. Because of particularistic recruitment patterns, socio-personal networks are important for getting entry into the urban job market (Holmstrom 1985). As a result, migrants of common origin tend to cluster in certain jobs and trades. In a survey of fourteen villages in West Java, Indonesia, Hugo found that two narrowly defined occupational categories most common among migrants from any one village accounted for over two-fifths to four-fifths of migrants and commuters (Hugo 1977). The timber market of Acra was controlled by immigrants from far away Niger in the 1950s (Rouch 1956). And in Mexico city the manufacture and sale of ice cream are found to be the monopoly of migrants from the community of Mextica clan (Rollwagen 1971).

The early migrants to the industrial and urban centres to establish their hold in the city and to develop a community life bring their relatives, caste-fellows, friends and acquaintances and help them in getting jobs through their personal and social networks they have established in the city's economic structure. More so, this type of recruitment mostly based on the recommendations of the old loyal workers is preferred by the management of private concerns especially as it helps them in ensuring some hold over the workers. In an earlier study, Sheth has shown how the factory management manipulated caste networks to recruit loyal workers (Sheth 1968). The study of Klass van der Veen in Bulsar region of Gujarat shows that unskilled workers get recruited to various jobs in the government and industry by articulating patron-client ties and neighbourhood ties (van der Veen 1979). Even the recruitment of *badli* workers in the textiles mills of Bombay is not free from primordial attachment. Holmstrom points out that a permanent worker of a factory usually recommends a person from his own caste or village to a *badli* position in the factory (Holmstrom 1985). Breman mentions that the recruitment of labour is invariably done through the labour contractors and middlemen, who mobilize workers from their own villages and neighbourhoods (Breman 1979). On account of use of these personal, kin, caste and primordial networks, it is not uncommon to notice the enclaves of Udupi hoteliers in Bombay, the Pahadi domestic servants in Delhi, the Oriya Maharaja (cook) in Calcutta and the Nepalese Bahadurs as watchmen in the factories and bungalows of various towns and cities in India (Panini 1986). Thus, observing such trends of migration of people to the industrial and urban centres of India and particularistic pattern of recruitment and employment of workers in the factories and their concerns, Holmstrom writes that most of the big industrial cities like Calcutta, Bombay and Bangalore have important ethnic minorities with pocket of employment for this or that group which can only be explained by fits and starts in industrial development and migration (Holmstrom 1985: 246).

The continuation of this sort of recruitment system based on caste, kinship and other primordial factors has enabled the migrant workers to entrench themselves in certain critical positions by strengthening their hold over the jobs in urban and industrial sector, especially when job opportunities are not growing commensurately with the population growth. The practice of taking workers' relative and friends as replacements of new workers has led to aggregation of people from particular castes, villages or linguistic groups in the same occupation often throughout an industry.

SOCIAL EFFECTS

In this situation, the urban society of Rourkela has started facing serious social disturbances due to increasing unemployment and restricted employment opportunities of the locals in the urban labour market, which is dominated by the early entrants to the city. *De facto* continuation of particuristic recruitment system based on kinship and other primordial factors has enabled a particular group or section, hailing from a particular caste, religion, language or region to strengthen its hold over the limited jobs available both in the organized and unorganized sectors of the city. Even in the informal sector, the job structure is governed more by primordial ties of caste, religion, language, village, kin and friendship. Most of the organized sector jobs and relatively better types of jobs in the unorganized sector are cornered by the outsiders, viz., the upper caste Oriya Hindus of the coastal belt and the non-Oriyas. The local tribals except a few displaced persons and also the migrant tribals of other adjacent districts such as Sambalpur, Kendujhar and Mayurbhanj in Orissa and Ranchi, Gumla and Singhbhum in Jharkhand earn their livelihood by working as contract labourers in the steel plant. It is found from a study of contract labour in Rourkela Steel Plant that based on a higher side of estimation the plant was employing around 11,656 persons as contract labourers in its various wings or departments in the 1980s (Sengupta 1983). Interestingly a majority of them is found to be local tribals and other low and scheduled castes people of Sundergarh, Sambalpur, Kendujhar and Mayurbhanj besides the tribals of Singhbhum and Gumla and they are found to be employed in such hazardous and lowly jobs, where the regular workers of the steel plant have refused to work. In the present employment situation when the members of the new generation of locals acquire higher education, they find their employment opportunities in the organized sector including the steel plant have become more restricted due to the domination of upper caste Oriya Hindus of the coastal belt and other non-Oriya upper caste people. As a result, of late, the locals have started feeling restless and they have started mobilizing themselves against the outsiders including the upper caste Oriyas of the coastal belt in the form of 'sons of the soil movements' like in various other parts of the country (Weiner 1978; Gupta 1977; Sharma 1976). It is observed that the local tribals are getting united under the banner of Jharkhand party and they have started developing militant attitude also. For instance, when a milk dairy was established in Rourkela by the Orissa Co-operative Milk Producers, Federation Ltd (OMFED) in the 1980s, the local tribals got mobilized under the guidance of Jharkhand party and demanded employment of the local tribals in all the available vacancies. They even threatened to kill the outsiders whosoever joined the co-operative.

On account of increasing population growth, agricultural backwardness of the region coupled with loss of agricultural lands, forests, displacement and disruption of tribal way of life in the wake of industrialization and urbanization, the tribals of the region are virtually reduced to the status of daily wage earners in an uncongenial environment of the industry and mining centres. Further the glaring disparities of life styles between the outsiders and the locals have made the tribals, especially those belonging to the younger generation more restless. However, at this critical juncture the city economy has reached its full potential of providing employment opportunities and day by day the level of unemployment and underemployment has started rising in the city.

It is seen from Table 5.12 that in our sample households out of a total of 590 able-bodied persons available for work, only 506 (87.76%) are found employed in various jobs in the city of Rourkela and 14.24 per cent is unemployed in true sense. Of the unemployed persons in the sample, only 2.38 per cent were in search of employment for less than one year, 40.48 per cent had remained unemployed for a period of one to three years, 36.90 per cent for a period of three to five years and 20.24 per cent were unemployed for more than five years.

It is further noticed from Table 5.12 that the rate of unemployment in the steel township is found to be higher than in the civil town area. This may be due to the strong preference for organized sector jobs among the unemployed people of steel township. The pattern of preference for jobs among the unemployed shows that government service is the most preferred one followed by jobs in Rourkela Steel Plant; whereas the least preferred employment is found to be service in private sector companies.

Thus, given the situation of growing unemployment and continuous inflow of migrants competition for jobs among the various ethnic groups and the native tribes has become intensive and finds expression in political mobilization along ethnic lines. Bose

TABLE 5.12: TOTAL NUMBER OF JOB SEEKERS, DURATION OF UNEMPLOYMENT AND THE JOB PREFERENCE OF THE UNEMPLOYED IN THE SAMPLE HOUSEHOLDS OF ROURKELA

Sl. No.	Locality	Total no. of persons available for work	Actual no. of earners	% of job seekers to total no. of persons available for work	Duration				Preference				
					Below 1 year	1 to 3 years	3 to 5 years	5 years and above	RSP jobs	Other Ind. jobs	Govt. service	Pvt. Comp. serv-ice	Self employ-ment
1.	Civil Town-ship	315	287	8.89	0	8 (28.57)	15 (53.57)	5 (17.86)	5 (17.86)	1 (3.57)	11 (39.29)	0 (0.0)	11 (39.29)
2.	Steel Town-ship	219	219	20.36	2 (3.57)	26 (46.43)	16 (28.57)	12 (21.43)	14 (25.00)	8 (14.29)	27 (48.21)	4 (7.14)	3 (5.36)
All Total		506	506	14.24	2 (2.38)	34 (14.48)	31 (36.90)	17 (20.24)	19 (22.62)	9 (10.71)	38 (45.24)	4 (4.76)	14 (16.67)

NOTE: Figures in brackets indicate percentage.

says that the migrant groups try to create the cultures of their places of origin at the place of destination which results in cultural pluralism and enrichment of the city culture (Bose 1968). However, in Rourkela urban centre one facet of cultural pluralism is ethnic tension. Electoral politics further amplifies these ethnic tensions. While there are several associations of castes, tribes, linguistic and regional groups such as Khandayat-Kshatriya Mahasabha, Bihar Rajputs Mahasabha, Adivasi Unnayan Sangha, Paschima Orissa Surakshya Samiti, Kurmi Mahasabha, Bihar Yadav Mahasabha, Nikhila Bharat Banga Sahitya Sammelan, Kerala Samskarika Samiti to articulate various types of groups' interests, there are broader associations like 'Nila Chakra' to project the interest of all Oriya speaking people including the Scheduled Tribes of Orissa vis-a-vis the outsiders, and the Jharkhand Mukti Morcha to articulate the political cause of all tribals of Chotanagpur plateau cutting across State boundaries. The situation has become so highly charged that in 1989 the Government of Orissa was forced to take a decision to make a residential certificate compulsory for those seeking to register themselves in the Employment Exchange of Rourkela. Consequently most of the second generation job seekers born and brought up in Rourkela were found ineligible for jobs in Rourkela because their parents did not possess the residential *patta* notwithstanding their stay in the city for more than two decades.

Thus, from our analysis of the growth and spatial organization of urban population at Rourkela it is noticed that the large scale inmigration of people to the city from different sociocultural backgrounds, proliferation of slums and informal sector economy and above all partial monopolization of various types of jobs in the plant and other industries including the informal tertiary activities by different ethnic groups have led to the formation of a typical urban social structure like many other Indian cities. Despite planned efforts to give the city a modern look, the nature of inmigration and the growth of urban economy accompanied by social, cultural and political factors play a crucial role in determining the land use pattern and social ecology of the city. In the next chapters, we make an attempt to analyse the development process at Rourkela in relationship with the ecology and urban-industrial society.

NOTES

1. The First Master Plan of Rourkela Civil Town mentions that in 1951 the total population of Rourkela was around four thousand. However, the *District Census Hand Book* of Sundergarh in 1961 reports that the total population of Rourkela village including *bustee* in 1951 was around 2.5 thousand only.
2. The districts cited here refer to the 13 old and undivided districts of Orissa.

CHAPTER 6

Industrial Urban Society and the Ecology: A Perspective of Development at Rourkela

Although industrialization and the application of modern science and technology has reduced the physical and cultural distance among the peoples in various countries of the world and has enriched the quality of human life, of late, it has been realized that reckless exploitation of both finite and infinite resources of the earth is slowly dragging the modern industrial civilization to a premature and early end. Large scale concentration of factories and human population coupled with the intensive use of inanimate sources of energy in urban industrial complexes lead to ecological imbalances mainly due to poisoning of earth through chemical dumps, the growth of slums, insanitary conditions, emission of poisonous gases into the atmosphere and the discharge of industrial effluents into water. Increasing pollution of the environment and destruction of the ecosystem generate several types of new diseases and health hazards. Epidemics caused by inadequate facilities in new and expanding cities; mass cyclical as well as structural unemployment resulting from insufficient control of the economy, oppressive conditions of work because of a lag between the break down of traditional regulations, and the emergence of modern legal regulations; certain types of crime directly attributed to poverty and unsettled conditions in cities and over population are some of the problems that developing countries are facing in the wake of rapid industrialization.

In the foregoing chapters I have discussed how the setting up of a large public sector plant suddenly unleashed the forces of modern industrialization and urbanization in this backward region of Chotanagpur. Rourkela was converted into a big class-I town of

Orissa within a very few years of the setting up of the steel plant. I have already mentioned earlier that how the functioning of the steel plant and the growth of a new township generated multiple linkage effects and rapid proliferation of informal sector has supported the large scale migration of people to the city, thereby contributing to the mushrooming of innumerable slums and squatter areas in which more than 30 per cent of the city population inhabit at present.

In this chapter my concern is about how the city of Rourkela is coping with the problems of economic development, social transformation and ecological stresses and strains. In order to get a clear view on the perspective of socio-economic development in the region and its associated ecological effects, I have made an intensive study of 316 households covering specific localities in both the civil and the steel township areas of Rourkela as explained in Chapter 2, besides using secondary data and available literature for the purpose.

THE URBAN SOCIETY AND ECONOMY

It is already discussed in Chapter 3 that before the establishment of the public sector steel plant the economy of Rourkela was a simple agricultural one following primitive methods of cultivation. The region was full of forests and sparsely populated mainly by the tribals like Oraon, Kharia, Munda and Bhuiyan. The location of the steel plant and concentration of other large, medium and small industries in Rourkela suddenly transformed the primitive agricultural economy into a modern industrial one.

According to the 1981 Census, Rourkela urban agglomeration had an all total of 96,172 main workers. Of this, 3,587 (3.73%) were found to be primary sector workers, 47,205 (49.08%) were secondary sector workers and the remaining 45,380 (47.19%) main workers were employed in the tertiary sector of the city economy. However, it is noticed that like other Third World cities, the economy of Rourkela has also become a dualistic one, although the public sector steel plant as well as its satellite industrial and tertiary units in the organized economic sector provides a major portion of employment and the share of informal sector employment in the city is only around 25 per cent as compared to 45 per cent in Bombay, Calcutta and Ahmedabad and 60 to 70 per cent in Valsad and Sambalpur

(Joshi and Joshi 1976; Bose 1978; Papola 1981; Breman 1977; Samal 1990).

There exists a wide disparity in the level of earning of organized and unorganized informal sector workers. Because of their better organizational strength and effective bargaining power, the organized sector workers always get higher wages and better service amenities from their employers than the unorganized and informal sector workers. Employment avenues for the unorganized and informal sector workers mostly exist in petty manual and menial occupations like scavenging, sweeping, plumbing, carpentry, masonry, vegetable-vending, rickshaw and cart pulling, minor electrical and mechanical repairing and servicing works, etc. The unorganized nature and ample supply of such works and services in the city in the wake of large scale exodus of unskilled and semi-skilled workers with low educational profile in many cases keep the wage at subsistence level only. Like the economy, the urban society also gets divided into two unequal worlds, one characterized by good residential localities of the organized affluent workers with all sorts of modern basic amenities and the slums and squatter areas resided mostly by workers engaged in the informal sector. Rourkela is not an exception to this type of socio-economic development that has occurred in the wake of large scale industrialization and unplanned urban growth of the city. So, in the following sections I make an attempt to assess the socio-economic development that is taking place in Rourkela.

SOCIAL CHARACTERISTICS OF THE HOUSEHOLDS

In Chapter 5, I have already discussed how the former 30 villages of Rourkela suddenly grew into a new town in the wake of setting up of the steel plant and resulting in a profound change in caste configuration and ethnic composition of population. From my survey of 316 households in various localities in both the civil and the steel townships, it is found that 73.10 per cent are Hindus, 16.46 per cent are Muslims, 5.06 per cent are Christians, 2.21 per cent are Sikhs and the remaining 3.16 per cent belongs to other unclassifiable religious groups. In the civil township out of a total sample of 150 households, 90 (60.00%) are found to be Hindus, 49 (32.67%) are Muslims, six (4.00%) are Christians and the remaining five (3.33%) belong to other religions; whereas in case of the steel township out of a total sample of 166 households 141 (84.94%) are Hindus, three (1.81%) are Muslims, 10 (6.02%) are Christians, seven (4.2%) are Sikhs and five (3.01%) belong to other religions (Table 6.1). It is further seen from the table that among the different caste Hindu and tribal households 18.99 per cent are found to be belonging to high castes, 20.89 per cent are from the middle castes, 8.86 per cent are from the low castes, 15.82 per cent are from the scheduled castes and the remaining 16.46 per cent are members of scheduled tribes.

The characteristics of family among the sample households in the city presented in Table 6.1 show that 95 (30.06%) of them are joint family households, 209 (66.14%) are nuclear family households and only 12 (3.80%) are single family households.[1] This shows that despite industry linked urbanization quite a substantial number of households in the new town of Rourkela still adhere to joint family norms. The average size of family in the sample is found to be 5.69 for the city as a whole; 5.57 in the case of the civil township and 5.81 in the case of the steel township. The average number of children per family is found to be 1.93-2.15 in the civil township and 1.74 in the steel township. The percentage of child population to total population in the sample is 33.91; whereas the percentage share of child population in the country is reported to be above 40.

At the time of 1981 census, it was found that the Rourkela city had a relatively higher percentage (59.63%) of literate population as compared to all the urban areas of Sundergarh district (57.37%) or of the Orissa State (54.79%). The field data collected during 1987-9 through my household survey clearly reveals the developed nature of the human capital in this industrial city. Even in the late 1980s the general literacy level of population in our sample households was found to be much higher than the present literacy level of population in Orissa (63.61%) according to 2001 census. It is found from Table 6.2 that excluding children below six years of age, the percentage of illiterate population among the sample households of the city as a whole is 17.45; 27.95 in the civil township sample and only 9.23 in the steel township sample. The overall percentage of people having education below Matric level is 41.13 and the percentage of matriculates and intermediates is 23.18 only. The

TABLE 6.1: SOCIAL CHARACTERISTICS OF THE SAMPLE HOUSEHOLDS AT ROURKELA

Indicators	Civil Township	Steel Township	Total
No. of Sample Households	150	166	316
RELIGION			
Hindu	90 (60.00)	141 (84.94)	231 (73.10)
Muslim	49 (32.67)	3 (1.81)	52 (16.46)
Christian	6 (4.00)	10 (6.02)	16 (5.06)
Sikh	0 (4.22)	7 (2.21)	7
Others	5 (3.33)	5 (3.01)	10 (3.16)
CASTE			
High	11 (7.33)	49 (29.52)	60 (18.99)
Middle	18 (12.00)	48 (28.92)	66 (20.89)
Low	9 (6.00)	19 (11.45)	28 (8.86)
S.C.	30 (20.00)	20 (12.05)	50 (15.82)
S.T.	33 (22.00)	19 (11.45)	52 (16.46)
FAMILY			
Joint	44 (29.33)	51 (30.72)	95 (30.06)
Nuclear	98 (65.33)	111 (66.87)	209 (66.14)
Single	8 (5.33)	4 (2.41)	12 (3.80)
Average size	5.57	5.81	5.69
No. of child per family	2.15	1.74	1.93

NOTE: Figures in brackets indicate percentage.

TABLE 6.2: LITERACY LEVEL AND EDUCATIONAL ATTAINMENT OF VARIOUS MEMBERS IN THE SAMPLE HOUSEHOLDS

Indicators	Rourkela Civil Township	Rourkela Steel Township	Total
Total no. of Households	150	166	316
Total population of the sample	835	964	1799
No. of illiterates	225	89	314
	(26.95)	(9.23)	(17.45)
EDUCATION			
Below Matric	363	377	740
	(43.47)	(39.11)	(41.13)
Matric & Intermediate	129	288	417
	(15.45)	(29.88)	(23.18)
General Graduate & Post Graduate	16	69	85
	(1.92)	(7.16)	(4.72)
Tech. Diploma & Certificate	0	42	42
	(0.00)	(4.36)	(2.33)
Technical Degree	0	15	15
	(0.00)	(1.56)	(0.83)

NOTES: 1. Figures in brackets indicate percentage of total sample population.
2. Children below 6 years of age are excluded and they do not form part of the illiterate population.

percentage of general graduates and postgraduates is 4.72, whereas technical degree holders constitute only 0.83 per cent and the percentage of technical diploma and certificate holders for the sample as a whole is 2.33 only. However, it is noticed from Table 6.2 that the level of literacy in the steel township is higher than in the civil township. Steel township being mostly inhabited by the organized sector steel workers the sample households have furnished higher percentage of matriculates and intermediates, general graduates and post graduates and above all technical degree, diploma and certificate holders as compared to the civil township sample.

OCCUPATION AND EMPLOYMENT

The economic survey of Rourkela region made by the Government of Orissa in 1954, on the eve of the establishment of the steel plant showed that the economy of the region was predominantly agricultural. However, after the establishment of the steel plant and the emergence of Rourkela as a big town, the economy of the region has become predominantly industrial. According to 1981 census, the city of Rourkela with an urban population share of more than 80 per cent in the district of Sundergarh had 41.88 per cent of all its total main workers in the non-household manufacturing industry sector alone as compared to only 15.74 per cent of such workers for the district as a whole and merely 3.63 per cent of such workers for the State of Orissa as a whole. It is seen from Table 6.3 that the average number of earners per household in my sample is 1.60 for the city as a whole. However, in the case of

TABLE 6.3: TYPES OF OCCUPATIONS FOLLOWED BY THE EARNING MEMBERS IN THE SAMPLE

Indicators	Rourkela Civil Township	Rourkela Steel Township	Total
Total no. of earners	287	219	506
	(100.00)	(100.00)	(100.00)
Avg. no. of earners per HH	1.91	1.32	1.60
PRIMARY SECTOR			
Organized	0	0	0
Unorganized	10	0	10
	(3.48)	(0.00)	(1.98)
SECONDARY SECTOR			
Organized (RSP)	31	140	171
	(10.80)	(63.93)	(33.79)
Organized (Others)	1	12	13
	(0.35)	(5.48)	(2.57)
Unorganized	91	16	107
	(31.71)	(7.31)	(21.15)
TERTIARY SECTOR			
Organized	25	31	56
	(8.71)	(14.15)	(11.07)
Unorganized	129	20	149
	(44.95)	(9.13)	(29.45)

NOTE: Figures in brackets indicate percentage.

the civil township sample the average number of earners per household is 1.91 as compared to 1.32 in the steel township sample. The sectoral distribution of earner workers in the table shows that the city has only 1.98 per cent of primary sector unorganized workers, who mostly reside in the civil township area. Employment in the secondary sector is found to be 57.51 per cent. This in total consists of 33.79 per cent of the sample workers employed in the steel plant, 2.57 per cent in other organized secondary sector establishments and remaining 21.15 per cent in the informal secondary sector establishments. Similarly, the tertiary sector provides an employment share of more than 40 per cent in the sample, of which the organized sector's share is found to be around 11 per cent. This means in our sample altogether around 45 per cent of worker earners are found employed in the organized sector and the unorganized sector has an employment share of the remaining 55 per cent. More so, it is noticed from the table that the steel township where a majority of the steel plant workers and their family members reside together has very high percentage of organized workers employed in both secondary and tertiary sectors; whereas in the civil township a majority of the workers earns its livelihood in the unorganized economic sector. Thus our sample has a higher proportion of workers in the unorganized sector as compared to the data for the whole city.

It is further noticed from Table 6.4 that, of the total number of organized and unorganized workers in the sample, 64.43 per cent are workers with regular employment and 35.57 per cent are casually employed mostly in the unorganized sector. The percentage of such casual workers in the civil township sample is 42.51; whereas it is only 26.48 in the steel township. On account of organized nature of employment of the main earners among the sample households of the steel township, the worker's participation rate is very low, i.e. 22.72 per cent as compared to 34.37 per cent in the civil township. However, for the sample as a whole it is 28.13 per cent, which is almost equivalent to the city's workers' participation rate of 29.81 per cent according to 1981 population census.

It is probably due to industrialization and improved economic conditions of the people in the region that the number of women and child workers in the sample is found to be very low. It is observed

TABLE 6.4: NATURE OF EMPLOYMENT AND NUMBER OF ADULT MALES, FEMALES AND CHILDREN IN THE SAMPLE EMPLOYED IN THE ORGANIZED AND UNORGANIZED SECTOR AT ROURKELA

Indicators	Rourkela Civil Township	Rourkela Steel Township	Total
EMPLOYMENT			
Total	287	219	506
Regular	165	161	326
	(57.49)	(73.52)	(64.43)
Casual	122	58	180
	(42.51)	(26.48)	(35.57)
% of workers to total sample population	34.37	22.72	28.13
ORGANIZED SECTOR			
Male	56	176	232
	(19.51)	(80.36)	(45.85)
Female	1	7	8
	(0.35)	(3.20)	(1.58)
Child	0	0	0
	(0.00)	(0.00)	(0.00)
UNORGANIZED SECTOR			
Male	187	29	216
	(65.16)	(13.24)	(42.69)
Female	40	7	47
	(13.94)	(3.20)	(9.29)
Child	3	0	3
	(1.04)	(0.00)	(0.59)

NOTE: Figures in brackets indicate percentage.

from Table 6.4 that the percentage of women workers is only around 11 and of child workers is only 0.59 per cent. Interestingly, it is the poor women who come forward to work with a view to improve the living condition of their families. As a result, out of a total of around 11 per cent of women earners in the sample, 9.29 per cent work in the unorganized sector and only 1.58 per cent work in the organized sector. The 1981 population census data also provide a similar picture of women's employment in the city. It has been worked out from the census data that the percentage of main woman workers to total main workers in Rourkela city was only 8.20 in

1981 as compared to 15.21 for the district of Sundergarh and 16.18 for the State of Orissa as a whole.

The processes of industrialization and urbanization help many people in achieving a high rate of occupational mobility. It is found that in this study sample, there are as many as 198 (62.66%) respondents whose previous occupation was different from the present occupation. It is seen from Table 6.5 that out of these 198 respondents, 78 (39.39%) were previously employed in the unorganized primary sector, i.e. in agriculture and allied activities, 48 (24.24%) and 34 (17.17%) respectively in unorganized secondary and tertiary sector activities and only 15 (7.58%) and 23 (11.62%) respectively in organized secondary and tertiary sector economic activities. At present only 1.51 per cent of them are working in unorganized primary sector, 18.69 per cent and 15.15 per cent respectively in the unorganized secondary and tertiary sector economy of the city. On the other hand, the percentage of such respondents presently employed in the organized secondary and tertiary sector economy of the city are 56.06 and 8.59 respectively. This clearly indicates that industrialization, especially the location of the steel plant has also attracted quite a few organized tertiary sector workers towards organized secondary sector employment besides attracting a large number of unorganized sector workers towards organized secondary sector employment.

Further, the trend of occupational mobility over three generations in the sample households reveals a remarkable occupational change of the ego, i.e. the head of the household as compared to the occupation adopted by his/her father and the grandfather. It is seen from Table 6.6 that at present, only 0.95 per cent, 20.57 per cent and 19.30 per cent heads of the sample households respectively derive their livelihood in the unorganized primary, secondary and tertiary sectors economy of the city; whereas 51.90 per cent and 7.28 per cent of them respectively are found to be employed in the organized secondary and tertiary sectors. In contrast to this, the occupations of their fathers and grandfathers were mostly agriculture and allied activities in unorganized primary sector. The respective percentages of employment of fathers and grandfathers in such occupations were 50.95 per cent and 68.04 per cent. The percentages of unorganized secondary sector employment in these two groups were respectively

TABLE 6.5: PREVIOUS AND PRESENT OCCUPATION OF THE RESPONDENTS IN THE SAMPLE HOUSEHOLDS

Indicators	Rourkela Civil Township	Rourkela Steel Township	Total
Total no. of Respondents	101	97	198
PREVIOUS OCCUAPATION			
PRIMARY SECTOR			
Organized	0 (0.00)	0 (0.00)	0 (0.00)
Unorganized	52 (51.48)	26 (26.80)	78 (39.39)
SECONDARY SECTOR			
Organized	1 (0.99)	14 (14.43)	15 (7.58)
Unorganized	18 (17.82)	30 (30.93)	48 (22.24)
TERTIARY SECTOR			
Organized	8 (7.92)	15 (15.46)	23 (11.62)
Unorganized	22 (21.78)	12 (12.37)	34 (17.17)
PRESENT OCCUPATION			
PRIMARY SECTOR			
Organized	0 (0.00)	0 (0.00)	0 (0.00)
Unorganized	3 (2.97)	0 (0.00)	3 (1.51)
SECONDARY SECTOR			
Organized	30 (29.70)	81 (83.51)	111 (56.06)
Unorganized	25 (24.75)	12 (12.37)	37 (18.69)
TERTIARY SECTOR			
Organized	13 (12.87)	4 (4.12)	17 (8.59)
Unorganized	30 (29.70)	0 (0.00)	30 (15.15)

NOTE: Figures in brackets indicate percentage.

TABLE 6.6: THREE GENERATION OCCUPATIONAL MOBILITY OF THE SAMPLE HOUSEHOLDS

(*in nos.*)

Occupation followed	Generational Category		
	Ego's Present Occupation	Father's Occupation	Grandfather's Occupation
PRIMARY SECTOR			
Organized	0 (0.00)	0 (0.00)	0 (0.00)
Unorganized	3 (0.95)	161 (50.95)	215 (68.04)
SECONDARY SECTOR			
Organized	164 (51.90)	24 (7.59)	0 (0.00)
Unorganized	65 (20.57)	35 (11.08)	26 (8.23)
TERTIARY SECTOR			
Organized	23 (7.28)	41 (12.97)	20 (6.23)
Unorganized	61 (19.30)	55 (17.40)	55 (17.40)

NOTE: Figures in brackets refer percentage share in the total sample.

11.08 and 8.23 and for the unorganized tertiary sector those were 17.40 in each case. In this situation it is obvious that organized sector employment among the fathers and grandfathers would be very low indeed. It is noticed that only 7.59 per cent of the fathers and none of the grandfathers had been employed in the organized secondary sector. The respective percentages of employment for these two groups in the organized tertiary sector were only 12.97 and 6.33.

Thus, it can be inferred from Tables 6.3 to 6.6 that the processes of industrialization and urbanization bring about radical changes in the occupational structure and employment pattern of the economy. The high degree of dependence of people in the unorganized primary sector with very low income base and uncertainty gives way to flourishing secondary and tertiary sector economy. People get absorbed in modern occupations in the organized secondary and tertiary sectors and acquire an urban way of life. When they fail to get employment in the organized industry and tertiary sector establishments they work in the unorganized and informal sector economy of the city with the hope of joining the organized sector economy at some future date.

The advent of modern industrial culture results in separation of work place from residence. The development of modern means of transport and communication system enables people to commute between their residence and work place and back every day. At the time of the field study it was observed that the workers of Rourkela regularly covered long distances while commuting between their places of residence and their work places located in various areas of the city. Moreover, many of the workers working in the unorganized and informal secondary or tertiary sector of the city did not have any fixed work place or site. It keeps on changing everyday.

It is found from Table 6.7 that in our sample households the majority of the main earners cover more than 2 km. daily while reaching their places of work. Only 24.68 per cent of the main earners reported that their work places were located within a distance of

TABLE 6.7: DISTANCE OF WORKPLACE OF THE MAIN EARNERS IN THE SAMPLE HOUSEHOLDS

Sl. No.	Distance	No. of main earners from Civil Township	No. of main earners from Steel Township	Total no. of main earners
1.	Below 2 km.	51	27	78
		(34.00)	(16.26)	(24.68)
2.	2 to 5 km.	38	48	86
		(25.33)	(28.92)	(27.21)
3.	5 to 8 km.	9	82	91
		(6.00)	(49.40)	(28.80)
4.	8 km. & above	0	9	9
		(0.00)	(5.42)	(2.85)
5.	Unfixed distance	52	0	52
		(34.67)	(0.00)	(16.46)
All Total		150	166	316
		(100.00)	(100.00)	(100.00)

NOTE: Figures in brackets indicate percentage.

2 km. from their residence. While 27.21 per cent of the main earners reported that their work places were located between 2 to 5 km., and 28.80 per cent of the earners had work places located between 5 to 8 km. Besides this, 16.46 per cent of the main earners mentioned that they did not have any fixed work place. As a result, the degree of dependence of workers on public or private transport vehicles has increased to a great extent. From Table 6.8 it is seen that only 75 (23.73%) of the main earners in our sample go on foot to their work places. A majority of them used bicycle (44.30%) followed by the two wheeler scooters or motorcycles (17.09%). Of the rest only 1.27 per cent of the earners use public transport and 5.70 per cent private hand drawn rickshaw/auto-rickshaw; whereas 7.91 per cent have the privilege of going to their work places by the institution's car or bus.

TABLE 6.8: MODE OF TRANSPORT USED BY THE MAIN EARNERS IN THE SAMPLE WHILE GOING TO THEIR WORKPLACE

	Rourkela Civil Township	Rourkela Steel Township	Total
No. of Main Earners	150 (100.00)	166 (100.00)	316 (100.00)
MODE OF TRANSPORT USED & NO. OF MAIN EARNERS			
Walk	59 (39.33)	16 (9.64)	75 (23.73)
Cycle	58 (38.67)	82 (49.40)	140 (44.30)
Scooter/Motor Cycle	8 (5.33)	46 (27.71)	54 (17.09)
Public Transport	4 (26.67)	0 (0.00)	4 (1.27)
Rickshaw/Auto-rickshaw	18 (12.00)	0 (0.00)	18 (5.70)
Institution's Car/Bus	3 (2.00)	22 (13.25)	25 (7.91)

NOTE: Figures in brackets indicate percentage.

MONTHLY INCOME AND ECONOMIC CONDITION

The annual per capita income of the people in this region of Sundergarh district in Orissa during 1954 was around Rs. 144 only, which was about one half of the per capita income for the whole of India (Misra 1958: 73-4). However, the onset of industrialization has changed the economy of the region and the economic condition of the people seems to have improved to a great extent. It is found out that in our sample of 316 households the per capita monthly income is Rs. 345.95 or say Rs. 4,151.40 per annum during 1988-9 (Table 6.9). When we convert this income to 1970-1 constant wholesale prices, this comes to Rs. 953.60 per capita per annum for our sample households and the per capita annual income of the region, which was Rs. 144 during 1954-5 becomes Rs. 334.88 in 1970-1 prices. This means if our sample holds true for the whole population of the region, within a period of 34 years the per capita annual income of the region has registered an increase of 184.79 per cent or at the rate of 5.43 per cent per annum.

Thus, the annual per capita income in the region after the functioning of the steel plant has increased at a rate of around 5.43 per cent. This is far higher than the average annual increase

TABLE 6.9: CASTE AND COMMUNITYWISE AVERAGE PER CAPITA MONTHLY INCOME OF THE SAMPLE HOUSEHOLDS

	Rourkela Civil Township	Rourkela Steel Township	Total
Avg. per capita income of the Sample Households	282.95	399.03	345.95
CASTE HINDUS			
High	350.00	401.14	392.60
Middle	275.78	470.96	417.73
Low	368.11	407.26	394.68
S.C.	276.67	322.40	294.90
S.T.	265.58	368.58	303.21
Muslim	289.88	231.33	286.50
Christian	–	1400.00	1400.00
Sikh	–	530.14	530.14

NOTE: Tribal Christian households are included under the category of Scheduled Tribes.

in per capita income for the country as a whole, which is around 1.50 per cent. In the wake of industrialization the region has witnessed significant change in its quality of population. People belonging to different ethnic groups and hailing from different parts of the country now reside at Rourkela. They either work in the steel plant or other flourishing sector of the city economy. So, the per capita income of people in Rourkela is much higher than many other urban centres of the State.

However, it is seen from Table 6.9 that the average per capita monthly income of the sample households in the civil township is Rs. 282.95; whereas it is Rs. 399.03 in the steel township. There is a disparity in the level of earnings of different castes and ethnic households. Although there is little difference in the monthly per capita income of the higher, middle and the low caste Hindu households, the monthly per capita income of the scheduled caste households is Rs. 294.90 only; for the scheduled tribes households Rs. 303.21 and for the Muslims it is Rs. 286.50 only as compared to more than Rs. 390.00 for the clean Hindu castes. Of course, our small sample was able to draw in only one non-tribal Christian household and a very few Sikh households. Hence the computed income for these two categories of households in fact does not reflect the actual income pattern of these communities in the city as such. Nonetheless, it is observed that a majority of Sikhs and non-tribal Christians in the city earn their livelihood in the organized economic sector. Many of them are highly skilled and well qualified. Also in the informal sector economy of Rourkela they are found to be working as big traders, retailers, garage mechanic and motor transport owners. Hence as such the average per capita income of people in these two communities is found to be much higher than the caste Hindus.

If the actual monthly per capita income of various sample households among the caste Hindus and other ethnic groups are considered (Table 6.10), it is found that none of the higher and middle caste households as well as the other minority households like Muslims, Christians and the Sikhs earned an income, which was below Rs. 100 per capita per month during 1988-9. On the other hand, the sample data shows that 7.14 per cent of the lower castes, 4.00 per cent of the Scheduled Castes and 1.92 per cent of the

TABLE 6.10: CLASSIFICATION OF THE SAMPLE HOUSEHOLDS ON THE BASIS OF THEIR PER CAPITA INCOME AND CASTE/COMMUNITY

Per Capita Income (in Rs.)	No. of Caste Hindu Households				No. of S.T. HHs	No. of Muslim HHs	No. of Christian HHs	No. of Sikh HHs	Total No. of House-holds
	High	Middle	Low	S.C.					
1	2	3	4	5	6	7	8	9	10
Below 100	0 (0.00)	0 (0.00)	2 (7.14)	2 (4.00)	1 (1.92)	0 (0.00)	0 (0.00)	0 (0.00)	15 (1.58)
100-150	2 (3.33)	3 (4.55)	3 (10.71)	6 (12.00)	4 (7.69)	5 (9.61)	0 (0.00)	0 (0.00)	23 (7.28)
150-200	9 (15.00)	7 (10.61)	3 (10.71)	7 (14.00)	9 (17.31)	4 (7.69)	0 (0.00)	0 (0.00)	39 (12.34)
200-250	10 (16.67)	9 (13.64)	3 (10.71)	11 (22.00)	14 (26.92)	14 (26.92)	0 (0.00)	0 (0.00)	61 (19.30)
250-300	6 (10.00)	11 (16.67)	1 (3.57)	3 (6.00)	6 (11.54)	9 (17.31)	0 (0.00)	1 (14.29)	37 (11.71)
300-400	4 (6.67)	18 (27.27)	2 (7.14)	7 (14.00)	6 (11.54)	11 (21.15)	0 (0.00)	2 (28.57)	50 (15.82)
400-500	8 (13.33)	5 (7.58)	2 (7.14)	5 (10.00)	4 (7.69)	3 (5.77)	0 (0.00)	1 (14.29)	28 (8.86)
500-600	10 (16.67)	4 (6.06)	6 (21.43)	6 (12.00)	3 (5.77)	4 (7.69)	0 (0.00)	1 (14.29)	34 (10.76)
600-700	3	2	3	2	2	1	0	0	13

	(5.00)	(3.03)	(10.71)	(4.00)	(3.85)	(1.92)	(0.00)	(0.00)	(4.11)
700-900	7	2	2	1	2	1	0	1	16
	(11.67)	(3.03)	(7.14)	(2.00)	(3.85)	(1.92)	(0.00)	(14.29)	(5.06)
900-1100	0	1	1	0	1	0	0	1	4
	(0.00)	(1.51)	(3.57)	(0.00)	(1.92)	(0.00)	(0.00)	(14.29)	(1.27)
1100-1300	1	0	0	0	0	0	0	0	1
	(1.67)	(0.00)	(0.00)	(0.00)	(0.00)	(0.00)	(0.00)	(0.00)	(0.32)
1300-1500	0	1	0	0	0	0	1	0	2
	(0.00)	(1.51)	(0.00)	(0.00)	(0.00)	(0.00)	(100.00)	(0.00)	(0.63)
1500 & above	0	3	0	0	0	0	0	0	3
	(0.00)	(4.55)	(0.00)	(0.00)	(0.00)	(0.00)	(0.00)	(0.00)	(0.95)
All Total	60	66	28	50	52	52	1	7	316
	(100.01)	(100.01)	(99.97)	(100.00)	(100.00)	(99.98)	(100.00)	(100.02)	(99.99)

NOTES: 1. Column 8 excludes tribal Christian households.

2. Figures in brackets indicate percentage.

Scheduled Tribes had a per capita monthly income of less than Rs. 100 during 1988-9. During the year 1988-9, if it is assumed that households having a monthly per capita income of less than Rs. 200 in Rourkela are in fact the poorer households, then around 18 per cent of the high castes, 15 per cent of the middle castes, 29 per cent of the lower castes, 30 per cent of the Scheduled Castes, 27 per cent of the Scheduled Tribes and 17 per cent of the Muslims in the sample were poor. Similarly, if it is assumed that households with a monthly per capita income of Rs. 500 and above during 1988-9 are regarded as being reasonably well-off, then around 35.00 per cent of the high castes, 20.00 per cent of the middle castes, 43.00 per cent of the low castes, 18.00 per cent of the Scheduled Castes, 16.00 per cent of the Scheduled Tribes, 11.00 per cent of the Muslims, and all the non-tribal Christians and 29.00 per cent of the Sikhs were found to be better-off in the sample.

This means the benefits accruing from the industrialization have been shared by all categories of the households with some minor variation of the gains among the various castes and communities. According to the Seventh Five Year Plan document an average Indian household consisting of 5.2 persons with an annual household expenditure of Rs. 7,200 in urban areas in the beginning of the Seventh Plan was considered to be living below the poverty line. On this basis, when we estimate the number of absolutely poor households in the Rourkela city as presented in Table 6.11 only 12 per cent of the households during 1988-9 were living below the

TABLE 6.11: MONTHLY INCOME RANGE OF THE SAMPLE HOUSEHOLDS

	Rourkela Civil Township	Rourkela Steel Township	Total
No. of Sample HHs	150 (100.00)	166 (100.00)	316 (100.00)
MONTHLY INCOME (in Rs.)			
Below 400	2 (1.33)	2 (1.20)	4 (1.27)
400 to 800	23 (15.33)	10 (6.02)	33 (10.44)

(contd.)

800 to 1200	54 (36.00)	7 (4.22)	61 (19.30)
1200 to 1600	31 (20.67)	32 (19.28)	63 (19.94)
1600 to 2000	7 (4.67)	30 (18.07)	37 (11.71)
2000 to 2400	9 (6.00)	32 (19.28)	41 (12.97)
2400 to 2800	4 (2.67)	16 (9.64)	20 (6.33)
2800 & above	20 (13.33)	37 (22.29)	57 (18.04)

NOTE: Figures in brackets indicate percentage.

poverty line. Further, it is found to be around 17 per cent in the case of the civil township sample and in the steel township sample it is as low as 7 per cent.

It is also noticed that the expanding nature of industrial and tertiary activities in the city has provided a steady source of livelihood to a large number of households. Many of them have developed regular saving habit due to their improved economic condition.

It is seen from Table 6.12 that around 40 per cent of the households

TABLE 6.12: AMOUNT OF REGULAR MONTHLY SAVINGS MADE BY THE SAMPLE HOUSEHOLDS

	Rourkela Civil Township	Rourkela Steel Township	Total
No. of Sample HHs	150	166	316
AMOUNT OF MONTHLY SAVINGS AND NO. OF HOUSEHOLDS			
Below Rs. 100	5 (3.33)	17 (10.24)	22 (6.96)
Rs. 100 to 200	23 (15.33)	27 (16.26)	50 (15.82)
Rs. 200 to 500	13 (8.67)	34 (20.48)	47 (14.87)
Rs. 500 & above	2 (1.33)	11 (6.63)	13 (4.11)

NOTE: Figures in brackets refer to percentage in the total sample households.

are taking part in regular monthly savings schemes although the proportion of such households in the case of the civil township is found to be much lower than that of steel township. Table 6.12 shows that 6.96 per cent of the sample households save below Rs. 100 per month; 15.82 per cent of the households save between Rs. 100 to 200 per month; 14.87 per cent save between Rs. 200 to 500 per month and the remaining 4.11 per cent of the households has a regular monthly saving of more than Rs. 500.

The improved economic condition of the households residing in this industrial city is reflected from the varieties of durable consumer goods possessed by the sample households. It is seen from Table 6.13 that around 89.56 per cent of the households possess bicycle, 91.77 per cent possess radio/tape recorder and 63.71 per cent possess electric fans, which may be regarded as basic comfort goods to provide a minimum level of comforts to the people residing in urban areas. Besides this, it is found that 41.46 per cent of the sample households possess television sets, 32.59 per cent possess

TABLE 6.13: TYPES OF CONSUMER DURABLES OWNED BY THE SAMPLE HOUSEHOLDS

	Rourkela Civil Township	Rourkela Steel Township	Total
Total no. of Sample HHs	150 (100.00)	166 (100.00)	316 (100.00)
% OF HOUSEHOLDS IN POSSESSION OF			
Radio/Tape Recorder	90.00	93.37	91.77
TV Set	28.00	53.61	41.46
Refrigerator	2.67	10.24	6.65
Sewing Machine	16.00	47.59	32.57
Fan	33.55	90.96	63.71
Dining Table	6.00	10.84	8.54
Dressing Table	16.00	11.45	13.61
Sofa Set	18.00	28.90	22.15
Bicycle	82.00	96.39	89.56
Scooter/Motor Cycle	15.33	45.18	31.01
Car/Jeep	2.00	1.20	1.58

sewing machines, 22.15 per cent possess sofa sets, 8.54 per cent possess dining tables, 6.65 per cent possess refrigerators, 31.01 per cent possess scooters/motor cycles and 1.58 per cent of the households are found to be in possession of cars/jeeps. However, when the ownership pattern of these types of consumer durable goods is analysed area-wise, it is found that the households in the steel township have better assets position than civil township households. This is mainly due to the large scale aggregation of the steel plant worker households in the steel township area of the city.

HOUSING AND LIVING CONDITIONS

Housing reflects conditions of living of people in urban areas. The visible dimension of poverty in many third world cities is, in fact, manifested in the housing conditions of the urban residents. As the growth of organized sector economy in the cities of the developing world is relatively slower than the rate of growth of population resulting from large scale migration of poor from the countryside, the unorganized sector economy becomes the main base of employment for a large section of the migrant population. However, due to low economic returns from the informal sector employment coupled with the irregularity of the nature of the jobs such people are forced to huddle themselves in shabby accommodation lacking basic civic amenities. On any index of service provision, household density or physical quality, majority of the urban population in developing countries is living at standards that are clearly unacceptable to the people of the developed countries. Many studies on the housing problems of urban India show that more than half of the urban households live in one room with an average occupancy of 4.4 to 5.3 persons per room in the metropolitan cities of Calcutta, Bombay, while many others sleep on the pavements at night (Misra 1978; Ramachandran 1974; Rosser 1972).

In the previous chapter, it has been shown that industrialization with the location of the steel plant led to the growth of Rourkela as a big class-I category of town and the growth of a substantial size of informal sector workforce resulting in the proliferation of slums and squatter areas in different parts of the city. It is seen from Table 6.14 that 49.37 per cent of the households live in kutcha houses and the remaining 50.63 per cent in pucca houses. The civil township

TABLE 6.14: TYPE OF SHELTER AND PHYSICAL LIVING CONDITION OF THE SAMPLE HOUSEHOLDS

(in nos.)

Sl. No.	Type of House	Rourkela Civil Township	Rourkela Steel Township	Total
1.	Own	110 (73.33)	46 (27.71)	156 (49.37)
2.	Rented	40 (26.67)	120 (72.29)	160 (50.63)
3.	Pucca	32 (21.33)	128 (77.11)	160 (50.63)
4.	Kutcha	188 (78.67)	38 (22.89)	156 (49.37)
5.	One room house	58 (38.67)	46 (27.71)	104 (32.91)
6.	Two room house	50 (33.33)	99 (59.64)	149 (47.15)
7.	Three room house	19 (12.67)	12 (7.23)	31 (9.81)
8.	More than three room house	23 (15.33)	9 (5.42)	32 (10.13)
9.	No. of houses with latrine facility	51 (34.00)	121 (72.89)	172 (54.43)
10.	No. of houses with bathroom facility	27 (18.00)	117 (70.48)	144 (45.57)
11.	No. of houses with electricity connection	87 (58.00)	136 (81.93)	223 (70.57)

NOTE: Figures in brackets refer to percentage share to the total sample households.

sample has a very high percentage of the households living in kutcha houses (78.67%) as compared to only 22.89 per cent of such houses in the steel township. However, the percentage of sample households owning their own house is only 49.37 and the remaining households stay in rented houses. As the steel township mostly consists of quarters supplied by the Rourkela Steel Plant, the number of tenants is found to be more than in the civil township area.

The availability of living space in these sample households reveals that 32.91 per cent of the households live in one-room houses,

47.15 per cent in two room houses, 9.81 per cent in three room houses and the remaining 10.13 per cent live in more than three room houses. According to the Indian standard of living and prescribed norm of civic authority, a family of five persons requires at least a two roomed house besides space for kitchen. On this basis, it can be stated that quite a substantial portion of the sample households (32.91%) in the city with an average size of 5.69 persons per household lives in a congested environment. It is further noticed from Table 6.14 that the percentage of such households in the civil township sample is found to be as high as 38.67 as compared to 27.71 of such households in the steel township.

The provision of basic civic amenities such as latrines, bathrooms, electricity, etc., is found to be highly inadequate. Only 54.43 per cent of the sample households are having latrine facility in their houses and the percentage of households with bathroom facility is only 45.57. The picture of availability of such facilities localitywise, as seen from Table 6.14 is that only 34.00 per cent and 18.00 per cent of the sample households residing in the civil township area are having latrine and bathroom facilities respectively in their houses; whereas as many as 72.89 per cent and 70.48 per cent of the households residing in the steel township area respectively are enjoying the facilities of latrine and bath-room in their dwelling units. Similarly, there is a disparity in the provision of availability of electricity connection in these two townships. Although the whole city sample shows that 70.57 per cent of the households have electricity connection, the percentage of such households in the civil township is 58.00 as compared to 81.93 in the steel township.

PATTERN OF SOCIAL INTERACTIONS

The industrial urban society is supposed to be relatively more open, universalistic and governed by achievement-oriented norms. It can be noticed that the onset of modern industrialization and urbanization has made the social system and structure more flexible. There are definite trends indicating that the urban society is gradually marching towards a universalistic, egalitarian and achievement-oriented social order. While discussing the process of industrialization and urbanization in Rourkela in the previous chapter, I have shown how the various particularistic social variables such as caste, kinship, language, region and religion predominated over secular social variables such as the process of migration and job recruitment in the organized and unorganized sectors and influenced settlement pattern in the city. However, the growth of a large, dense and permanent settlement of heterogeneous individuals tends to break down rigid social structures, produces increased mobility, instability, insecurity and above all wide interactions with a variety of intersecting and tangential social groups. The rigidity of the caste system and the notions of purity and pollution are gradually losing their importance and in many cases the formation of close social groups and community level interactions take place on the basis of pecuniary nexus, similar socio-economic status and spatial proximity.

It is seen from Table 6.15 that although around 56.96 per cent of our sample households in the city of Rourkela are still found to be keeping close friendship and social interactions with the people of same caste or community, the remaining 43 per cent of the households have developed close friendship and social interactions with the people of other castes and community groups. This is quite substantial percentage-wise to judge the degree of fluidity and change in our age-old particularistic social behaviour. It is further noticed that in the steel township locality of Rourkela, predominantly resided by the steel plant workers hailing from various parts of the country only 51.81 per cent of the sample households are found to be having close friendship and social interactions with the people of same caste or community; whereas in case of the civil township, the figure is as high as 62.67 per cent. The households in our sample, which have developed close friendship with the people of other castes or ethnic and linguistic groups reveal up the following patterns: lower caste vis-a-vis upper caste friendship (12.66%), upper caste vis-a-vis lower caste friendship (9.49%), parallel or similar caste group friendship (12.34%), caste Hindu vis-a-vis Scheduled Caste friendship (1.90%), caste Hindu vis-a-vis Scheduled Tribe (3.1%) and friendship between the households of heterogeneous religions and ethnic groups (3.48%). Of this the friendship between the households of dissimilar linguistic groups comprises 11.39 per cent only and the remaining 88.61 per cent of the households have close friendship and social interaction with the people of same linguistic class.

TABLE 6.15: CLOSE FRIENDSHIP AND SOCIAL INTERACTION PATTERNS OF THE SAMPLE HOUSEHOLDS

	Rourkela Civil Township	Rourkela Steel Township	Total
CLOSE FRIENDSHIP & SOCIAL INTERACTIONS WITH			
Same Caste Community	94 (62.67)	86 (51.81)	180 (56.96)
Upper Caste	17 (11.33)	23 (13.86)	40 (12.66)
Lower Caste	7 (4.67)	23 (13.86)	30 (9.49)
Similar Caste	16 (10.67)	23 (13.86)	39 (12.34)
S.C.	3 (2.00)	3 (1.81)	6 (1.90)
S.T.	4 (2.67)	6 (3.61)	10 (3.16)
Other Ethnic & Religious Groups	9 (6.00)	2 (1.20)	11 (3.48)
LANGUAGE			
Other Linguistic Groups	15 (10.00)	21 (12.65)	36 (11.39)
Same Linguistic Groups	135 (90.00)	145 (87.35)	280 (88.61)

NOTE: Figures in brackets refer to percentage share to the total sample households.

Although the experiences of industrialization in many Asian countries including Japan, China and India reveal that there is no linear sequence of industrial development and there is no pre-condition for the replacement of traditional social orders and institutions, yet it is noticed that the progress of science and technology affects the social institutions of these countries in various ways. The factory is not merely a place of work but also a community. Informal relationships develop among the workers because of close and constant interaction in and outside the factory premises. Relationships among the workers develop more on the basis of occupation than on the basis of caste or any other primordial identity. The workers belonging to similar trades or occupations form their own associations to protect their professional interests. This leads to the formation of classes thus breaking the traditional social order. Because of specific types of skills and technical knowledge required for the various types of jobs in the factory, the traditional caste or family based occupations lose their significance and workers are recruited in an achievement oriented framework based on their education, skill and merit rather than on the basis of their primordial identity (Ramaswamy and Ramaswamy 1978).

In the sample out of 316 households, the respondents of 145 (45.89%) households were workers in the Rourkela Steel Plant. From the interaction pattern of these workers in their work places inside the steel plant, it is noticed that factory system of production affects the traditional caste or ethnic based relationships to a great extent. It is seen from Table 6.16 that the respondent workers of the steel plant have developed a broad-based pattern of friendship and social interactions at their work places in comparison to the friendship and social interactions patterns of the total sample households in

TABLE 6.16: FRIENDSHIP PATTERNS OF THE RESPONDENTS IN THEIR WORKPLACE AT ROURKELA STEEL PLANT

	Rourkela Civil Township	Rourkela Steel Township	Total
Total no. of respondents	32	113	145
FRIENDSHIP WITHIN			
Same caste only	13 (40.62)	37 (32.74)	50 (34.48)
Same religious group only	18 (56.25)	61 (53.98)	79 (54.48)
Same language group only	18 (56.25)	65 (57.52)	83 (57.24)
Same regional grouping only	15 (46.87)	45 (39.82)	60 (41.38)
Others	14 (43.75)	58 (51.33)	72 (49.65)

NOTE: Figures in bracket indicate percentage of respondents.

the whole city. It is found that only 34.48 per cent of the workers have developed close friendships with the workers within their own caste. 54.48 per cent of the workers have confined their friendships to same religious or ethnic group, 57.24 per cent within the same linguistic group and 41.38 per cent within the same region; whereas there are as many as 72 (49.65%) worker respondents, whose friendship and close interpersonal interactions at their work places are not based on any sort of primordial identity such as caste, religion, language or region. This clearly shows that modern industrialization and large factory based production system is likely to have a deeper impact on the society and interpersonal interaction patterns than the process of urban growth alone occurring due to expansion of informal sector economic activities in the city.

From the intensive study of the sample households in various localities of the city, it is observed that the process of industrialization and urbanization in this tribal belt of Chotanagpur has generated profound changes in the traditional social institutions, values and norms. Untouchability in any form is rarely practised. The Scheduled Caste members, especially the workers of the steel plant freely intermix and inter-dine with the people of caste Hindu community both at occupational and at familial levels. In quite a few cases even intercaste and inter-community marriages are found to be taking place smoothly with the approval of parents, although such types of social alliances might not have social sanctions of the caste or community leaders of either side. Social friendship and close interactions of many households including the tribals has become more wide and open cutting across the boundaries of caste, language, region, religion or any other primordial identity.

ECOLOGY *VS* INDUSTRIAL URBAN SOCIETY

As discussed earlier, industrialization generates four types of 'stresses' on the environment such as (i) eutrophic, (ii) exploitative, (iii) disruptive and (iv) chemical and industrial stress (Dasgupta 1978). Eutrophic stress arises from the decomposition of wastes produced by consumption and production. Exploitative stress is a result of cropping of plants, extraction of minerals, hunting of animals and felling of forests. The rate of exploitation of the natural resources should not exceed nature's capacity to reproduce. Disruptive stress may arise due to the physical changes brought about by forest clearance, construction of a high way or the setting up of a new township. Chemical and industrial stress is mainly a product of technological development—heavy concentration of lead, mercury or radioactive substances.

The process of industrialization in Rourkela and the functioning of many large, medium and small industries including the giant public sector steel plant in a large urban complex, of late, have started generating these four types of 'stresses' on the environment. As a result, although the industrialization of the region has produced improvement in the state of economy and society in the short run, it is likely to generate ecological degradation of the region in the long run. The city has started experiencing a high rate of environmental pollution resulting in deterioration of quality of life due to the concentration of engineering and metal based industries including the giant public sector steel plant and the proliferation of slums and squatters, which is a byproduct of the brisk growth of informal sector economy. Further, the lack of a developed infrastructural base and scarcity of basic amenities for a large section of people residing in slums and other low income localities of the civil township aggravates the living conditions of the people residing in the city and its periphery.

INDUSTRIES AND POLLUTION

According to a study made by an engineering student of Regional Engineering College, Rourkela the steel plant produces 50-60 kg. of dust per tonne of steel produced (Mahapatra 1988). It leaves huge amount of dust in the exhaust from LD furnace containing 7.30 grams of flue gas per cubic metre and the dust size ranging from 6 mm to 200 mm. This dust causes potential health hazard and contributes to air, land and water pollution. The flue gas containing carbon monoxide, nitrogen oxide etc. causes air pollution too. Besides this, the plant produces a huge amount of blast furnace slag (12.15%) which creates a disposal problem and water pollution problem too when rainwater passes over it to the river. The captive thermal power plant produces 30,000 tonnes of fly ash per year, which is solid waste byproduct and a potential health hazard. The power plant itself emits 40 to 50 per cent of the sulphur dioxide (SO_2) into the air through the chimney besides the release of arsenic and other radioactive gases. From nitric acid plant, huge amount of nitrogen oxide is emitted into the atmosphere. The emission of hydrogen sulphide (H_2S) from the ammonia plant turns river water into a 'milky coffee' colour. Added to this, release of a huge amount of waste steam cooling water and hot liquid steam from the byproducts and the fertilizer plants contributes to both water and soil pollution in the region. From the LD converters of the steel melting shop of Rourkela Steel Plant every day huge quantity of brown coloured iron dust is released into the atmosphere. The plant has 5 LD converters of 40/50/60 tonnes each and each converter is blown for 50 times a day on an average. When the converter is blown off, it releases 10 kg. of iron dust per one tonne of steel and the amount of iron oxide in this dust is found to be 72 per cent according to the information given by a retired chief chemist of the Rourkela Steel Plant. The quantity of iron dust released by the LD converters is so high and heavy that because of huge deposits the roof of the steel melting shop collapsed in 1972. After that the plant has been spending in lakhs by employing around 100 contract workers in cleaning jobs alone. Besides this, huge quantity of dust is released by the coke ovens, sintering plant and the blast furnaces. At the time of my field study it was noticed that although the steel plant had the provision to lessen the degree of air pollution through its various pollution controlling instruments, unfortunately none of them was functioning. The dust controlling instruments, like the dust catchers and electrostatic precipitators had gone out of order. The amount of coal and iron dust released within a radius of 5 km. is so high that the city dwellers get coal dust or iron dust in their eyes while moving in the busy market area or while passing through the ring road on foot, bicycle or two-wheelers like scooter or motor cycle. Apart from that many times the atmosphere of the city gets polluted by the leakage of various poisonous gases like carbon monoxide, hydrogen sulphide, carbon disulphide, hydrogen, cyanide, etc., from the steel plant and the fertilizer plant. Blast furnace gas contains 25 to 27 per cent carbon monoxide and the coke oven gas and mixed gas of the plant contains 9 to 13 per cent carbon monoxide. If only 0.5 per cent carbon monoxide is found in the air, man will become unconscious and will die within two minutes. So, one can well imagine the situation when there is any leakage of either blast furnace or coke oven or mixed gas inside the steel plant's working zone. According to investigative news of an Oriya daily, *Sambad*, eight persons have died while working in the steel plant due to leakage of carbon monoxide gas at different times (Mishra 1988). The coke oven gas as well as the hydrogen sulphide gas of the sulphuric acid plant is a colourless gas. However, when this gas enters into the body through respiration, men develop respiratory troubles and the nerves of the brain become impotent. There was acid rain in Udit Nagar area in 1972 as there was leakage of sulphuric acid gas from the byproducts plant unit of the Rourkela Steel Plant. C. Mishra, the representative of *Sambad* at Rourkela in his investigative report writes that in 1986, Dr A.N. Tiwari of Regional Engineering College, Rourkela had made a survey of different localities in the city apprehending acid rain due to high rate of environmental pollution caused by the industries of the region. Out of his 20 sample units of rainwater, he found acid portion in two units only and the remaining 18 had alkali in it. On this basis, Dr Tiwari has written in his article that Rourkela is experiencing alkali rain these days. Mr Mishra further writes that according to the environmental pollution study of Prof. M. Ali of Regional Engineering College, Rourkela in Rourkela-Rajgangpur industrial belt around 75 per cent of the people have developed asthma, lungs diseases and other respiratory troubles due to high level of air pollution. Many people in Rourkela have been affected by cinderosis, benzene and tuberculosis due to the huge deposit of iron dust in the atmosphere beyond its permissible limit of 10 mg. per cubic metre. Many people also develop eye troubles as iron dust enters into the eyes and affects the eyeballs and lenses (Mishra 1988).

Besides the public sector steel plant the other major polluting industries located in and around Rourkela are (i) Orissa Industries Limited, Lathikata producing all types of refractory materials, (ii) Suidihi Distillery, Lathikata, (iii) Indian Detonators Ltd, Sonaparvat, Rourkela, (iv) various mini cement plants located at Kalunga, Kanshbahal, (v) medium size metal finishing industries located at Rourkela, Vedavyas, (vi) Kalunga Industrial Estate area and above all (vii) Orissa Cement Limited, Rajgangpur located at a distance of 30 km. away from Rourkela.

According to the investigative report of C. Mishra, *Sambad* representative cited above, besides the giant public sector steel plant the private sector cement industry of Rajgangpur is the major polluter of the environment in Rourkela region. The level of dust pollution caused by this cement plant is so high that the villages located within a radius of 10 km. are deeply affected by it. Incessant fall out of huge quantity of cement dust in a radius of 10 km. to 15 km. has converted tree leaves, soil and roof top of the houses in this locality into brown. Around 60,000 people living in 52 nearby villages are the main victims of this pollution. Many of them are getting affected by the diseases like asthma, bronchitis, tuberculosis and above all pneumoconiosis or siliocosis type of diseases. Domestic animals like cows and goats are also found to be getting affected by dust related diseases to a great extent. Because of the regular fall of cement dust the soil of the region is gradually losing its fertility and it has become very hard also. Many people have stopped cultivating their lands and the productivity of paddy crop has gone down considerably. According to the official record of the Agricultural Extension Officer (AEO) of the Rajgangpur block, in the year 1984-5 a total 8,099 ha of cultivable land in this circle was reported to be under different crops; it went down to 7,487 ha in the year 1987- 8. It is found from reliable source that the two kilns of the cement factory at Rajgangpur release around 70 to 80 tonnes of cement dust into the atmosphere, although the management authority of the factory does not admit to this fact.

Besides causing soil and air pollution while releasing various types of poisonous gases and dust into the atmosphere most of these industries discharge their effluents into the various water bodies of the city and nearby villages without getting them properly treated, thereby causing high level of water pollution also. The sewage treatment plant of the steel plant is found to be in a defunct state. Effluents of the steel plant are though discharged into the *Guradinala* by sedimentation process, this procedure does not check the flow of coaltar, benzene, oil and other acidic elements into the water. People living at the confluence point of the *Guradinala* and the river

Brahmani report that because of the poisonous elements of the steel plant discharge into the water through the Gurudinala every day large number of fish, snails, frogs, etc., are put to death and found floating in the river. Various skin diseases affect people bathing downstream in the river Brahmani often, when the plant releases huge amount of effluents water in the *Guradinala*. It is reported that in the past there used to be good number of fish and prawns available in the downstream of river Brahmani and this was a good source of earning for the traditional fishing community. However, of late the rate of yield of fish and prawns at the downstream of river Brahmani has dwindled to a greater level due to increasing pollution of water. Similarly, the municipal wastes and sewages of the city are discharged into the various water bodies such as into the river Koel near Hamirpur village in case of the steel township and to the agricultural fields of village Deogaon and also to the river Brahmani in case of the civil township. It is to be noted that the localities in the civil township neither have proper drainage system nor any sewage treatment plant to treat the domestic effluents. However, although the steel township has a proper drainage system and sewerage network, the sewage treatment plant located near Hamirpur village was also not found in proper working order at the time of our field study. As a result, people residing downstream of the Koel river, especially the villagers of Luakera, Tumkela, etc., reported a high intensity of skin diseases while taking their baths in the river water. Although the test of groundwater in the various localities of the city by scientists of the local Engineering College has not revealed the presence of arsenic, the water bodies of Rourkela have been contaminated to a great extent with elements like copper, zinc, lead, mercury, iron oxide, benzene, oil, coaltar, etc. As a result, people using polluted water often suffer from various water borne diseases like dysentery, diarrhoea, jaundice, gastroenteritis, skin irritation and premature hair fall.

MINING AND ENVIRONMENT

Although mining activities were started in the district of Sundergarh with the opening of railways during the colonial rule, they were not so extensive. Before setting up the steel plant the area of mining in the district was confined to a few limestone and dolomite quarries.

The first lease of iron ore mines was granted in 1955 only (Senapati 1975). However, after the functioning of the steel plant and several other industries in the Rourkela-Rajgangpur industrial belt including the private sector cement plant, Orissa Cement Limited, Rajgangpur, the mining activities in the region have been intensified. The steel plant alone has several captive iron ore mines and limestone and dolomite quarries in various places close to Rourkela such as Barsuan and Kalta Iron Ore Mines, Purunapani Limestone Quarry and Ispat Dolomite Quarry. According to the annual statistics 1987-8, published by the Rourkela Steel Plant, since inception till the year 1978-9 the plant alone had extracted from its Barsuan mines 10.33 million tonnes lump iron ores and 9.25 million tonnes of fine ores and another 4.19 million tonnes of iron ores from its mines at Kalta. Thus, all total 23.77 million tonnes of iron ores were extracted from the local captive mines of the Rourkela Steel Plant till the year 1978-9. Further, between 1979-80 to 1987-8 another 15.17 million tonnes of iron ore was extracted from these mines. Owing to the expansion of production capacity of the steel plant, the consumption of iron ore from the captive mines of the plant have increased over the years and during 1987-8 production year, the plant had extracted 1.97 million tonnes of iron ores from these mines. Similarly, the amount of limestones extracted from the captive quarry of the steel plant at Purunapani was 6.93 million tonnes till the year 1978-9 and by the end of 1987-8 this amounted to 11.55 million tonnes. Till the year 1978-9 dolomite ore consumption from the captive mines was 0.91 million tonnes and by the end of 1983-4 this had further increased to 1.89 million tonnes.

It is found from the *District Statistical Handbook* of Sundergarh that between 1978-9 to 1987-8 the total amount of iron ore extracted from the various mines of the district was 19.86 million metric tonnes or 1.99 million tonnes per annum on an average. The amount of manganese ore extracted during the said period is found to be 1.33 million metric tonnes at the rate of 0.13 million tonnes per annum on an average. The amount of limestone and dolomite extraction from the mines of the district during 1978-9 to 1987-8 was 31.54 million metric tonnes at an annual average extraction rate of 3.15 million tonnes. Fire clay and quartz extraction from the mines of the district during the said period were respectively of 0.23 million metric tonnes and 0.10 million metric tonnes or say an average annual extraction rate of 0.023 million metric tonnes and 0.01 million metric tonnes respectively. According to latest available data the total land area covered under the mines in Sundergarh district was 20,606 ha or 206.06 sq. kms. in the year 1985-6 and this was 2.10 per cent of the total land area.

Although precisely the amount of agricultural and forest lands lost to mining in the district is not known from the latest available data of total land area under the mines, a conservative estimate would be that around 5 to 6 per cent of the total land area must have been spoiled due to mining which started in the later part of the nineteenth century. Mining ruins the land, water, forests and air, whether it is open cast mining or underground mining. The loss or pollution of natural resources degrades the quality of human life. It is observed at the dolomite quarries and limestone quarries of Biramitrapur, Purunapani and Hathibari in Rourkela-Rajgangpur region that the level of dust pollution is very high and the land site is totally barren due to large scale felling of trees and loss of topsoil. Similarly, the intensification of mining activities in Kalta, Barsuan, Tensa, Koida, etc., of Bonai subdivision has resulted in loss of dense forest area, drying up of many streams, displacement and disruption of tribal life. The working of many small iron and manganese ore mines in the private sector on leased basis has accentuated the socio-economic conditions of the tribals living in the border areas of Sundergarh and Keonjhar districts of Orissa. The tribals of the region, who were leading a simple life by doing subsistence cultivation and by collecting forest produce from the dense forests of the region are now reduced to the status of daily contract wage earners. They have lost their right over their forestlands. In the mining sites of Koida region, it is observed that every day truckloads of tribal men, women and children are brought like animals to work in the manually operated small mines and quarries. They are not covered under any type of industrial benefits such as ESI, Provident Fund, etc., as provided to other workers working in the organized sector. The wage rate is found to be far below the statutorily fixed wage rate. In many cases, in order to extract more work from the tribal workers the mine contractors have introduced wage on a piece-rate basis. The tribals work for long hours. Their wives and small children are also employed in such work. After blasting, they manually crush the ores into small pieces with the help of big and small hammers.

Despite hard work, the tribals lead a very poor life, which is clearly indicated from the emaciated bodies of expectant mothers and small children. Quite a high proportion of their earning is spent on the consumption of country liquor and *handia* (liquor made from rice). On account of blasting and manual crushing of mineral ores a huge amount of mineral dust is generated in the process, which pollutes the environment. Respiratory diseases such as asthma, tuberculosis, bronchitis, etc. affect workers working in these mines mostly. Large scale felling of trees in the mines area coupled with total neglect of the land sites after the exhaustion of mineral ores has converted many patches of land in this deep forest area of Bonai into dry and barren land. Because of careless mining the ground water of the region has been contaminated by ferrous and iron oxide. Goitre disease to a very large extent is affecting the local tribals, especially the women.

FOREST COVER AND RAINFALL

Before the advent of industrialization and the growth of a large urban-industrial complex such as Rourkela the total forest area of Sundergarh district was around 70 per cent of the total land area. However, in the year 1958-9—the year of construction of Steel Plant and the township—this had come down to 56.75 per cent. It is reported by the local elders in Rourkela that before the setting up of the steel plant the area was full of *sal* forests and the tribals residing in this region were left free by the feudal chiefs to clear any part of the forest for agricultural purposes. So to say land was made available to them as a free gift of nature in the old Princely States of Gangpur and Bonai. But the functioning of the steel plant and expansion of the urban boundary activated the destruction of forest by large scale felling of trees to meet the growing needs of urban and industrial markets. Though the commercial exploitation of forests in the district was started with the coming of the railways in the 1920s, deforestation had not assumed such gigantic proportion as it has today (Senapati 1975).

It seems, the major decline in forest cover started with the industrialization and urbanization of Rourkela-Rajgangpur region in the early 1960s. From the data presented in Table 6.17, it is found that the total forest area of Sundergarh district registered a decline from 54.18 per cent in 1965-6 to 38.18 per cent in the year 1985-6. By applying simple linear regression method Y = a + bX, when we estimate the value of 'b' it is found to be (-) 1.12 and the 't' value of 'b' is (-) 5.38, which is significant at 1 per cent level of significance and R^2 value is 0.60, thereby indicating a good measure of fit. Hence, we can forcefully say that since the year 1965-6 the forest area of the district has registered a declining trend and the average decline is estimated to be 1.4 per cent per year. Coincidentally modern industries in Sundergarh district started growing with the setting up of the private sector cement factory at Rajgangpur in the year 1951

TABLE 6.17: YEARWISE AREA UNDER FOREST IN THE DISTRICT OF SUNDERGARH DURING 1965-6 TO 1985-6

Sl. No.	Year	Total forest area (in sq. km.)	Percentage of forest area to total land area
1.	1965-6	5,325	54.28
2.	1966-7	5,744	58.55
3.	1967-8	5,760	58.71
4.	1968-9	6,487	66.12
5.	1969-70	5,437	55.42
6.	1970-1	5,437	55.42
7.	1971-2	5,437	55.42
8.	1972-3	5,296	53.98
9.	1973-4	3,308	33.72
10.	1974-5	4,234	43.16
11.	1975-6	4,539	46.26
12.	1976-7	4,539	46.26
13.	1977-8	4,815	49.08
14.	1978-9	4,816	49.09
15.	1979-80	3,733	38.05
16.	1980-1	3,535	36.03
17.	1981-2	3,535	36.03
18.	1982-3	4,171	42.51
19.	1983-4	4,171	42.51
20.	1984-5	4,171	42.51
21.	1985-6	3,746	38.18

SOURCE: District Statistical Office, Sundergarh.

and the commencement of production at the Rourkela Steel Plant in 1960 and the functioning of a growing number of large, medium and small industries mostly in Rajgangpur-Rourkela industrial belt after 1960.

It is established from the findings of many studies in India and other countries of the world that with the spread of modern industrial civilization, the earth has witnessed a large scale decline of forest, increasing environmental pollution and erratic rainfall. According to the Second Citizens Report, *The State of India's Environment 1984-5*, prepared by the Centre for Science and Environment, New Delhi, on account of growing needs of woods and trees by the urban markets and their industries, India is losing 1.3 million hectares of forest a year nearly eight times the annual rate put out by forest departments of the country. There is a close association between the forest and rainfall because it is the forest which provides adequate moistures for precipitation. So, with the fall of forest area the district of Sundergarh has started showing an erratic trend and high rate of fluctuation in its annual rainfall also (Fig. 6.1). The normal annual rainfall of the district is found to be 164.76 cm. However, it is seen from Table 6.18 that in between 1965 to 1987 period, the annual rainfall of the district was within the range of normal rainfall only during 1968, 1971, 1973, 1984 and 1985. Otherwise, during all other years the deviation of actual recorded rainfall from the normal rainfall of the district was more than minus 25 cm. every year, thereby indicating a secular decline and a high rate of fluctuation in the rainfall with the decline of forest coverage and increasing environmental pollution resulting from the growth of industry and urban area in the district. The recorded actual average annual rainfall of the district for the whole period 1965 to 1987 is found to be only 123.43 cm. and the 'X^2' value of the actual recorded rainfall for the above time period is as high as 491.16, which is significant at 1 per cent level of significance, thereby indicating a high rate of deviation of the actual rainfall from the normal rainfall.

QUALITY OF LIFE

Over the years Rourkela has grown into a big class-I town of Orissa and functionally it is classified mainly as an industrial city. Apart from this, in recent years the city has started gaining importance as

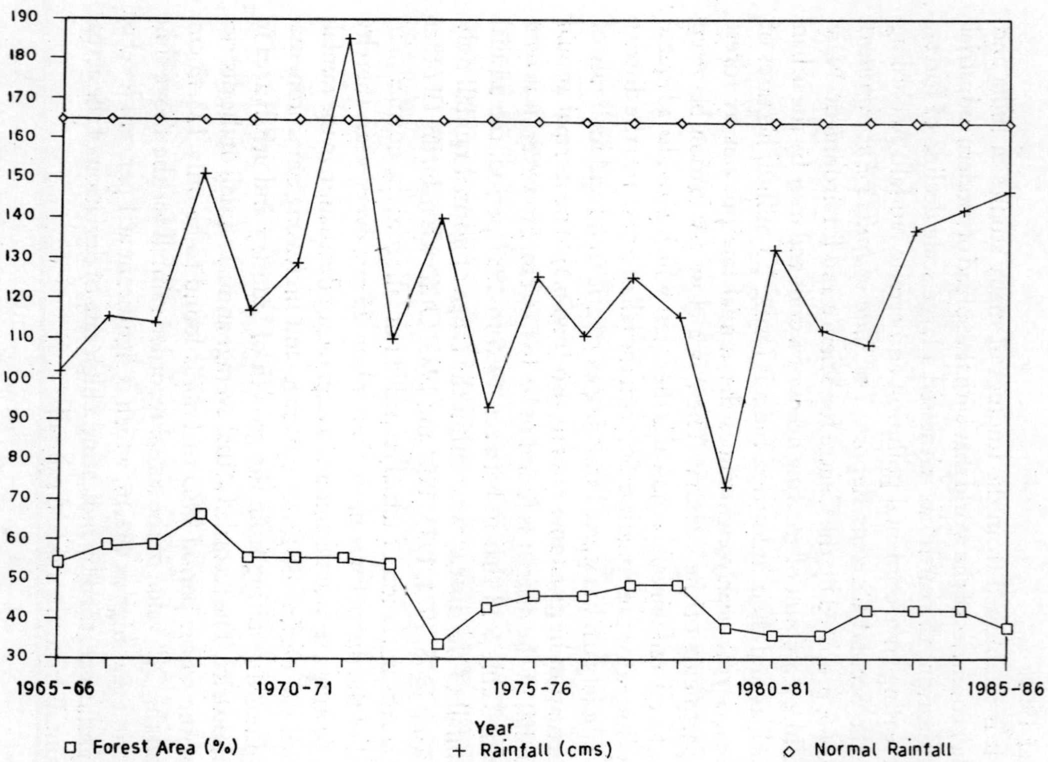

Fig. 6.1: Forest Area and Rainfall

TABLE 6.18: YEARWISE NORMAL AND ACTUAL RAINFALL RECORDED IN THE DISTRICT OF SUNDERGARH DURING 1965-87

(in cm)

Sl. No.	Year	Normal rainfall	Actual recorded rainfall	Deviation from normal rainfall
1.	1965	164.76	101.63	(-) 63.13
2.	1966	164.76	115.29	(-) 49.47
3.	1967	164.76	113.87	(-) 50.89
4.	1968	164.76	150.88	(-) 13.88
5.	1969	164.76	116.86	(-) 47.90
6.	1970	164.76	128.89	(-) 36.07
7.	1971	164.76	185.00	(-) 20.24
8.	1972	164.76	110.00	(-) 54.76
9.	1973	164.76	140.00	(-) 24.76
10.	1974	164.76	93.29	(-) 71.47
11.	1975	164.76	125.63	(-) 39.14
12.	1976	164.76	110.82	(-) 53.94
13.	1977	164.76	125.85	(-) 35.91
14.	1978	164.76	115.83	(-) 48.93
15.	1979	164.76	73.65	(-) 91.11
16.	1980	164.76	132.65	(-) 32.11
17.	1981	164.76	112.55	(-) 52.21
18.	1982	164.76	109.04	(-) 55.72
19.	1983	164.76	137.56	(-) 27.20
20.	1984	164.76	142.57	(-) 22.19
21.	1985	164.76	147.47	(-) 17.29
22.	1986	164.76	139.27	(-) 25.49
23.	1987	164.76	107.59	(-) 57.17

NOTES: $\bar{x} = 123.47$

Chi-square value $= \Sigma \frac{(o - e)^2}{e} = 491.16$

SOURCE: District Statistical Office, Sundergarh.

the main commercial centre of the region also. It may be recapitulated that when the Master Plan of the city was finalized the planners thought that the total population of this man-made industrial town would be around 2 to 2.5 lakh in future and accordingly necessary provisions were made for adequate basic infrastructures and civic amenities of the urban residents.

However, India is still found in the second stage of demographic transition characterized by high birth rate and low death rate with its developing nature of the economy. It is observed that in this situation of swelling population, innumerable growth of industries and many other commercial and service establishments in a dualistic economic frame of organized and the unorganized sectors, the latter mostly being the linkage and propulsive effects of the former and accompanied by the slums and squatters, the quality of life in the city, of late, has started showing a deteriorating trend. Over the years the civic bodies of the city have failed to maintain and develop the supply base of its infrastructure and basic civic amenities to the urban residents vis-a-vis the population growth. It is seen from Table 6.19 that due to high population growth the city is not only failing to provide adequate basic amenities to its residents, but also it has failed to maintain its earlier supply position of such amenities. Except the facilities of higher and vocational education, the availability rate of all other amenities in the city has shown marked deterioration after 1971. The percentage of pucca road to total road length in the city agglomeration area came down from 99.19 in 1971 to 81.95 in 1981 and marginally increased to 82.45 in 1991. The number of latrines per 100 households came down from 57 in 1971 to 45 in 1981 and further to 38 in 1991. The per capita availability rate of potable water in the city although improved from 44.84 litres to 380.17 litres during 1971-81, in 1991 this slid down to 113.68 litres per head. The overall position of domestic electrical connection in the urban agglomeration decreased to 38.86 per cent from 46.38 per cent, during 1971-81, although during the period domestic connection in the civil town area increased from 13.91 per cent to 25.80 per cent and in the case of the steel township, the decline was from 58.21 per cent to 46.94 per cent. In 1991 possibly due to regularization of the slum areas in the city the percentage figure for domestic electricity connection increased to 52.41 in the urban agglomeration area of Rourkela. The number of road-light points, which was 22.64 per km. of road in the whole city in 1971 however, slid down to 16.69 in 1981 and further to 13.81 in 1991. The number of hospitals/dispensaries per 10,000 population was 0.81 in 1971 for the urban agglomeration area and this came down to 0.77 in 1981 and to 0.65 during 1991. Similarly, the number of beds available per 10,000 population in these hospitals/dispensaries for the treatment of indoor patients went down from 33.40 in 1971 to 19.09 in 1981 and to 16.10 in 1991. The facility of availability of number of primary and middle schools per 10,000 population was 2.61 in the city agglomeration area in 1971 and as high as 4.25 in the civil town area. But, although the availability of such provision improved in case of the steel township from 1.99 to 2.10 in 1981, the overall availability in the whole city slid down to 2.36 and to 2.70 in the civil town locality. In 1991 the situation was worsened further in both civil and steel township localities. But there was an overall improvement in the availability rate of vocational and higher educational institutions in the whole city and also in its two segments.

The worsening situation of the three main civic amenity indicators like, (i) percentage of pucca road to total road length, (ii) number of latrines per 100 households, and (iii) number of road-light points per km. of road length clearly show that the city has recorded a high rate of growth of slums and squatter areas during 1971-91 accompanied by the proliferation of unorganized and informal nature of economic activities. This type of high growth of migrant population accompanied by the proliferation of slums and squatters has put a great strain in the supply of basic civic amenities by the urban local body of Rourkela to all categories of population residing in different localities of the city. Since the city continues to grow at an alarming rate fed by the stream of poor and lowly qualified people from the countryside and the investible funds with the government are limited to develop basic infrastructure and civic amenities in all parts of the city, the desired level of environmental support is assured only to a small fraction of the population. This has resulted in spatial division and segmentation of the population, polarized on the basis of caste, region, language and ethnicity and operationalized through the ecological factors like competition and dominance besides institutional dictates like land use restrictions and building bye-laws. Like all other cities of the developing world, the limited development of infrastructural facilities and basic civic amenities in this city are distributed in favour of the relatively affluent localities.

It is seen from Table 6.19 that with regard to the availability of various basic amenities in the twin townships of the city, the steel township is relatively better than the civil town area. Further, according to my observation there is a wide difference in the rate of availability of such basic services among the various localities of

TABLE 6.19: AVAILABILITY OF BASIC AMENITIES AT ROURKELA DURING 1971, 1981 AND 1991

Sl. No.	Amenities	Rourkela U.A.			Rourkela civil Town			Rourkela Steel Town		
		1971	1981	1991	1971	1981	1991	1971	1981	1991
1	2	3	4	5	6	7	8	9	10	11
1.	% of pucca road to total road	99.19	81.95	82.45	85.71	81.19	–	100.00	82.19	–
2.	Population density per sq. km. (in thousand)	1.42	2.32	2.54	2.14	–	–	1.26	–	1.78
3.	No. of latrines per 100 HHs	57	45	38		28	21	–	56	56
4.	Per capita availability of potable water (in litres)	44.84	380.47	113.68	48.33	615.62	–	43.56	296.69	–
5.	% of domestic connection of electricity to total number of households	46.38	38.66	52.41	13.91	25.80	30.00	58.21	46.94	67.24
6.	Number of road light points per 1 km. of road	22.64	16.69	13.81	40.71	8.17	10.80	21.55	19.37	26.72

7.	No. of hospitals/dispensaries per 10,000 population	0.81	0.77	0.65	1.06	0.94	0.71	0.72	0.75	0.65
8.	No. of beds availability for patients per 10,000 population	33.40	19.90	16.10	19.10	12.20	8.33	38.70	24.50	24.36
9.	No. of general colleges per 10,000 population	0.17	0.22	0.55	0.00	0.10	–	0.24	0.28	–
10.	No. of vocational schools/institutions per 10,000 population	0.23	0.46	–	0.42	0.31	–	0.16	0.56	–
11.	No. of secondry schools per 10,000 population	0.46	0.96	–	0.70	0.73	–	0.32	1.12	–
12.	No. of primary and middle schools per 10,000 population	2.61	2.36	1.88	4.25	2.70	2.14	1.99	2.10	1.81

SOURCE: Census of India, 1971, 1981 and 1991, *Town Directory*, Series 16, Part X A, Directorate of Census Operations, Orissa.

these townships. Within the steel township boundary the sector areas and the fertilizer township area are infrastructurally developed with underground sewerage and drainage system, neat and clean asphalt roads, wide coverage of trees, gardens, parks and playgrounds. All the staff quarters accommodating plant employees and their families in these localities are provided with all modern basic amenities such as latrine, bathroom, underground sewerage, tap water and electricity connection. However, within the various sectors of the localities there is a further discrimination in the rate of availability and maintenance conditions of such amenities. The sectors like Sector Nos. 1 and 2 and various other localities of the remaining sectors accommodating low graded plant workers look to be shabbily maintained than the Sector Nos. 3, 4, 5 and 19 mostly accommodating executives and higher officials of the steel plant. It is unfortunate to note that the lower grade workers are provided with one bedroom houses with asbestos roof, where they find it difficult to stay in the sweltering heat of hard summer at Rourkela. Asbestos roofing is also supposed to be harmful to health. Apart from this the conditions of unorganized and informal sector workers living in the unauthorized slums and lower grade workers' colonies of the steel township area such as Khariabahal, Modern India Labour Colony, Gaja Laxmi Market, Construction Colony, Golghar, Captive Power Plant Jhonpri, Tarapur, Kalinga Auto Colony, Lal Tanki, etc., encircling the steel plant and its township are bad beyond description. Hardly any provision of basic amenities is made for these colonies except a few bore wells or broken public water stand posts, cycleable kutcha roads and a few poorly maintained street light points. A majority of the houses does not have electricity connection, no provision of drainage or sewerage. The workers and their families residing in these colonies use open space for defecation and take their bath in nearby ponds, wells, or at the leakage points of the water supply pipes and public water stand posts. The environmental surrounding of these localities is worsening day by day. People residing at the boundary wall of the steel plant in Modern India Labour Colony are also exposed to poisonous gases such as benzene, anthracine vapour, carbon monoxide, iron oxide, etc., which get leaked and are occasionally discharged from the coke ovens and the byproducts plant located nearby. The level of concentration of coal dust, iron dust, iron oxide, sulphur oxide, benzene, anthracine vapour, nitric oxide, etc., in the air of these adjacent localities of the plant especially the Modern India Labour Colony, Gaja Laxmi Market, Lal Tanki, Tarapur, Construction Colony, etc., is found to be very high. The leaves of the trees in Modern India locality prematurely get yellow and many of the trees here look dull and are leafless even in the spring season. People residing here since early 1960s say that only of late, they have started feeling acute health problems caused by dust and air pollution. Diseases like jaundice and malaria have taken an endemic form. Besides, quite a few residents in these localities are found to be suffering from various eye ailments, hypertension and paralysis of the face and limbs, gastroenteritis, asthma, tuberculosis, etc., due to acute environmental pollution caused by the steel plant. The living condition of the people residing in the Construction Colony which houses around 500 workers of the steel plant, is so acute due to environmental pollution that once some of the residents had sent a representation to the then Prime Minister, Mrs Indira Gandhi in the early 1980s with a hope of getting quick environmental relief. The colony, surrounded by the steel plant, fertilizer plant and Indian Detonators Limited is situated next to the route of the main drain of the fertilizer and the byproducts plants. These plants release liquid naphtha, various non-degradable chemicals and contaminated water in this drain, which acutely affects the environment of this locality. In 1981, a fire broke out in the main drain as the naphtha released by the plant caught fire and three persons of the colony were burnt to death, besides heavy loss of property. The effluents discharged by the water treatment plant as well as the waste treatment plant of the Rourkela Steel Plant have formed a lagoon in the vicinity of this colony and the hot slag dumping ground of the blast furnace is also located nearby.

While the supply of basic amenities and the quality of life of the people residing within various localities of the steel township are highly uneven, for those residing outside the steel township the situation is worse. In civil township the localities like Udit Nagar and Basanti Colony near the Central Business District of the city and the Area Nos. 7 and 8 near Panposh are found to be well developed and better served with basic amenities than the old residential localities like Oraon Para mainly resided by the local tribals such as Oraon and Kharia, Kumbhar Para, Gandhi Road,

Bhatti Road, Plant Site Road, etc. Adjacent to the Central Business District, Railway Station and the main gate of the Rourkela Steel Plant the process of urban growth in the civil town has led to the formation of many slums and squatter areas such as Malgodam, Madhusudanpalli, Kavisamratpalli, Gopabandhupalli, Nala Road, Mohulpali, etc. Here the living condition of the people is found to be worse than the unauthorized slums and squatter areas of the steel township. These localities are found to be densely populated with a very low supply provision of basic amenities. Further, as they are located nearer to the steel plant as well as to the Central Business District Zone, the dwellers here are found to be the worst victims of land, air, water and dust pollution caused by the giant steel plant and many other commercial and small industrial establishments. Also, smoke caused due to the plying of a large number of motor vehicles in busy market areas of the city add to their miseries.

Except Nala Road area resided mostly by the Muslims, the other slum localities of the civil town mostly consist of one room jhonpris with no separate kitchen accommodating 6 to 7 persons. In some of the jhonpris of Malgodam it is observed that even 10 to 12 persons are huddled together in one room. People residing in such localities are the poor informal sector migrant workers with an unsteady source of income. Excluding a few families where the small children are incapable of looking after themselves and there is no other elderly person to take care of the small children, in rest of the families both the husband and wife and also their grown-up sons and daughters work as daily wage earners. The employment patterns of these workers reveal that some of them work as construction workers in various work sites of the city and also in the steel plant as contract labour. Some others work as unskilled and semi-skilled workers of the small and unorganized sector industries including garages and petty commercial and service establishments; whereas the rest others are self-employed rickshaw pullers, vegetable vendors, plumbers, carpenters, masons, painters and the like.

None of the houses in these slums and squatter settlements possesses latrines except a few service latrines available for the Muslim households of the Nala Road. None of these localities has piped water supply. There are a few bore wells or hand pumps and their availability rate works out to one bore well for every 150 families. However, people report that the water of the bore well is hard and unpalatable to drink, which may be due to the contamination of groundwater with iron oxide and other undissolved and untreated chemicals released by the steel plant and various other industries. There is no drainage and sewerage facility. There are very few street light points and only a lucky few have provision of electricity in their self-acquired unauthorized huts. Domestic waste is scattered over the roads covered by dirt and dust. Added to this, in the absence of private or community latrines people use the nearby open space across the railway line for defecation purpose.

Virtually people in these slum localities live like animals. The over-crowding polluting environment coupled with unsteady source of earning and fluctuating income level has led to disruption of community life, social disorganization, intensification of crimes and development of rebellious attitude, among a large section of the people. Malgodam, the biggest slum of the city, which houses migrants from Madhya Pradesh, Bihar, West Bengal and also from the eastern and western parts of Orissa, is notorious for the frequent social disturbances and for crimes. There is a high level of marital breakdown in the family. According to a young educated Oriya of Malgodam locality, many children hardly know the names of their fathers as their mothers switch two to three male partners and in some cases even more during their life time. Elopement among the young boys and girls is found to be more frequent cutting across the boundary of caste, community, language and region. Drinking of country liquor among the men and women is quite common and a significant portion of their earning is spent on alcohol. The general living condition of these slum dwellers is very poor. They survive only on rice, salt, onion, potato and cheap pulses. From rice the tribal slum dwellers prepare a type of liquor called *handia*, which is food and drink to everybody at home including the children. Because of malnutrition and high level of environmental pollution many people suffer from tuberculosis and other lungs related diseases. Besides this, quite a significant number of young and middle-aged people especially the tribals and migrant workers of Bilaspur region of Madhya Pradesh are reported to be suffering from venereal diseases because of their promiscuity.

On account of the deterioration in the supply of basic civic services, proliferation of overcrowded slums and a high rate of environmental pollution caused by the steel plant and many other large, medium and small industries of the city, the urban dwellers are getting affected by the many types of environment related diseases such as asthma, tuberculosis, respiratory disorder, cancer, leprosy, heart diseases, paralysis, jaundice, skin and eye diseases and the like. Workers in the steel plant suffer from various types of occupational health hazards and many of the workers working in small and unorganized sector engineering and metal-based units are compelled to work in an unprotected environment with little medical benefits, though they equally face similar health hazards like the steel plant workers. Especially those who work at the coke ovens, blast furnaces, steel melting shop, sintering plant, byproducts plant and the fertilizer plant encounter severe health hazards due to acute dust as well as the air pollution. As there is no provision of intershop transfer, many of the workers in those departments are getting affected by diseases like tuberculosis, asthma, paralysis, neurological disorder, cataract of the eyes, hypertension and rheumatic diseases. There is a high level of dust pollution in this zone, which is encountered by me personally for several days while observing the working condition of the steel workers at their work places. Because of insufficient light in the blast furnaces and the coke ovens area, workers in the night shift virtually are at the risk of losing their lives while at work. Although there are many posters directing the workers to wear safety goggles, gas mask, ear plug and the like while working, the workers complain that they are hardly provided with such types of safety equipments except boots, helmet and a pair of hand gloves. Frequent inhalation of coal dust and tar gas make coke oven workers prone to diseases like asthma and tuberculosis. When anthracine vapours are released from the byproducts plant, the workers working in the nearby coke ovens develop breathing problems and continuous cough. The workers report that during 10.00 p.m. to 6.00 a.m., it becomes difficult to work in the coke ovens zone because of the leakage and concentration of benzene, anthracine vapours and other poisonous gases from the byproducts plant. The workers working in the coke ovens complain that they frequently fall sick and remain absent from duty on medical grounds many times during the year.

Like the coke ovens zone, the blast furnace zone is equally hot, dusty and gas affected. According to the information provided by the old workers since the day of functioning of the plant around 10 to 12 workers of the blast furnaces have died on the spot due to occasional leakage of poisonous gases like carbon monoxide, sulphur dioxide, nitric oxide, etc. Many of the workers after working for 10-15 years get affected by the diseases like gastric, asthma, tuberculosis, high blood pressure, loss of eye sight, paralysis, continuous headache, mental disorder and deafness. The lighting system is also found to be bad like in the coke ovens zone. A major portion of the railway track remains under darkness and the road is watery and slippery.

The other highly polluting zones of the steel plant are found to be the sintering plant, steel melting shop and the byproducts plant. The level of dust pollution in sintering plant and steel melting shop areas is found to be especially very high. According to the workers' report, these days the management is not taking any step such as watering, etc., to bring down the level of dust pollution caused by the use of lime stone in steel melting. The shop area is found to be accident prone because of the poor visibility caused by the dust. Around 20 people have died in accident since the functioning of the shop. Further, as the machines have worn out there is frequent leakage of gas at many points in the shop floor area and when the workers come in contact with such poisonous gases they fall unconscious and in a few cases have died as well. Owing to the high level of dust pollution, excessive heat and slow poisoning of the body caused by exposure to poisonous gases, quite a few workers of this shop are reported to be suffering from asthma, tuberculosis, high blood pressure, paralysis, mental disorder and gastric troubles.

Although the byproducts plant looks neat and clean outwardly, leakage of gas from the byproducts plant is found to be very frequent. So to say, this is the number one culprit insofar as the pollution generated by the steel plant is concerned. The machineries of the plant have become very old and worn out. In chemical plants normally they are replaced after every 15 or 20 years; whereas the management authority of the Rourkela Steel Plant have never bothered to replace the machineries for the last 25 years or so. The workers report that the leakage of gas from sulphuric acid plant makes them unconscious on the working spot quite often. The leakage of anthracine vapours irritates eyes and nose and the leakage of benzene vapours makes workers giddy and sleepy. Since the day of its commissioning around 10 workers have died of gas explosion and fire in byproducts plant. Workers of this plant generally suffer from gastric, skin disease, loss of appetite, headache, giddiness and paralysis after working here for a long time.

The workers complain that they are not provided with adequate safety equipments to protect their body from the exposure to gases and chemicals. Use of gas mask is very rare, the gloves are of sub-standard types and they are not provided with apron to cover their bodies while working. Although the level of sound pollution is also very high, workers rarely use earplugs. Moreover, the spread of coke ovens dust makes their life most uneasy. One Sikh worker of this plant was so obsessed with pollution that he told to me that he would never advise his off-springs to work in any industrial unit of this type at any cost.

Besides the steel plant, the growth of many other large, medium, small and informal sector industrial units in and around Rourkela, which are in fact the creation of the steel plant, abets unchecked and growing rate of pollution of the environment. In the absence of a proper environmental pollution controlling mechanism, weak or nonexistent municipal laws and regulations, these industries were virtually left free to grow anywhere in and around Rourkela in the initial years of growth of the city. It is observed that there are many fabrication and machining units besides garages and small workshops functioning in the busy market area and densely populated localities of the civil town. These industrial units freely discharge their gaseous and liquid effluents to the atmosphere and to the open fields or normal sewerage channels of the city respectively, thereby exposing people, animals and vegetation in the neighbourhood to serious health problems. Moreover, the proliferation of densely populated slum and squatter areas, a product of the informal sector economy, brings out glaringly the differences between the 'haves' and the 'have-nots'. The unhealthy livings of the 'have-nots' further generates 'spill over effects' on the society of the 'haves' and multiply the level of environmental pollution in the city.

With the loss of forests and erratic rainfall, the level of industrial pollution generated by the industries seems to have increased manifold in recent years. It seems because of increasing industrialization and urbanization of the region, i.e. the Rourkela-Rajgangpur belt with a high location quotient of pollution causing industries like iron and steel, cement, refractory, engineering and

TABLE 6.20: NUMBER OF PATIENTS TREATED DUE TO VARIOUS DISEASES PER THOUSAND POPULATION IN THE GOVERNMENT HOSPITALS/DISPENSARIES OF THE DISTRICTS IN ORISSA DURING 1980-1

Sl. No.	Districts	All Types of Diseases	Tuberculosis & Respiratory diseases	Syphlis	Dysentry	Leprosy	Infection hepatitis	Malaria	Filarisis	Others
1.	Baleswar	1963.42	2.64	0.35	150.37	0.92	0.52	18.69	25.23	1764.70
2.	Bolangir	1139.29	1.78	0.48	63.06	1.40	0.55	10.58	3.84	1057.60
3.	Cuttack	1613.88	3.42	0.34	111.45	2.85	2.21	9.51	17.95	1466.15
4.	Dhenkanal	1639.91	2.03	1.79	92.53	2.72	1.19	40.77	9.47	1489.41
5.	Ganjam	647.24	3.89	1.20	106.22	1.76	2.37	28.55	14.85	488.38
6.	Kalahandi	1344.48	4.78	1.65	76.22	0.34	0.58	26.49	0.88	1233.54
7.	Kendujhar	1446.68	2.60	0.78	82.73	0.41	1.07	57.03	5.47	1296.59
8.	Koraput	841.41	1.52	0.80	61.53	0.42	0.80	27.14	1.33	747.86
9.	Mayurbhanj	1554.28	3.49	0.48	97.62	1.15	0.78	10.55	4.88	1435.32
10.	Phulbani	1809.12	1.27	0.76	95.75	0.35	0.65	77.67	1.19	1631.49
11.	Puri	1958.18	3.51	0.94	126.35	2.22	2.98	17.26	26.86	1778.05
12.	Sambalpur	1424.80	4.17	0.56	83.73	4.14	1.49	41.55	2.47	1286.69
13.	Sundergarh	2276.74	7.28	1.25	178.11	3.65	1.95	63.47	13.65	2007.39
	All Orissa	1484.81	3.30	0.80	104.11	1.94	1.55	26.97	12.20	1333.94

SOURCE: Govt. of Orissa (1985), *Statistical Abstract of Orissa, 1981*, Bhubaneswar, Bureau of Statistics and Economics, Table 5.02, pp. 165-77.

chemicals, the whole district of Sundergarh has started facing severe ecological consequences in recent years. As shown earlier, since 1965 the district has been losing a total forest cover of around 1.4 per cent per annum coupled with an erratic level of precipitation far below the normal level of rainfall. It is seen from Table 6.20 that because of increasing environmental pollution the government hospitals and dispensaries of the district are reportedly treating the largest number of patients, i.e. 2,276.74 per one thousand population as compared to any other district of Orissa or the State as a whole. So, it may be assumed that the morbidity rate of people residing in the district of Sundergarh is much higher than the people of any other district in the State. It may be mentioned here that the high rate of reporting of diseases by the hospitals and dispensaries of the district is not due to better access to the health services. The tribal highlands districts like Phulabani, Koraput and Sundergarh due to low population density report a relatively higher rate of availability of hospitals and dispensaries per lakh population than the advanced coastal districts like Cuttack, Puri, Baleswar and Ganjam in Orissa. Further, during 1980-1 the availability of hospitals and dispensaries per lakh population in Sundergarh was only 1.27. This was 2.09 for Phulbani, 1.64 for Mayurbhanj, 1.69 for Koraput, 1.37 for Bolangir, 1.34 for Kalahandi and 1.19 for the State as a whole. From the recorded diagnosis report of the patients affected by various diseases in the old and undivided 13 districts of Orissa during the year 1980-1, it is found that the prevalent rate of pollution related diseases like tuberculosis and respiratory diseases, dysentery and malaria in the district of Sundergarh is highest among all the districts of Orissa. Besides, the district has a very high number of cases of syphilis, leprosy and infection hepatitis and filariasis also. Thus, although the year-wise data on occurrence of various diseases in the different districts of Orissa was not available for a long period from the *Annual Statistical Abstract of Orissa*, it may be inferred from Table 6.20 and my field data analysed later that because of increasing environmental pollution the district of Sundergarh has become more susceptible to particular types of diseases than any other district of the State.

It is found from the health survey of our 316 sample households in the city presented in Table 6.21 that during the past ten years on an average 14.8 persons per thousand people annually have suffered from various types of serious water borne diseases such as diarrhoea, gastric, jaundice and the like. The rate for respiratory diseases like tuberculosis, asthma is 4.8, heart diseases 1.2, cancer 0.2, malaria 5.8, persons from eye diseases 2.6, paralysis 1.2, rheumatism 2.2 and other serious diseases 3.2. The table reveals that on an average 39 persons out of every 1,000 persons in the sample have suffered from various types of serious ailments traceable to water and air pollution in the city. This sort of health scenario approximately corroborates the findings of Dr T.K. Bose, Chief Medical Officer of the Ispat General Hospital, Rourkela (Bose 1987). According to him a random study of health status of 1,500 workers in the Rourkela Steel Plant revealed that 6.0 per cent of them suffered from respiratory diseases and 14.9 per cent showed high eosinophil content. A follow up study of 1,113 workers working in the dusty areas of the steel plant further

TABLE 6.21: NO. OF PERSONS PER THOUSAND POPULATION IN THE SAMPLE AFFECTED BY VARIOUS POLLUTION RELATED DISEASES AT ROURKELA EVERY YEAR

Sl. No.	Name of the Diseases	No. of affected persons per 1,000 population
1.	WATER BORNE DISEASES	14.8
	(a) Diarrhoea	4.0
	(b) Gastric	6.2
	(c) Jaundice	3.5
	(d) Typhoid	0.4
	(e) Skin diseases	0.7
2.	RESPIRATORY DISEASES	4.8
	(a) Tuberculosis	1.8
	(b) Asthma	2.7
	(c) Others	0.3
3.	Heart diseases	1.2
4.	Cancer	0.2
5.	Malaria	5.8
6.	Chickenpox	1.7
7.	Eye diseases	2.6
8.	Blood Pressure	1.4
9.	Paralysis	1.2
10.	Rheumatism	2.2
11.	Other diseases	3.1
Total		39.0

SOURCE: Field Data 1988-9.

revealed that 3.2 per cent suffered from asthma, 4.8 per cent suffered from chronic respiratory diseases and 3.3 per cent suffered from tuberculosis (Bose 1987: 8).

Similarly, in the total sample population of 1799, 64 persons were reported to have died due to various diseases including old age during 1984-9 period. Thus, the annual death rate per one thousand of the sample population was 7.11 only as compared to around 13 to 14 for the country as a whole in the late 1980s. This means there has been considerable improvement in the availability of health services in the city of Rourkela. However, the causes of death in the sample households presented in Table 6.22 shows that of the 64 recorded deaths only 15.62 per cent have died due to old age, 4.60 per cent due to accidents and 17.19 per cent due to high fever. Of the others, 17.19 per cent have died due to respiratory and lung diseases, 7.81 per cent due to heart diseases, 9.37 per cent due to paralysis, 1.56 per cent due to jaundice, 4.69 per cent due to cancer, 10.94 per cent due to dysentery and another 10.94 per cent have died due to various other unclassifiable diseases at the age of less than 50 years.

TABLE 6.22: TOTAL NUMBER OF DEATHS IN THE SAMPLE HOUSEHOLDS DURING LAST FIVE YEARS (1984-9) AND THEIR CAUSES

	Rourkela Civil Township	Rourkela Steel Township	Total
Total no. of deaths	29	35	64
	(100.01)	(99.99)	(100.00)
DEATH DUE TO			
Old age	5	5	10
	(17.24)	(14.29)	(15.62)
Accidents	1	2	3
	(3.45)	(5.71)	(4.69)
DISEASES RELATED			
Fever	8	3	11
	(27.59)	(8.57)	(17.19)
Respiratory & Lungs diseases	8	3	11
	(27.59)	(8.57)	(17.19)
Heart diseases	2	3	5
	(6.90)	(8.57)	(7.81)
Paralysis	0	6	6
	(0.00)	(17.14)	(9.37)
Jaundice	0	1	1
	(0.00)	(2.86)	(1.56)
Cancer	0	3	3
	(0.00)	(8.57)	(4.69)
Diarrohea & Dysentry	5	2	7
	(17.24)	(5.71)	(10.94)
Other diseases	0	7	7
	(0.00)	(20.00)	(10.94)

NOTE: Figures in brackets indicate percentage.

This shows that pollution related diseases cause early death of people residing in the city and such deaths are more frequent than the deaths caused due to accidents and old age. Further, it is observed from Table 6.22 that although the civil town has a very low number of steel plant workers and their families, the percentage of deaths due to respiratory and lung diseases, fever including malaria and dysentery and diarrhoea is found to be higher than in the steel township sample. This implies that the level of air and water pollution in the civil town area are more acute than in the steel township area and this may be due to inadequate provision of basic infrastructure and civic amenities in the civil town area vis-a-vis the planned steel township.

It seems due to increasing industrial pollution and hostile environment the average life expectancy rate of human population in the district of Sundergarh is probably much lower than the many other districts of Orissa. It is found out from 1981 census data that the district of Sundergarh had only 4.80 per cent of population in the 60 plus age group as compared to 6.39 per cent of such category population in the State of Orissa at the aggregate level.[2]

Thus, the analysis of the state of development of industrial urban society at Rourkela in the previous sections shows that industrialization and urbanization of the region have led to different types of development (both positive and negative) in social, economic and ecological fronts. Firstly, it has led to the growth of a modern industrial economy, change in land use pattern, diversification of the occupational structure and a general rise in the level of earning of the people. Secondly, in the wake of industrialization and urbanization resulting from large scale migration of people from various parts of the country as well as from foreign countries at a very limited level, the new urban society that grew up at Rourkela has earned pluralistic and cosmopolitan characters. The region (which was once found to be mainly resided by the tribal people only with a simple agricultural economy of subsistence nature) is now resided by the people of various ethnic, caste and religious groups hailing from different States of the country. However, the nature of development of economy and urban society is not a linear one. It is observed that the very process and nature of industrialization and urbanization in a developing society like India (embodied with particularistic and ascriptive values) has led to the degradation of ecology, misuse of resources and large scale environmental pollution of the region. As the planners have not paid due attention towards the maintenance of necessary ecological balance between industry, ecology and society, there is a deterioration of general urban environment. The functioning of a giant iron and steel unit and also many other large, medium and small industries without proper environmental safeguards has led to large scale pollution of land, air and water. Added to this, there is large scale destruction and depletion of natural resources, displacement of tribals and other vulnerable sections from their traditional ecological base and subsistence production.

Like in other parts of the country the modern industrial-urban society that grew up at Rourkela has more or less finally taken the shape of traditional, particularistic and hierarchical caste society. The resource and income distribution arising from industrialization and urbanization is skewed in favour of the upper castes and privileged sections of society. There is a positive correlation between the level of income and caste status of the individuals and despite adoption of a universalistic, achievement oriented norm, the pattern of distribution of population, jobs and occupations in the city are mainly oriented towards traditional caste society. The large scale migration and rural exodus of people to this urban-industrial complex is not only due to push and pull factors; on the other hand, in many cases they are found to be network based migration leading to partial monopolization of different types of jobs in the city by different types of castes, ethnic, linguistic or regional groups.

More so, in this situation of quasi-particularization of jobs and resources, the distribution of inadequate civic amenities gets distorted and compounds the skewed distribution of such amenities and the slums and the localities resided by the poor informal sector workers become the main victims. As the urban body of the city has failed to assure the regular and adequate supply of basic civic services to its all categories of growing population the urban poor and tribals have been deprived of minimum basic amenities of life in the city. As they are less resourceful they are made to pay a heavier price of industrialization and urbanization of the region. They face more pollution hazards, job insecurity, low income, which further weakens their competitive capability, although it is true that environmental problems affect every one; some are more affected than others.

NOTES

1. In this study I have defined those sample households as joint family, where the family members of three generations such as ego and ego's wife, their married son(s) and daughter-in-law(s) and the grand son(s) and grand daughter(s) live together under one roof. Nuclear family here refers to ego, ego's wife and their offsprings and the single family household basically refers to those sample respondents, who were staying alone in the city at the time of my survey irrespective of their marital status.
2. The respective percentage of 60 plus age group of population in the old and undivided 13 districts of Orissa according to 1981 census data is as follows: (i) Balasore (6.53%); (ii) Bolangir (6.77%); (iii) Cuttack (7.86%); (iv) Dhenkanal (6.05%); (v) Ganjam (6.73%); (vi) Kalahandi (5.44%); (vii) Keonjhar (5.44%); (viii) Koraput (4.58%); (ix) Mayurbhanj (5.21%); (x) Phulbani (5.48%); (xi) Puri (7.10%); (xii) Sambalpur (7.16%) and (xiii) Sundergarh (4.80%). For detail see Census of India, 1981, *General Economic Tables*, Part III-A & B(i), Series 16, Directorate of Census Operations, Orissa.

CHAPTER 7

Summary and Conclusion

The developing countries pinned their hopes on modern industrialization to provide the impetus for accelerating economic growth. Till the 1970s the concept of development and human welfare was predominantly based on the economic criterion of rise in per capita income and gross national product. However, in recent years the fallout of rapid industrialization and urbanization has been realized. Human beings are now confronting the threat of global warming caused by accumulation of poisonous gases such as carbon monoxide and carbon dioxide in the atmosphere resulting in the depletion of the ozone layer. Therefore, realizing that there is close linkage between development patterns and global environmental problems the 1992 Earth Summit at Rio de Janerio, held under the auspices of United Nations Conference on Environment and Development (UNCED) gave a call to identify environmental and economic linkages thereby arrive at a worldwide consensus on a most judicious use of global resources and achieving sustainable development.

Till the 1970s the ecological fallout of modern urban-industrial society was almost entirely ignored. Earlier studies of industrialization and urbanization mainly focused on socio-economic transformation, ecology of human settlement patterns in the cities, patterns of urban land use and the like. It is only since the mid-1970s that any study of urban-industrial society with the focus on ecological degradation and negative aspects of urban-industrial development has gained importance. It is true that the production patterns and life styles of people, particularly in developed countries contribute greatly to the present eco-crisis, but in the case of developing countries increasing pressure of population and social inequalities brought about by economic development contribute to ecological decay (Gadgil 1991). In these countries much attention is paid to economic parameters so as to rapidly catch up with the level of economic development of advanced countries. This has detracted attention from social and organizational issues that are more important and relevant in equal distribution of the benefits of economic growth in these developing countries. Consequently, the emphasis on capital intensive industrialization has promoted progressive segmentation of the labour market in such a way that vast masses of the poor have to eke out their livelihood in the so-called 'informal sector', marked by low wages, poor living and working conditions, long hours of work drudgery, uncertainty of income and the like. The push of the distressed poor towards urban centres has contributed to slums cropping up in urban areas, resulting in decayed urban services, traffic congestions, scarcity of water and electricity and insufficient supply of basic amenities. Cheap labour supply has often encouraged the use of obsolete technology even in some of the large public sector undertakings. In many cases these industries do not pay adequate attention towards the maintenance of clean environment. In such a situation urban-industrial development has promoted inequities and ecological degradation. Even the planned urban-industrial complexes are not free from these problems as the investible funds for the development of basic infrastructure and civic services are limited, the municipalities try to cope with such problems by resorting to the supply of basic services and amenities in such a manner which favour the areas inhabited by the rich and more powerful people. Consequently the poor residing in the slums become the worst affected. Thus, in this transition to a modern urban-industrial social set-up it is usually the poor and vulnerable sections of the society who bears the brunt of massive environmental pollution.

The focus of the present chapter is to recapitulate the main findings of the study in order to provide a holistic view of the inter-relationships between industry, ecology and society in Rourkela. Based on these findings certain conclusions on the implications of industrialization and urbanization at a micro and macro level have been drawn.

ECOLOGICAL STUDY OF THE URBAN SOCIETY

The growth and development of modern urban society is certainly a product of the industrial revolution in the seventeenth century. Many social scientists have attempted to study the causes and nature of growth of urban centres. Adna Weber's study of urban centres stands out for its systematic approach. According to Weber, the causes of concentration of people in cities were primarily a product of economic forces such as the invention of steam and machinery, improved transport and communication networks, expansion of trade and commerce and factory-based production system. In contrast to this approach Josiah Strong developed theoretical interest on the moral effects of the city. He believed that modern civilization is based on a materialistic orientation and outlook towards life and the city symbolizes it.

However, such studies did not offer any theoretical explanation of the city. They only accounted for its size, growth and location. It was in fact a group of social scientists which later came to be identified as the Chicago School of Sociology in the earlier part of the twentieth century, sought to develop a systematic theory of the city based on ecological principles of biotic growth. The researchers of the Chicago School led by Park, Burgess and Mckenzie, believed that just as plant species adapt themselves to their environment by distributing themselves over a localized area in a pattern that enables them to have complementary uses of the habitat's resources, the various subpopulation in the city compete for spatial positions from which they perform diverse functions in an unfolding division of labour. This gave rise to the proposition that the various segments of urban community were systematically arranged in space, due to certain ecological processes. The study of the urban structure in its spatial dimension came to be known as human ecology theory of the city.

Based on such premises Burgess developed his concentric zone model of city growth. According to him the natural growth of the city takes the form of radial expansion from its central business district. This is the first area and it is normally encircled by a second area, mostly inhabited the slum dwellers and transient population and invaded by business and light manufacturing units. The third zone is the area of industrial workers who have escaped from the area of deterioration but retain an easy access to their place of work. Beyond this zone there is the residential area of higher income groups in the form of either apartment buildings or single family dwellings. Still farther out, beyond the city limits but within thirty to sixty minute ride to the central business district is the suburban areas or the commuter's zones. However, Park and Burgess only made a physical portrait of typical areas and zones but the fuller explanation of these so-called ecological laws or processes was provided by their colleague Mckenzie. Mckenzie translated various concepts of plant ecology such as competition, dominance, segregation, invasion and succession into human terms. According to him man competes for the limited space in the city to gain access to the most desirable location for his residence and his economic activities. Such competitive activity is reflected in land values, through which the market mechanism sorts out similar types of persons. Competition leads to differentiation and specialization of urban land use and this in turn leads to segregation of neighbourhoods. The second process is dominance, which is intimately connected with the concepts of invasion and succession. In the plant world, the dominant plants by their activities in changing the micro-environment in which they live, create conditions in which other less tolerant species are also able to thrive. The latter species then begin to invade the environment, eventually establishing themselves as dominant elements. As the process continues, these species which have now become dominant allow other vulnerable species to thrive, and become dominant and the succession process is thus continuously replicated. In the development of human communities constituting the city such processes of dominance, invasion and succession can be identified. Invasion of the residential areas by the industries and commercial or business undertakings, and of higher status residential areas by the lower status groups are delineated. The major ecological processes that contribute to the formation of the city are, in order of importance, competition, concentration, centralization, segregation, invasion and succession. Their operation creates the 'natural areas that form the physical structure of the city'.

The human ecology theory of the city, which proved to be highly influential in the 1920s and 1930s, gradually came under searching critical scrutiny. On the basis of rental data collected from a large number of cities, Hoyt evolved a new model of urban structure, which differed from the zonal pattern postulated by Burgess. The Chicago School confined its attention to the investigation of subsocial, spatial and competitive aspects of human society and tacitly assumed that social, economic, political and moral life in the city was determined by ecological process. Hence, several scholars including Radhakamal Mukerjee, Hawley, Duncan and others sought to modify the theory. Mukerjee and Hawley emphasized competition as well as cooperation in the study of human communities. Duncan evolved a set of four 'variable concepts', viz., population, environment, organization and technology to understand the human ecological process.

Such criticisms, however, have strengthened the human ecology approach to the study of cities. Reviewing the progress of human ecology theory, Hawley in the 1980s identified two distinct though related lines of investigation that have now emerged. One line pertains to the form and development of urban organization, and the other line investigates how human social systems of various types develop in different environmental settings. Burgess' concentric zone model still exhibits a remarkable persistence. The findings of many studies confirm that the distribution of the housing types, occupational, educational and family characteristics of the residents broadly exhibit a graded pattern of variation from lower to higher values as distance from the city centre increases.

However, the pattern of growth of cities in the developing countries including India, is remarkably different from the pattern postulated by the ecology model. Gist, from his study of Bangalore city, concludes that in India, high income and high status residents live nearer to the centre of the city which is the social and institutional heart of the community, whereas the low income and low status residents are located near the periphery. Economic establishments are highly dispersed and suburban growth and residential decentralization are limited. Moreover, they do not show any distinct functional division in their land use. It is important to note that quite a large number of Indian cities and towns and their internal socio-cultural and economic organizations have been investigated using this perspective and the methodology of the urban ecological theory.

The one deficiency of the human ecology approach of the Chicago School is its silence on the effects of urban settlement pattern and growth on quality of life and the physical environment of the city. Intensive industrialization followed by consequent urbanization in India and other developing countries has now attracted the attention of urban ecologists to the issues of ecological degradation. An attempt has been made in this study to examine not only the patterns of human settlement and land use in the city, but also to investigate the processes that have contributed to the deteriorating quality of life in the Indian cities. This study demonstrates how the social structure of the city also contributes to environmental decay. The focus of this research has been on Rourkela, which as a city planned to support the Rourkela Steel Plant and its ancillary industrial units, provides a unique opportunity to examine the linkages between industrialization, patterns of urbanization and environmental degradation.

INDUSTRIALIZATION, URBANIZATION AND ECOLOGY

Industrialization and urbanization are considered synonymous to development in the materialistic world. Although industrialization is considered as mainly an economic process, it generates profound changes in polity and society. There is a close interrelationship between industrialization and urbanization. Basically, the pattern of growth of various industries determines the formation of urban social structure, and land use and settlement patterns in the city. In India jobbers and middlemen from various backgrounds have often influenced the movement of labourers in and out of a region. Besides jobbers, other sociopolitical networks have been articulated in inducing the cityward migration of people. Thus since the social corridors of migration are structured by ascriptive and particularistic loyalties of caste, kinship, religion, region and language, urban centres are dotted with ethnic enclaves. Apart from ethnic heterogeneity of the city caused by the forces of industrialization, another factor that needs to be considered is the pattern of industrialization itself. In a labour surplus economy such as in India, even planned industrialization with emphasis on basic and heavy industries tends to favour the process of segmentation of labour and of markets. Segmentation expresses itself in the spread of and multiplication of economic activities in the informal sector, which are invariably located near slums and squatter settlements in the city. Mushrooming of such slums and squatter settlements put severe pressure on the distribution of urban services and amenities.

Recent ecological studies have investigated the close interrelationships that occur between industry, ecology and society. Ecology means the ecosystem or natural environmental surroundings which is the store house of natural resources and above all energy accommodating various patterns of interactions between the living and nonliving organisms. It is observed that human settlement patterns and the economic and social systems are usually evolved in accordance with the natural surroundings and resource endowment of the region. The ecological system provides raw materials to the economic system, of which industry is an important part and absorbs the wastes generated by the economic system. There is, however, a limit to the carrying capacity of an ecological region in terms of population pressure and economic activities. The limit to its carrying capacity is exceeded when the symbiosis between industry, ecology and society breaks down. Such a breakdown leads to cumulative environmental pollution, ecological degradation and deterioration in the quality of human life in the city.

ENVIRONMENTAL CRISIS AND THE ORETICAL DEBATE

The current debate on ecological crisis arising from large scale industrialization and urbanization revolves around the role of the market. According to the Marxists, the capitalist mode of production, free market economy and increasing consumerism are mainly responsible for the present eco-crisis. They hold that the imbalance between ecology and society is not created by technology *per se*, but by technology operating within the regime of capitalism. As opposed to this approach, some social scientists point out that the eco-crisis is not restricted to capitalist societies alone. They point out that in the former socialist countries the degree and scale of ecological crisis was even more acute than in capitalist societies, which tended to contain ecological degradation by strict monitoring of industrial houses and limiting pollution. They hold the view that the present ecological crisis or environmental degradation is a product of wrong choice of modern technology. The situation can be rectified, according to these thinkers, by evolving institutions, which can regulate and control pollution causing activities and encourage the development of right technologies that could consume non-polluting sources of energy. Implicit in this approach is the recognition of social and political processes, which would recognize the man-nature relationship.

There is, to be sure, a third approach which holds that modern science and technology and the very foundation of modern society is so deeply flawed that regulatory coping mechanisms are no longer helpful to avert the impending crisis. Hence, this approach recommends a wholesale rejection of modern science and technology and the search for alternative solutions rooted in traditional knowledge systems. Since traditions articulate a worldview based on man living in harmony with nature rather than man as a conqueror of nature, it is argued that a rejection of modernity and all its vestiges is called for. The approach adopted in this study is, however, a pragmatic one, which realizes that rejection of modernity is not practicable given the altered gestalt of man today. Simply put, traditional knowledge systems alone are not in a position to cope with the population problem, poverty, hunger and disease. Hence, instead of rejecting modern industrialization as such the approach adopted here seeks to explore ways by which the resulting ecological damage can be reduced, if not entirely eliminated. This calls for the development of sustainable technology, which can substitute non-polluting renewable sources of energy for highly polluting non-renewable sources, which are in use today (Postel 1992).

MAJOR FINDINGS OF THE STUDY

Pre-Industrial Rourkela

The city of Rourkela was a part of the erstwhile Gangpur State of the Chotanagpur plateau. Years before the location of the steel plant the region was dotted with tree clad isolated peaks, vast inaccessible deciduous forests and extensive river valleys. It was the home of several tribes such as the Oraons, the Kharias, the Bhuiyans, the

Mundas, the Kisans, the Bhumijs and the like. Quite a few of the tribal households were food gatherers and hunters. The socio-economic survey of 92 revenue villages in Rourkela made by the Government of Orissa in 1954, the year preceding the commencement of the construction of the Rourkela Steel Plant and township revealed that the region composed of 26.6 per cent of Hindus, 9.6 per cent scheduled castes, 45.3 per cent scheduled tribes and the remaining 18.5 per cent comprising of Muslims, Christians and other ethnic groups. Of the latter group, 83.7 per cent were Christians—most of them converted tribals. As compared to 82.9 per cent of the families in rural Orissa, earning their livelihood from agriculture during the year 1954, 84.8 per cent of the families in this region were engaged in agricultural pursuits. Of the remaining 15.2 per cent of the families pursuing non-agricultural occupations, 5.9 per cent were working as non-agricultural labourers, 3.9 per cent were in trade and transport, 3.6 per cent in production other than cultivation and only 1.8 per cent of the families were engaged in service and professions. The condition of the people was generally poor with a per capita income of Rs. 144 per annum. This was about one half of the per capita income for the whole of India during that year.

However, although the region was economically underdeveloped due to its subsistence agriculture and food gathering economy, it was ecologically rich and sustainable for the local people. The region was dominated by the tribals and there was hardly any unequal distribution of wealth and income. There was very little manifestation of social inequality as practised in the caste system of contemporary Orissa or other parts of the country in general.

Industrialized Rourkela

Before the establishment of the public sector steel plant at Rourkela, the district of Sundergarh was one of the least industrialized districts in the state of Orissa despite its rich mineral resources. The private sector cement factory at Rajgangpur was the only major industry of the district. However, with the Government of India's decision to set up its first public sector steel plant at Rourkela, in the late 1950s in collaboration with the Krupp-Demag of the then West

Germany, the landscape of the region soon began to change. As construction work for the steel plant and township began, infrastructural facilities such as metalled roads, rapid transport and communication networks, electricity, potable water supply, drainage and sewerage were also created to support the construction activities. Consequently, by the time the Rourkela Steel Plant became operational the sleepy, isolated village of Rourkela acquired the status of a class-II category town. The steel plant generated its propulsive and multiple effects in the regional economy and several other large, medium and small scale industries cropped up in the organized sector. The forward and backward linkage effects generated by the steel plant resulted in the growth of engineering and metal based industries in the small scale sector as well. These industries in turn generated their own propulsive effects thereby supporting a wide range of tiny units in the informal sector.

The cumulative spread effects of the Rourkela Steel Plant on the economy has been so dramatic that according to the annual survey report of the organized factory sector industries, Sundergarh district has now acquired the status of being the most industrialized and developed district in Orissa. Further, from the analysis of recently available data on the State's industrial scenario, it is found that the district of Sundergarh, has a higher location quotient of engineering and metal-based industries in the large, medium and small scale sectors as compared to other districts in the state. In the organized factory sector the district's share of such groups of industrial units is as high as 43.98 per cent, and its share of persons employed in engineering and metal-based industries is as high as 75.11 per cent. The data on small scale industries including units in the unorganized sector provide a similar picture regarding the location quotient of engineering and metal-based industries.

The 1981 census data reveal that Sundergarh district, with a share of only 5.07 per cent of the total population of Orissa, provided 12.69 per cent of employment in the State's secondary sector and accounted for 21.78 per cent of the State's employment in the non-household manufacturing industries. Moreover, Rourkela being the largest urban industrial complex in Sundergarh district and in the State as well, shared 24.11 per cent of the district's total population, 53.58 per cent of the district's employment in the secondary sector,

59.00 per cent of employment in the non-household manufacturing industry sector and also 53.81 per cent of the district's employment in the tertiary sector.

These findings demonstrate that with the setting up of the steel plant, Rourkela has now become the leading industrial centre in Orissa.

Urban Growth and the Urban Structure

As construction work for the steel plant and the steel township began, the stream of migration towards Rourkela gradually swelled up. The blueprint of the project covered an area of 207.37 sq. km. of which an area of 61.97 sq. km. was specifically marked for the growth of steel township, to house the industrial workers of the steel plant and their families. The Master Plan of the township made provisions for the supply of potable water and electricity, proper drainage and sewerage system for houses, schools, colleges, hospitals, post and telegraph offices and the like. Thus with the full-fledged functioning of the steel plant the population of the township registered spectacular growth. The growth of Rourkela city acquired a cumulative nature when several medium and small industries came up to meet the demand for goods and services generated by the huge urban population. Rapid industrialization further attracted several poor migrants from the countryside. This resulted in proliferation of slums and of the informal sector, thereby distorting the city's Master Plan and replicating the typical experience of several growing cities in the developing countries.

In the large scale immigration into Rourkela in the wake of industrialization, jobbers, middlemen and the contractors played an important role. They were responsible for recruiting both skilled and unskilled labour. In mobilizing labour they relied mainly on their kinship and caste affiliations and on their social networks with their native villages. Consequently, due to this process of linked migration many pockets of ethnic communities sprang up in various parts of the civil and steel township. Several groups and communities belonging to certain regions, castes and religions have become so prominent in certain occupations and trades in Rourkela, that they now exercise a quasi-monopolistic control over recruitment in these occupations and trades.

Another finding of the study is that the location of the Rourkela Steel Plant has influenced the land use pattern and the pattern of settlements in the city. Broadly the spatial structure of the city concurs with Burgess's concentric zone model. However, various socio-cultural forces such as caste, community, region, and linguistic origin of the population have also strongly affected the formation and composition of the city's neighbourhoods.

Industry, the City and the Ecology

Rapid industrialization of Rourkela has transformed a predominantly subsistence but sustainable agricultural economy into an industrial economy and has resulted in significant increase in the level of per capita real income in the region. According to the 1981 census, Rourkela had 41.88 per cent of its total main workers engaged in the non-household manufacturing sector alone; whereas in the district as a whole, the non-household workers comprised only 15.74 per cent of the total workers and in the State of Orissa, this was as low as 3.63 per cent. Because of increasing employment opportunities in the industrial sector very few households in the sample study live below the poverty line. It is found from the sample data that only about 20 per cent of the households in the city with a per capita monthly income of less than Rs. 200 in late 1980s could be regarded as the poor households.

The rapid growth of the city has led to a significant change in the ethnic composition of the population. The urban social structure of the city is marked by caste and regional heterogeneity. The city is mainly inhabited by workers from numerous States of India. The growth of an urban industrial culture has reduced the social barriers and interaction patterns cutting across caste, community, language and region. Untouchability is no more prevalent and communal relationship between various castes and communities has increased to a large extent. Even the primitive tribals like Oraons, Mundas, Kharias, Bhuiyans and Kisans have become aware and enlightened and therefore gradually becoming a part of the urban industrial culture of Rourkela.

There are, however, contradictory pressures, which are working against the relatively open, universalistic urbanism emerging in

Rourkela. The recent slowing down of the pace of industrialization in Rourkela is creating various kinds of social turmoils and disturbances. The level of unemployment among the younger generation is becoming acute. Loss of agricultural land coupled with growing unemployment and the quasi-monopolistic hold over the limited job opportunities exercised by certain communities and groups, who migrated into the region in the early phase of industrialization, is making the local tribal youths and the native Hindu residents restless. Nativism and 'Sons of the soil movement' have gained momentum, threatening the cosmopolitan culture of Rourkela.

These problems are getting aggravated everyday. There is evidence of disharmony in the society. The discord has happened not only because of runaway industrialization and modernization but also because residents of the city have neglected the serious fallouts of such rapid changes. It is astonishing to observe that very few of the city dwellers are aware of the state of ecology and the urban environmental decay. Although many of the workers suffer from occupational health hazards, caused by the arsenic elements discharged by the steel plant, very few talk about environmental pollution and address the problem. Perhaps in the present level of economic development, the immediate issue of bread and butter is more important than the issue of survival of the entire community. Even the major trade unions of the city keep silent about the health hazards generated by the steel plant and the resultant ecological degradation of the city. Of late, only a few of the conscious citizens have formed associations to prevent the high level of environmental pollution caused by the giant steel plant. They are raising the issues of land, air and water pollution in various forums and congregations. Often the local newspapers of the city bring to the limelight the problems of pollution, abnormal weather phenomena, and deforestation and denudation caused by mining activities.

It is mainly because of the pressure exerted by this environmental lobby that the plant started taking necessary steps for the installation of essential pollution controlling equipments for effluent treatment under its modernization programme. Around Rs. 500 crore was earmarked for the purpose. But this is unlikely to drastically reduce current pollution levels in the plant, if one goes by the attitude of the plant's management. The management, in order to minimize the production cost deliberately avoids the adoption and installation of pollution controlling technology. Further, even the existing facilities are not utilized because it would increase the cost of production. For the same reasons machines are not repaired in time, as was the case with the dust catchers and electrostatic precipitators. The incessant emission of various types of poisonous gases into the atmosphere such as carbon dioxide, carbon monoxide, sulphur dioxide, nitrogen oxide from the steel plant and other industrial units, coupled with increasing vehicular pollution, the release of untreated effluents and inadequate sewerages disposal have created massive health hazards apart from polluting the land, air and water.

Increasing growth of slums and proliferation of informal sector economic activities in the wake of a large scale migration of lowly skilled and distressed people from various parts of the State and the neighbouring States of Bihar, Madhya Pradesh and West Bengal, has distorted the planned growth of the city. The city is facing an acute supply scarcity of basic civic amenities such as potable water, and electricity. The city's drainage and sewerage systems, roads, public transport, schools, parks and playgrounds have become congested. This has further resulted in discriminatory distribution of such basic services to the various localities and various categories of the population. The poor informal sector workers have become the main victims of the situation and those living in the slum areas of the city are more acutely exposed to pollution hazards than those who live in better off localities.

High population growth has led to distortion in urban land use patterns, and many localities of the city depict a mixed pattern of land use, where the small and tiny informal sector industries and commercial undertakings are interspersed together with high level population density. Owing to the proliferation of informal sector activities the foot-paths in the Central Business District of the city have been encroached by a variety of vendors, hawkers and petty traders. The roads of the main market area are congested with mixed movement of both high and slow speed vehicles such as motor vehicles, bicycles, cycle rickshaws and handdrawn carts. All this has led to increasing road accidents and noise pollution.

Even though Rourkela came up as a planned town, urban planning authorities were unable to anticipate the ecological degradation and decay that could follow in future. Increasing pressure of population and growth of informal sector economy operating hand in glove with the formal sector enterprises affect the existing infrastructure and services to a great extent. As the supply position of the basic infrastructure and services in the city is not expanding to keep pace with population growth and the growth of economic establishments in the city, it has contributed to the discriminatory supply of basic services and amenities to different categories of population and establishments located in different localities of the city. There is hardly any municipal law or regulation to check the level of pollution caused by such spontaneous growth of human settlements and informal sector establishments.

There is a large scale destruction and depletion of natural resources and displacement of tribals and other vulnerable sections of the population from their traditional ecological base. It is found that although quite a few among the scheduled tribes have benefited from the region's industrialization, a number of them have become the worst victims as well. Owing to improper land revenue record of the ex-Princely State of Gangpur, many of the displaced tribals could not be rehabilitated adequately. More so, due to the dominating nature of the upper castes in the organized sector economy of the region, from their independent self-employed status, the tribals have been exploited and are wandering as wage earners in the informal sector economy of the city because of the loss of their traditional source of livelihood. It has been observed that due to extensive mining activities, the entire Panposh and Bonai subdivisions of Sundergarh are losing their forest cover and fertile agricultural lands. The tribals who were dependent on sustainable forest based food gathering and primitive agricultural economy for their livelihood, are now banking upon the insecure mining activities by engaging themselves as daily wage earners. When they fail to get any work they migrate to Rourkela as turnover and seasonal migrants to work either as contract labour in the steel plant or as informal sector workers such as *coolies*, rickshaw pullers, unskilled construction workers, domestic help and the like.

Like in any other parts of the country the modern urban society that emerged at Rourkela, has more or less finally taken the shape of traditional, caste based particularistic and hierarchical society.

The resource and income distribution arising from industrialization and urbanization is skewed in favour of the upper caste and privileged sections of society. There is a positive correlation between the level of income and caste status of the individuals and despite adoption of a universalistic, achievement oriented norm, the pattern of distribution of population, jobs and occupations as well as wider level social interactions in the city are mainly favouring traditional caste oriented society. The large scale migration and rural exodus of people to this urban-industrial complex is not only due to push and pull factors; but in many cases they are found to be network based migration leading to partial monopolization of different types of jobs in the city by different types of caste, ethnic, linguistic or regional groups.

More so, in this situation of quasi-particularization of jobs and resources, the distribution of inadequate civic amenities compounds the skewed distribution of such amenities and the slums and the localities resided by the poor informal sector workers become the main victims. As the urban body of the city has failed to assure regular and adequate supply of basic civic services to its all categories of growing population, the urban poor and tribals have been deprived of minimum basic amenities in the city. As they are less resourceful they are made to pay a heavier price of industrialization and urbanization and therefore they face more pollution hazards, job insecurity and low income, which further weakens their competitive capability.

The experience of industry led development and change in Rourkela region clearly show that the present model which is based on GNP led growth of the economy, is unable to maintain the symbiosis between industry, ecology and the human society which may ultimately prove to be a failure in the long run. The development model of the present day exposes several contradictions. Free market economy oriented towards accumulating individual profits at the cost of societal loss; use of improper technology to reap high level individual profits under the capitalistic production system; inappropriate shared social values facilitating structural differentiation of society, universalistic achievement oriented social order while promoting the culture of an over-aggressive individualism and an uncritical view of economic expansion at the cost of depletion of scarce resources, deprivation and displacement of the weaker sections from their traditional ecological base of livelihood are some of the negative aspects.

Whatever the case may be, it is to be admitted that to solve the problem of poverty there is no alternative to industrialization in the contemporary world. For an over-populated developing country like India, the best solution lies in judicious utilization of resources in the process of industrialization. The planners and policy makers have to bear in mind the multi dimensional problems and prospects of technology, energy consumption pattern, growth of informal sector economy, slums, pressure of population and the multiple effects of industry and urban proliferation. It is beyond doubt that wherever a giant steel plant is established, it will pose an ecological threat to the region. However, such problems could easily be tackled if the planners foresee the possible ecological damage and take necessary corrective measures for the conservation of the eco-system. In the 1960s and 1970s the industrial cities of the developed countries were enmeshed with acute environmental problems but they could successfully avoid the crisis by devising appropriate technology and proper planning. By installing pollution controlling instruments and by reducing the level of consumption of fossil fuel along with making a judicious utilization of renewable and non renewable resources, ecological balance of a region can easily be maintained. Society and the quality of life are to be given prime importance before seeking a 'growthist' solution to human miseries and poverty.

Urbanization in developing countries creates several contradictions, such as increasing industrial growth is accompanied by an inadequate urban infrastructure and grinding poverty of much of the urban population. The process of capital accumulation is based on exploitation of cheap and abundant labour. Such contradictions are not only an internal situation in industry but also they appear in many facets of urban life. The city must provide for the public services, markets, transport and basic medical facilities to all categories of population who reside in it (Roberts 1978; Castells 1977). Otherwise, it is likely to cause ecological degradation due to heavy and large concentration of population and industries in a limited space and inadequate infrastructure.

IMPLICATIONS OF THE PRESENT STUDY FOR URBAN PLANNING AND POLICY

It is clear from the study that the Master Plan of Rourkela has failed in many respects. It could not anticipate the multiplier effects of rapid urbanization; land use, migration pattern and the proliferation of economic activities both in the formal and informal sectors. The city gives a dualistic look; one section of it is planned and the other a product of spontaneous and haphazard growth of the informal sector economy. It becomes clear that the city planners and architects did not pay sufficient attention to the provision of basic services and housing facilities for the poor and distressed migrant population. As a result, slums, and spontaneous squatter settlements have sprung up in vacant and unauthorized public or private lands like cancerous growths. All these further complicate the environmental problems of an industrial city like Rourkela, where in the absence of proper environmental auditing, the public sector steel plant pollutes the entire biosphere of the region. Hence, the city planners and architects have to look for alternative options and devise new strategies for tackling the city's problems. The town planning authorities should pay adequate attention to the needs of growing informal sector economy, which supports a large section of population. Therefore, a sustainable strategy in urban planning is requirement of the day.

Bibliography

Abuughod, J. and R. Hay (eds.) (1977). *Third World Urbanization*, Ma'aroufa, Chicago.

Agarwal, A. et al. (1985). *No Place to Run—Local Realities and Global Issues of the Bhopal Disaster*, Highlander Centre and Participatory Research in Asia, New Delhi.

Agarwal, P.C. (1976). 'Durg-Bhilai Urban Complex: Its Morphology, Growth and Regional Relations', in S.M. Alam and V.V. Pokshishevsky (eds.), *Urbanization in Developing Countries*, Osmania University, Hyderabad.

Akinchan, S. et al. (1974). 'Industrialization and Urbanization in India: Indices and Variable Measurement', *Journal of Social and Economic Studies*, Vol. 2, No. 1, pp. 11-24.

Alam, S.M. (1976). 'Indian Cities, and Western Theories of Urban Growth: An Empirical Appraisal', in S. Manzoor Alam and V.V. Pokshishevsky (eds.), *Urbanization in Developing Countries*, Osmania University, Hyderabad, pp. 513-42.

Alihan, M.A. (1938 and 1964). *Social Ecology: A Critical Analysis*, New York.

Anal, A.K.S. (1972). 'Begusarai: A Study in Urban Morphology' *Deccan Geographer*, Vol. 10, No. 1, pp. 40-7.

Babu, V. (1959). *Report on a Preliminary Inquiry on the Growth of Steel Towns in India*, UNESCO Research Centre, Calcutta.

Bagchi, A.K. (1975). *Private Investment in India, 1900-39*, Cambridge University Press and Orient Longman, Madras.

Bandyopadhyay, J. et al. (eds.) (1985). *India's Environment: Crises and Responses*, Natraj Publisher, Dehradun.

Bandyopadhyay, J. et al. (1984). 'Planning for Underdevelopment', *Economic and Political Weekly*, Vol. 19, No. 4, 28 January 1984.

Berry, B. and J.D. Kasarda (1977). *Contemporary Urban Ecology*, Macmillan, New York.

Berry, B. and P. Rees (1969). 'The Factorial Ecology of Calcutta', *American Journal of Sociology*, Vol. 74, pp. 445-91.

Bhattacharjee, S. and T.N. Basak (1970). 'The Morphology of Chittaranjan Township', *Geographical Review of India*, Vol. 32, pp. 256-68.

Bhattacharya, N. and A.K. Chatterjee (1974). *Some Characteristics of Jute and Engineering Industry Workers in Greater Calcutta*, Research and Training School, Indian Statistical Institute, Calcutta (Mimeo).

Bladden, W.A. and P.P. Karan (1977). 'Environmental Pollution and its Perception in the Calcutta-Hooghlyside Area', in A.G. Noble and A.K. Dutt (eds.), *Indian Urbanization and Planning: Vehicles of Modernization*, Tata McGraw-Hill, New Delhi, pp. 281-93.

Bonarjee, V.S.C. (1973). 'Calcutta's Environmental Pollution: The Canker and Its Cure', *Civic Affairs*, Vol. 20, No. 10, pp. 75-86.

Bose, A. (1969). 'The Future of Chandigarh', *Civic Affairs*, Vol. 17, No. 4, pp. 9-11.

Bose, A.N. (1978). *Calcutta and Rural Bengal: Small Sector Symbiosis*, Minerva, Calcutta.

Bose, N.K. (1966). 'Calcutta: A Premature Metropolis', *Scientific Americana*, Vol. 213, pp. 236-40.

Bose, S.K. (1960). *Rourkela Township*, Indian Institute of Public Administration, New Delhi.

Bose, T.K. (1987). 'Occupational Health and Hazards in Steel Industry', *Souvenir—Indian Association of Occupational Health*, 37th All India Conference, January 1987.

Boyden, S. et al. (1981). *The Ecology of a City and its People: The Case of Hongkong*, Australian National University Press, Canberra.

Boyden, S. (1979). *Integrative Ecological Approach to the Study of Human Settlments*, UNESCO, Paris.

Breese, G. (1969). *Urbanization in Newly Developing Countries*, Prentice Hall, I, New Delhi.

Breman, J. (1979). 'The Market for Non-agrarian Labour: The Formal Versus the Informal Sector', in S.D. Pillai and C. Baks (eds.), *Winners and Losers: Styles of Development in an Indian Region*, Popular Prakashan, Bombay.

——— (1977). 'Labour Relations in the "Formal" and "Informal" Sector: Report of a Case Study in South Gujarat', *The Journal of Peasant Studies*, Vol. 4, Nos. 3 and 4, April and July 1977.

Brush, J.E. (1977). 'Growth and Spatial Structure of Indian Cities', in A.G. Noble and A.K. Dutt (eds.), *Indian Urbanization and Planning: Vehicles of Modernization*, Tata McGraw-Hill, New Delhi, pp. 64-92.

——— (1973). 'Application of a Model to the Analysis of Population Distribution in Indian Cities', in R.L. Singh (ed.), *Urban Geography in Developing Countries: Proceedings of I.G.U. Symposium*, No. 15, National Geographical Society of India, Varanasi.

——— (1970). 'The Growth of the Presidency Towns', in Richard G. Fox (ed.), *Urban India: Society, Space and Image*, Duke University, Durham, Programme in Comparative Studies on Southern Asia, Monograph and Occasional Papers Series No. 10.

——— (1968). 'Spatial Pattern of Population in Indian Cities', *Geographical Review*, Vol. 58, No. 3, pp. 362-91.

Bulsara, J.F. (1969). 'How to Save Bombay City?' *Civic Affairs*, Vol. 17, No. 4, pp. 13-15.

Caldwell, K.K. (1970). 'Authority and Responsibility for Environmental Administration', *Annals of the American Academy Political and Social Science*, Vol. 389, pp. 107-15.

Carlson, R. (1970). *Silent Spring*, Penguin, Harmondsworth.

Catton, W. (1978). 'Carrying Capacity, Overshoot and the Quality of Life', in J.M. Yinger and S.J. Cutler (eds.), *Major Social Issues: A Multidisciplinary View*, The Free Press, New York.

Centre for Science and Environment (1985). *The State of India's Environment 1984-85—The Second Citizen's Report*, New Delhi.

Chatterjee, R.M. and D. Ghosh (1973). 'Calcutta and its Population', *Civic Affairs*, Vol. 20, No. 10, pp. 71-3.

Cobden-Ramsay, L.E.B. (1910). *Feudatory States of Orissa*, Bengal Secretariat Book Depot, Calcutta.

Commoner, B. (1971). *The Closing Circle*, Alfred A. Knoff, New York.

Dagli, V. (ed.), (1982). *Ecological Imbalances and Quality of Life*, Commerce Publications, Bombay.

Dasgupta, B. (1978). 'The Environment Debate: Some Issues and Trends', *Economic and Political Weekly*, Annual Number, 1978.

de Souza, A. (ed.), (1978). *The Indian City: Poverty, Ecology and Urban Development*, Manohar, New Delhi.

Devi, S. (1982). *Revive Our Dying Planet—An Ecological, Socio-Economical and Cultural Appeal*, Gyanodaya Prakashan, Nainital.

Dhabriya, S.S. (1973). 'Evolution of KUJBAJ cities of Rajasthan', in R.L. Singh (ed.), *Urban Geography in Developing Countries: Proceedings of I.G.U. Symposium*, No. 15, National Geographical Society of India, Varanasi, pp. 109-15.

D'Monte, D. (1985). *'Temples or Tombs'—Industry Versus Environment: Three Controversies*, Centre for Science and Environment, New Delhi.

——— (1984). 'A Question of Survival', *The Illustrated Weekly of India*, 20-26 May 1984.

Douglas, I. (1981). 'The City as an Ecosystem', *Progress in Physical Geography*, Vol. 5, No. 3, pp. 315-67.

D'Souza, V.S. (1978). 'Socio-Cultural Marginality: A Theory of Urban Slums and Poverty in India', paper presented at the 8th World Congress of Sociology, Uppsala (Sweden).

——— (1970). 'Slums and Social Structure', *Urban and Rural Planning Thought*, Vol. 8, Nos. 1-2, pp. 70-4.

Duncan, O.D. (1959). 'Human Ecology and Population Studies', in P.M.

Hauser (ed.), *The Study of Population*, The University of Chicago Press, Chicago.

Ehrlich, P. and A. Ehrlich (1972). *Population, Resources and Environment*, W.H. Freeman, San Francisco.

England, R. and B. Bluestone (1973). 'Ecology and Social Conflict', in H.E. Daly (ed.), *Towards a Steady State Economy*, W.H. Freeman, San Francisco.

Enzenberger, H.M. (1974). 'A Critique of Political Ecology', *New Left Review*, Vol. 84, pp. 3-31.

Fox, R.G. (ed.) (1970). *Urban India: Society, Space and Image*, Duke University, Durham.

Fyodorov, Y. and I. Novik (1977). 'Ecological Aspects of Social Progress', in *Society and the Environment: A Soviet View (Current problems)*, Progress Publishers, Moscow.

Gadgil, D.R. (1972). *The Industrial Evolution of India in Recent Times, 1869-1939*, Oxford University Press, New Delhi.

Gadgil, M. (1991). 'Ecological Organization of the Indian Society', Vikram Sarabhai Memorial Lecture, ICSSR, New Delhi (unpublished).

George, J.J.S. (1971). 'Calcutta: A City of Fear', *Far Eastern Economic Review*, Vol. 71, No. 2.

Ghosh, B. and K.C. Mago (1971). 'Srirangam: Urban Form and Pattern of an Ancient Urban Town', *Urban and Rural Planning Thought*, Vol. 14, No. 2, pp. 95-126.

Gilbert, A. and J. Gugler (1981 and 1987). *Cities, Poverty, and Development—Urbanization in the Third World*, English Language Book Society, Oxford University Press, Oxford.

Gist, N.P. (1955). 'Selective Migration in South India', *Sociological Bulletin*, Vol. IV, No. 2, pp. 147-60.

—— (1957) 'The Ecology of Bangalore, India: An East-West Comparison', *Social Forces*, Vol. 35, pp. 356-65.

Goldthorpe, J.E. (1984). *The Sociology of the Third World—Disparity and Development*, Cambridge University Press, Cambridge.

Gore, M.S. and J.C. Sharma (1976). 'Dispersal of Urbanization, Industrialization and Tertiary Employment', in P.K. Muttagi (ed.), *Urban Development: A Perspective*, Tata Institute of Social Sciences, Bombay, pp. 108-12.

Gorizontov, B. (1985). *Capitalism and the Ecological Crisis*, Progress Publishers, Moscow.

Government of India (1961). *District Census Hand Book, Sundergarh*, Census of India 1961, Series 15, Orissa, Part X-A.

—— (1959). *Rourkela*, Publications Division, New Delhi.

Government of Orissa (1991). *Annual Survey of Industries in Orissa (Organized Factory Sector), 1983-84 and 1984-85*, Directorate of Economics and Statistics, Bhubaneswar.

Gupta, D. (1977). 'The Causes and Constraints of Urban Social Movement', *Contribution to Indian Sociology* (New Series), Vol. 2, No. 1, pp. 69-90.

Hanspal, R. (1977). *Urban Structure of Bangalore City: A Spatial Analysis*, Institute for Social and Economic Change, Bangalore.

Hardesty, J.N., C. Clement and C.E. Jenks (1971). 'The Political Economy of Environmental Destruction', in W.A. Johnson and J. Hardesty (eds.), *Economic Growth Versus the Environment*, Wadsworth, Belmont, California.

Harriss, J. (1982). 'Character of an Urban Economy: Small Scale Production and Labour Market in Coimbatore', *Economic and Political Weekly*, 5 June and 12 June 1982, pp. 945-54 and 993-1002.

Hauser, P.M. and L.F. Schnore (eds.), (1965). *The Study of Urbanization*, Wiley, New York.

Hawley, A.H. (1981). 'Human Ecology, Persistence and Change', in J.E. Short Jr. (ed.), *The State of Sociology—Problems and Prospects*, Sage Publications, Beverly Hills, London, pp. 119-40.

——— (1971). *Urban Society: An Ecological Approach*, The Ronald Press, New York.

——— (1950). *Human Ecology: A Theory of Community Structure*, The Ronald Press, New York.

Holmstrom, M. (1985). *Industry and Inequality: The Social Anthropology of Indian Labour*, Cambridge University Press, Cambridge and Orient Longman, Hyderabad.

House, P. (1973). *The Urban Environmental System*, Sage Publications, London.

Hoyt, H. (1964). 'Recent Distortions of the Classical Models of Urban Structure', *Land Economics*, Vol. XL, pp. 199-212.

———. (1939). *The Structure and Growth of Residential Neighbourhoods in American Cities*, Federal Housing Administration, Washington, D.C.

Hugo, G.J. (1977). 'Circular Migration', *Bulletin of Indonesian Economic Studies*, Vol. 13, pp. 57-66.

Hunter, A. (1971). 'The Ecology of Chicago: Persistence and Change', *American Journal of Sociology*, Vol. 77, pp. 925-44.

International Labour Office (ILO) (1972). *Employment, Income and Equality: A Strategy for Increasing Productive Employment in Kenya*, I.L.O., Geneva.

Jagmohan (1984). *The Challenge of Our Cities*, Vikas Publishing House, New Delhi.

Jauhari, A.S. (1973). 'Urban Development in Sutlej-Yamuna Divide', in R.L. Singh (ed.), *Urban Geography in Developing Countries: Proceedings of I.G.U. Symposium*, No. 15, National Geographical Society of India, Varanasi, pp. 65-71.

Joshi, H. and V. Joshi (1976). *Surplus Labour and the City: A Study of Bombay*, Oxford University Press, New Delhi.

Kasarda, J.D. (1980). 'A Human Ecological Theory or Organisational Structuring', in M. Micklin (ed.), *Sociological Human Ecology*, The Academic Press, New York.

—— (1972). 'The Theory of Ecological Expansion: An Empirical Test', *Social Forces*, Vol. 51, pp. 165-75.

Kayastha, S.L. and V.K. Kumra (1984). 'An Appraisal of Urban Environment and Suggestions for Improvement of Kanpur Region: A Case Study', in I.P. Gerasimov et al. (eds.), *Problems of Environment in Urbanized Regions*, Nauka, Moscow.

Kayastha, S.L. (1973). 'Trend of Urbanization in the Himalayan Beas Basin', in R.L. Singh (ed.), *Urban Geography in Developing Countries: Proceedings of I.G.U. Symposium*, No. 15, National Geographical Society of India, Varanasi.

Klausner, S.Z. (1971). *On Man in his Environment*, Jossey-Bass, San Francisco.

Kolbasov, O. (1983). *Ecology: Political Institutions and Legislation*, Progress Publishers, Moscow.

Kopardekar, H.D. (1986). *Social Aspects of Urban Development*, Popular Prakashan, Bombay.

Kulkarni, M.G. (1976). 'Spatial Distribution of Some Population Characteristics in Aurangabad City', in J.V. Fereira and S.S. Jha (eds.), *The Outlook Tower: Essays on Urbanization in the Memory of the Patrick Geddes*, Popular Prakashan, Bombay, pp. 339-61.

Kundu, A., G.K. Misra and R.K. Meher (1986). *Location of Public Enterprises and Regional Development*, Concept Publishing Company, New Delhi.

Kundu, A. (1984). 'Urban Planning at Crossroads', *Economic and Political Weekly*, October.

—— (1980). *Measurement of Urban Process—A Study in Regionalization*, Popular Prakashan, Bombay.

Kurien, C.T. and J. Josef (1975). 'Urbanization and Economic Change: A Pre-theoretic Investigation of Tamil Nadu', *Economic and Political Weekly*, Vol. 10, No. 8, pp. 359-70.

Landix, P.H. (1949). *Man in Environment*, Y. Crowell, New York.

Lee, J.A. (1985). *The Environment, Public Health and Human Ecology—Considerations for Economic Development*, The Johns Hopkins University Press, Baltimore.

Lincoln, J.R. (1979). 'Orgaizational Differentiation in Urban Communities: A Study in Organizational Ecology', *Social Forces*, Vol. 57, pp. 915-30.

Lomnitz, L.A. (1985). *Network and Marginality: Life in a Mexican Shanty Town*, Academic Press, New York.

Love, G.A. and R.M. Love (eds.) (1970). *Ecological Crisis—Readings for Survival*, Harcourt Brace, New York.

Lynch, O.M. (1974). 'Rural Cities in India: Continuities and Discontinuities', in M.S.A. Rao (ed.), *Urban Sociology in India*, Orient Longman, New Delhi.

Mahapatra, S. (1988). 'Pollution in and around Rourkela', *Utkal Chemical Engineer*, Regional Engineering College, Rourkela.

Mark, H. and K.P. Schwirian (1967). 'Ecological Position, Urban Central Place Function and Community Population Growth', *American Journal of Sociology*, Vol. 73, pp. 30-41.

Mathur, S.P. (1973). 'Growth and Functional Structure of Dehra Dun: A Case study of an Indian Resort Town', in R.L. Singh (ed.), *Urban Geography in Developing Countries Proceedings of I.G.U. Symposium*, No. 15, National Geographical Society of India, Varanasi, pp. 234-43.

McGee, T. (1971). *The Urbanization Process in the Third World*, Bell and Sons, London.

McKenzie, R.D. (1971). 'The Ecological Approach to the Study of the Human Community', in J.E. Short, Jr. (ed.), *The Social Fabric of the Metropolis: Contributions of the Chicago School of Urban Sociology*, The University of Chicago Press, Chicago, pp. 17-32.

Meadows, D.F. et al. (1972). *The Limits to Growth*, Universe Books, New York.

Michelson, W.H. (1970). *Man and His Urban Environment—A Sociological Approach*, Addison Wesley, Massachusetts.

Mishra, C. (1988). 'Mrudu Mrudu Mrityu', *Sambad*, Sunday Special, 28 February 1988 (Oriya).

Misra, G.K. and R. Gupta (1981). *Resettlement Colonies in Delhi*, Indian Institute of Public Administration, New Delhi.

Misra, R.P. (ed.) (1978). *Million Cities of India*, Vikas Publishing House, New Delhi.

Misra, S. (1958). *Rourkela: An Economic Survey*, Finance Department, Govt. of Orissa, Bhubaneswar.

Mohsin, Mohammad (1964). *Chittaranjan—A Study in Urban Sociology*, Popular Prakashan, Bombay.

Morris, M.D. (1965). *The Emergence of an Industrial Labour Force in India: A Study of the Bombay Cotton Mills, 1854-1947*, University of California Press, Berkeley.

Mukerjee, R. (1942). *Social Ecology*, Longmans Green, London.

——— (1940). *Man and His Habitation*, Longmans Green, London.

——— (1932). 'The Ecological Unbalance of Man', *The Sociological Review*.

Mukherjee, R. (1965). *The Sociologists and Social Change in India Today*, Prentice Hall of India, New Delhi.

Mumford, L. (1955). *Technics and Civilization*, Routlege and Kegan, London.

Muttagi, P.K. (1976). 'Urban Social Tensions', in P.K. Muttagi (ed.), *Urban Development: A Perspective*, Tata Institute of Social Sciences, Bombay, pp. 59-66.

Mythili, K.M., (1974). '"Little Madras" in Bombay City', in M.S.A. Rao (ed.), *Urban Sociology in India*, Orient Longman, New Delhi, pp. 241-50.

Narain, V. and M.K. Jain (1976). 'Metropolitan City Structure: An Indian Study', in J.V. Fereira and S.S. Jha (eds.), *The Outlook Tower, Essays on Urbanization in the Memory of Patrick Geddes*, Popular Prakashan, Bombay.

Odum, E.P. (1983). *Basic Ecology*, Saunders College, Philadelphia.

——— (1975). *Ecology: The Link Between the Natural and the Social Sciences*, Oxford & IBH, New Delhi.

——— (1969). 'The Strategy of Ecosystem Development', *Science*, Vol. 164, pp. 262-70.

Osburn, W.F. (1948). *Our Plundered Planet*, Little Brown, Boston.

——— (1945). *Green Belt Cities*, Faber & Faber, London.

Pal, A. (1972). 'India's Stinking Cities', *Civic Affairs*, Vol. 20, No. 5, pp. 17-22.

Panini, M.N. (1986). 'Industrialization and Social Stratification in India', in K.L. Sharma (ed.) *Social Stratification in India*, Manohar, New Delhi.

——— (1979). A Sociological Study of Entrepreneurs in an Urban Setting, University of Delhi, Delhi (unpublished Ph.D thesis).

Papola, T.S. (1981). *Urban Informal Sector in a Developing Economy*, Vikas, New Delhi.

Pappenfort, D.M. (1959). 'The Ecological Field and the Metropolitan Community: Manufacturing and Management', *American Journal of Sociology*, Vol. 64, pp. 380-5.

Park, R.E. (1936). 'Human Ecology', *American Journal of Sociology*, Vol. 42, pp. 1-15.

Park, R.E., E.W. Burgess and R.D. Mckenzie (1925). *The City*, The University of Chicago Press, Chicago.

Patel, K.M. (1963). *Rural Labour in Industrial Bombay*, Popular Prakashan, Bombay.

Pathak, C.R. (1983). 'Environmental Hazards and the Low Income Groups in the Slums of Calcutta Metropolis', *Indian Journal of Regional Science*, Vol. 15, No. 1, pp. 89-95.

Postel, S. (1992). 'Future of Earth—It is Now or Never', *Survey of the Environment 1992*, The Hindu, Madras.

Prakasa Rao, V.L.S. and V.K. Tewari (1979). *Structure of an Indian Metropolis: A Study of Bangalore*, Allied Publishers, New Delhi.

Preston, S.H. (1979). 'Urban Growth in Developing Countries: A Demographic Reappraisal', *Population and Demographic Review*, Vol. 5, No. 2, pp. 195-215.

Punekar, S.D. (1970). 'The Problem of Commercial Prostitution in Bombay', *Bombay Civic Journal*, Vol. 17 (9), pp. 6-8.

Quinn, J.A. (1950). *Human Ecology*, Prentice Hall Inc., New York.

——— (1940). 'Burgess Zonal Hypothesis and Its Critics', *American Sociological Review*, Vol. 5, pp. 210-18.

Rajagopalan, C. (1963). 'An Ecological Analysis of the Growth of Bombay City', *Geografica*, Vol. 2, pp. 99-105.

Ramachandran, P. (1974). *Pavement Dwellers in Bombay City*, Tata Institute of Social Sciences, Bombay.

Ramaswamy, E.A. and U. Ramaswamy (1978). *Industry and Labour*, Oxford University Press, New Delhi.

Rao, M.S.A. (ed.) (1986). *Studies in Migration: Internal and International Migration in India*, Manohar, New Delhi.

——— (ed.) (1974). *Urban Sociology in India*, Orient Longman, New Delhi.

Rao, M.S.A. (1976). 'Migration and Urban Area Development', *Social Change*, Vol. 6, Nos. 3 and 4, pp. 3-7.

——— (1974). 'The Migrant to the City', *Yojana*, Vol. 18, No. 20, pp. 7-13.

Redfield, R. and M. Singer (1954-5). 'The Cultural Role of Cities', *Economic Development and Cultural Change*, Vol. 3.

Reissman, I. (1964). *The Urban Process—Cities in Industrial Societies*, The Free Press of Glencoe, Collier Macmillan Ltd., London.

Ridgeway, J. (1971). *The Politics of Ecology*, Dutton, New York.

Roberts, B. (1978). *Cities of Peasants: The Political Economy of Industrialization in Latin America*, Arnold, London.

Robson, B.T. (1971). *Urban Analysis—A Study of City Structure with Special Reference to Sunderland*, Cambridge University Press, Cambridge.

Rollwagen, J.R. (1971), 'Region of Origin and Rural-Urban Migration in Mexico: Some General Comments and a Case Study of Entrepreneurial Migration from the West', *International Migration Review*, Vol. 5, pp. 277-338.

Ross, A.V. (1969). *Vice in Bombay*, Tallis Publishing, London.

Rosser, C. (1972). 'Housing and Planned Urban Change: The Calcutta Experience', in D.J. Dwyer (ed.), *The City as a Centre of Change in Asia*, University of Hongkong Press, Hongkong.

Rouch, J. (1956). 'Migration au Ghana (Gold Coast): Enquete 1953-5', *Journal de la Societe des Africanistes*, Vol. 26, pp. 133-96, quoted in Allan Gilbert and Josef Gugler (1987), *Cities, Poverty, and Development—Urbanization in the Third World*, English Language Book Society, Oxford University Press, Oxford.

Roy Burman, B.K. (1968). *Social Processes in the Industrialization of Rourkela*, Vol. 1, Monograph Series, Monograh No. 1, Part XI-E, Census of India, 1961, Government of India, New Delhi.

Ruff, L.E. (1972). 'The Economic Common Sense of Pollution', in R. Dorfman and N.S. Dorfman (eds.), *Economics of the Environment*, W.W. Norton, New York.

Saarinen, E. (1971). *The City—Its Growth, Its Decay, Its Future*, Scientific Book Agency, Calcutta.

Saberwal, S. (1978). *Process and Institution in Urban India*, Vikas Publishing House, New Delhi.

——— (1976). *Mobile Men: Limits to Social Change in Urban Punjab*, Vikas Publishing House, New Delhi.

Salgo, H. (1973). 'The Obsolescence of Growth: Capitalism and the Environmental Crisis', *Review of Radical Political Economics*, Vol. 5, pp. 26-45.

Samal, K.C. (1990). *Urban Informal Sector*, Manak Publications, New Delhi.

Samantrai, R.K. (1981). 'Social Integration in Rourkela Region', paper presented at the Seminar on *Problems of Integrated Development of the Steel Region*, Asian Workers' Development Institute, Rourkela (Cyclostyled).

Schnore, L.F. (1958). 'Social Morphology and Human Ecology', *American Journal of Sociology*, Vol. LXIII.

——— (1954). 'The Separation of Home and Work: A Problem for Human Ecology', *Social Forces*, Vol. 32, pp. 336-43.

Schumacher, E.F. (1973). 'Modern Pressures and the Environment', *Christian Action Journal*, Summer 1973.

Senapati, N. (1975). *Orissa District Gazetteers—Sundergarh*, Government of Orissa, Gazetteers Unit, Cuttack.

Sengupta, N. (1983). *Contract Labour in the Steel Region, Rourkela*, Asian Workers' Development Institute, Rourkela (Mimeo).

Shah, A.M. (1988). 'The Rural-Urban Networks in India', *South Asia*, Vol. XI, No. 2, pp. 1-27.

Sharma, K.L. (1976). 'Jharkhand Movement in Bihar', *Economic and Political Weekly*, Vol. 11, No. 2, 10 January 1976.

Sharma, R. (1984). 'Urban Environment Problems of Highly Congested Areas of Delhi Metropolis', in I.P. Gerasimov et al. (eds.), *Problems of Environment in Urbanized Regions*, Nauka, Moscow.

Sheth, N.R. (1968). *Social Framework of an Indian Factory*, University of Manchester Press, Manchester.

Shiva, V. and J. Bandyopadhayay (1986). 'Environmental Conflicts and Public Interest Science', *Economic and Political Weekly*, Vol. 21, No. 2, 11 January 1986, pp. 84-90.

—— (1982). 'The Political Economy of Technological Polarisations', *Economic and Political Weekly*, Vol. 17, No. 45, 6 November 1982.

Singh, A.M. (1978). 'Women and the Family: Coping with Poverty in the Bastis of Delhi', in Alfred de Souza (ed.), *The Indian City: Poverty, Ecology and Development*, Manohar, New Delhi.

Singh, H.H. et al. (eds.) (1986). *Geography and Environment—Issues and Challenges*, Concept, New Delhi.

Singh, R.L. (1976). 'Origin, Growth and Morphological Structure of Varanasi', in S.M. Alam and V.V. Pokshishevsky (eds), *Urbanization in Developing Countries*, Osmania University, Hyderabad.

—— (1973). 'Social Factors in the Morphogenesis of Varanasi: A Suggestion in Techniques for Form Evaluation', in R.L. Singh (ed.), *Urban Geography in Developing Countries: Proceedings of I.G.U. Symposium*, No. 15, National Geographical Society of India, Varanasi, pp. 3-27.

Sivaramakrishnan, K.C. (1971). 'Hope for a Better Calcutta', *Civic Affairs*, Vol. 18, No. 9, pp. 17-18.

Slater, D. (1978). 'Towards a Political Economy of Urbanization in Peripheral Capitalist Societies', *International Journal of Urban and Regional Studies*, Vol. 2, No. 1, pp. 26-52.

Sly, D. (1977). 'Ecological Approach to Migration Re-examined', *American Sociological Review*, Vol. 42, pp. 783-93.

Smith, D.M. (1983). *Where the Grass is Greener—Living in an Unequal World*, Penguin Books.

Southwick, C.H. (1972). *Ecology and the Quality of our Environment*, D. van Nostrand Reinhold, New York.

Sovani, N.V. (1981). 'The Role of Urbanization in Asia', *Artha Vijnana*, Vol. 23, No. 2, June 1981.

Spodek, H. (1965). 'The Manchesterization of Ahmedabad', *Economic and Political Weekly*, 13 March 1965.

Srivastava, S.S. (1963). *Juvenile Vagrancy: A Socio-Ecological Study of Juvenile Vagrants in the Cities of Kanpur and Lucknow*, Asia Publishing House, New York.

Strong, J. (1898). *The Twentieth Century City*, Baker and Taylor, New York.

Tewari, V.K., J. Weinstein and V.L.S Prakasha Rao (eds.) (1986). *Indian Cities: Ecological Perspectives*, Concept, New Delhi.

The Hindu (1992). *Survey of the Environment*, The Hindu, Madras.

Turwhitt, J. (ed.) (1974). *Patrick Geddes in India*, Lund Humphries, London.

UNESCO (1956). *Social Implications of Industrialization and Urbanization in India*, UNESCO Research Centre, Calcutta.

Ursul, A.D. (ed.) (1983). *Philosophy and the Ecological Problems of Civilization*, Progress Publishers, Moscow.

van der Veen, K. (1979). 'Urbanization, Migration and Primordial Attachments', in S.D. Pillai and C. Baks (eds.), *Winners and Losers: Styles of Development in an Indian Region*, Popular Prakashan, Bombay.

Vann, A. and P. Rogers (1974). *Human Ecology and World Development*, Plenum Press, London.

Venkatarayappa, K.N. (1957). *Bangalore: A Socio-Ecological Study*, University of Bombay, Bombay.

Viswanadham, G. (1979). *Urban Demography and Ecology—A Case Study of an Indian City, Hyderabad*, Life and Light, New Delhi.

——— (1977). 'The Ecological Structure of Hyderabad: A Study in Comparative Urban Ecology', *Indian Journal of Social Work*, Vol. 38, No. 3, pp. 205-13.

Weber, A.F. (1899). *The Growth of Cities in the Nineteenth Century*, Macmillan, New York.

Weber, M. (1968). *The City*, The Free Press, New York.

Weiner, M. (1978). *Sons of the Soil*, Oxford University Press, New Delhi.

Weinstein, J.A. (1974). *Madras: An Analysis of Urban Ecological Structure in India*, Sage Publications, London.

Wengert, N. (1972). 'Environmental and Political Decisions: The Reconciliation of Facts, Values and Interests', in P.O. Foss (ed.), *Politics and Ecology*, Duxbury, Belmont, California.

White, R. and I. Burton (eds.) (1983). *Approaches to the Study of the Environmental Implications of Contemporary Urbanization*, UNESCO, Paris (MAB Technical Notes 14).

Wilkinson, R.G. (1973). *Progress and Poverty: An Ecological Perspective on Economic Development*, Praeger, New York.

World Commission on Environment and Development (1987). *Our Common Future*, Oxford University Press, New Delhi.

Worster, D. (1985). *Nature's Economy—A History of Ecological Ideas*, Cambridge University Press, Cambridge.

Index